W9-DHG-279

LIFTING THE VEIL

The New Energy Apocalypse

Kryon
Book 11

165 International Kryon Books

in 23 Foreign Languages

Spanish - 8

Kryon Books - One, Two, Three, The Parables, The Journey Home, Kryon Book Six, Seven, and eight

Spanish - 5

Kryon Books Eight, Nine, Ten, Eleven and The Indigo Children books

Hebrew - 3

Kryon Books - One, Two, Three

Hebrew - 10

Kryon Books - The Parables of Kryon, The Journey Home, Books Six, Seven, Eight, Nine, Ten, Eleven, and The Indigo Children 1 and 2

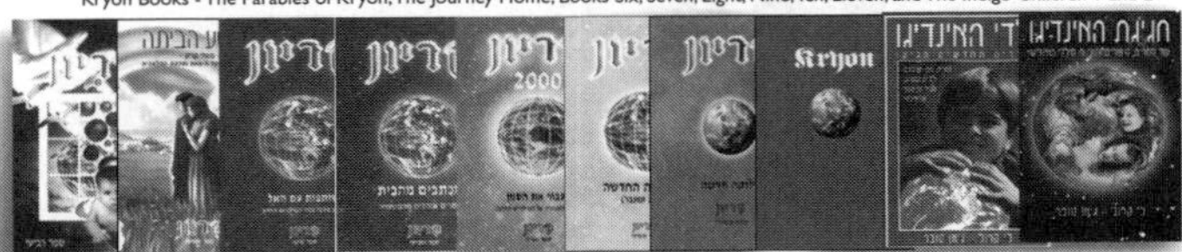

Slovene - 1

Indigo Children

Italian - 7

Kryon Books - One, Parables, Indigo Children, Book Seven, Eight, Ten, and Eleven

Estonian - 6

Kryon Books - One, Two, Seven, Parables + 2 Indigos

Turkish - 7

Kryon Books - One, Two, Three, Six, Seven, Eight, Nine and Ten

Turkish - 5

Kryon - Parables, Journey Home, Indigo Children & Book Eleven

Chinese - 4

Kryon Books - One, Two and Three & Parables

Portuguese - 6

Kryon Books - Indigo, Books One, Two, Three, Eleven & The Journey Home

Latvian - 7

Kryon Books - Seven, Eight, Nine, Ten, Eleven, Parables, Journey Home

165 International Kryon Books
in 23 Foreign Languages

French - 12
Kryon Books - One, Two, Three, Journey Home, Six, Seven, and Eight, Nine, Ten, The Indigo Children books, Kryon book 11

Russian - 4
Indigo One and Two - Books 4 and 5

Russian - 9
Kryon Books - One, Two, Three, Six, Seven, Eight, Nine, Ten, and Eleven

Danish - 1
Kryon Book One

Japanese - 3
Kryon Book - One, Five & Indigo Children

Hungarian - 13
Kryon Books - One, Two, & The Indigo Children 1 & 2, Books Three through Eleven

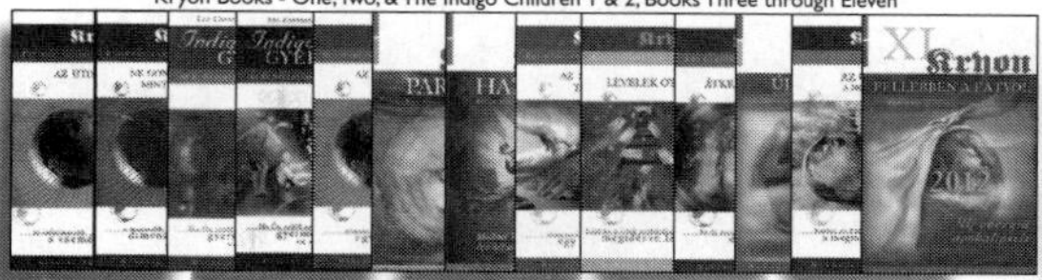

Bulgarian - 6
Kryon Books - One, Two, Four, Six, Seven & Eight

German - 13
Kryon Books - One, Two, Three, Journey Home, Parables, Six, Seven, Eight, Nine, Ten, Eleven, and Indigo 1 & 2

Romanian - 1
Indigo Children

Finnish - 10
Kryon Books - One, Two, Three, Four, Five, Six, Seven, Eight, Nine, and the Indigo Children

Greek - 4
Kryon Books - One. Two, Three, and Five (The Journey Home)

Greek - 4
Kryon Books - Six, Seven, Eight, and the Parables of Kryon

Dutch - 3
Kryon Books - Journey Home - Parables of Kryon - Indigo Children

Latvian - 6
Kryon Books - One, Two, Three, Six + Indigo 1 and 2

Korean - 1
The Indigo Children

Indonesian - 2
The Indigo Children

Lithuanian - 4
Kryon Book One and Five

Apocalypse -

(Greek: αποκαλυψις, literally: the lifting of the veil) is a term applied to the disclosure to certain persons of something hidden from the mass of humankind.

Dedicated to

Luise Hansen
Our living angel
in Japan

also in memory of...

Carey Norby
San Luis Obisbo, CA
You left us way too soon
Always beautiful
Always remembered

Petra Ostergaard
Our "rose" in Germany
Translator of the Kryon books
for the German language
who left us suddenly
but who is now
with us forever

Sheri Pari
She loved Kryon and fun!
We were with her on our
Mediterranian cruise, and then
she was gone. We love and
miss her!

LIFTING THE VEIL

The New Energy Apocalypse

Kryon Book 11

Publisher: The Kryon Writings, Inc.

1155 Camino Del Mar - #422
Del Mar, California 92014
[www.kryon.com]

Kryon books and tapes can be purchased in retail stores, by phone or on the Internet at [www.kryon.com/store].
(800) 352-6657 - E-mail <kryonbooks@kryon.com>

Written by Lee Carroll
Editing by Dawne Brooks
Copyright © 2007—Lee Carroll
Printed in the United States of America
First Edition—First Printing—April 2007
Second printing - February 2009

All rights reserved. Portions of this book may be freely quoted or reprinted up to 500 words without permission, provided credit is given to The Kryon Writings—LIFTING THE VEIL, Copyright © 2007.

The Kryon® logo is a registered trademark with the United States Patent and Trademark office.

ISBN# 1-888053-19-4 : $14.98

Table of Contents

Table of Contents... continued

From the Writer

Introduction

Kryon Book 11

Lee Carroll

Introduction

Introduction
Kryon Book 11
by Lee Carroll

It has now been 18 years since I began this journey and time has passed by like so many birds in a synchronized grouping, passing by all at once in the dimness of the afternoon. Like any life, you perceive it in hindsight – not a year at a time, but as an experience that has happened slowly yet somehow all at once.

The work that Jan Tober and I created in 1989 has sustained itself and grown into a worldwide effort. Jan still presents all over the globe with me, bringing healing energies to our meetings with her superb vocals (check out the Mt. Shasta videos sometime), and she continues to play a part in the day-to-day Kryon energy.

More and more, however, I find myself presenting Kryon alone, without the team we often bring to the very large meetings in Europe, Asia and South America. My energy remains high, even at age 62, and I present Kryon about 50 times a year this way in small, intimate meetings, mostly in the U.S.A.

The meetings we have had overseas and south of our border in the last decade or so have been amazing, with thousands in attendance. I wanted to share some of the snapshots of these meetings with you in this book (the first time!), so every so often you will see a page with photos of these experiences. If you wish to see them larger and in color, go to [www.kryon.com/countries].

Each photo has a story to it, sometimes amazing or humorous. Some of the most memorable are the ones where there were unusual circumstances... like the time in Segovia, Spain, where we fit 1,300 people into a hotel area that seated 800 (page 142). Talk about crowded! We couldn't believe that this was legal, but hey, it was Spain and they really wanted to be there! There were lines out of the hotel so long that the police were called to direct traffic. The photo doesn't do it justice, since there was no way we could photograph the whole seating.

That was also the time where Robert Coxon, our world-class Canadian musician and composer (part of the permanent Kryon team), had his "plug pulled" at the beginning of his first concert piece. There he was, frantically playing a difficult passage, but without any sound at all! It was surreal, with no audio happening but the sound of his fingers thumping the keys in front of this huge audience. He, on the other hand, was hearing it loudly and completely, in glorious stereo, through his earphones! He had his eyes closed and was concentrating on the moment – a moment of virtuosity and passion – with his piano swaying with the force of his performance on the unstable, make-shift platform we were placed on. But the audience heard nothing but the thumping of his fingers and the creaking platform. I had to get up from my chair and slowly interrupt him to start over and get the audio corrected. You should have seen the look on his face when I tapped him on the shoulder during this grand performance. I thought he was going to have a heart attack!

One of the photos looks like we are in a church (page 142). It's in Pont A Mousson, France, in the Abbaye de Prémontrés. We put more people into that abbey cathedral than seemed possible. The one you see presenting is guest speaker **Ronna Herman**, international channel for Archangel Michael. We have featured Ronna many times in the past, and she is a friend and world-class channel. [www.ronnastar.com]

Folks were everywhere, many even behind posts! You know, the European audiences are like that... they are often very patient with circumstances and situations that would be unacceptable to audiences in the states. But that's mainly due to the fact that they realize we might not be back, and they want to sample the energy of Kryon no matter what. In the states, they know we live there, and will be back. (yawn)

Our Kryon seminar in Austria featured a huge crowd (page 82). It was a very energetic meeting and we ended up producing a commercial video of it [www.kryon.com/videos]. I'll tell you what went on right after that seminar (see "Into the Breach" later in this chapter), but this particular meeting had a unique surprise. You can also see that photo in color on the back of this book.

I've had many hecklers before, and I know what to do. But I never had anyone decide to come up on stage during the meeting and begin to channel an entity of their own in a language that was a combination of German and English. Of course, the audience didn't know and thought it was part of our program. It wasn't, and it occurred while I was at the lectern. I was lecturing and about to introduce Todd Ovokaitys, and a man casually comes down the aisle from where he was seated, climbs the stairs to the stage, and takes a seat facing the audience and begins to channel! There I stood at the lectern, with some guy I didn't know, sitting in *my* channelling chair a few feet from me, going at it. In addition, his message was anti-American! Yikes... what do I do? His microphone was on, which was also odd. But the tech crew thought he was part of the program and had turned it on. (sigh)

I spoke to him from the lectern and informed the audience that it was not part of our presentation, but he kept going. It was the inappropriateness of what was occurring that I was aware of, not anything else. There is a time and place for all messages, but a universal rule of courtesy is that you don't take advantage of one person's venue to give your own message. I knew it and the audience now realized it. He had to go.

I was just about to go over to him and unplug his microphone (I would have done it!), when two young women came on stage and spoke to him gently, got him out of the chair, and walked him out of the auditorium! These were part of a team of young people who I really respect, and who had met with me several times in the past. They are all Indigos. (Remember, Jan and I wrote the original book on Indigo Children, and we know what they look like.) They were in good front-row seats and had come out of them quickly and were on this guy immediately. Leave it to the Indigos! Kryon has called them the future "peace makers." These young women did what two big muscle men would have probably had trouble with… they removed him from the stage gently, keeping his dignity intact. I was so impressed!

What took place was out of the paradigm of what any of us would have thought could happen. A seemingly belligerent, unbalanced person, who had come with intent to interrupt the meeting, had been subdued and neutralized by the energy of these two young women. I'm not certain how many in the audience really knew what had happened.

By the way, this man wasn't crazy. He was just overwhelmed with a spiritual experience at that moment. Later he apologized to our Austrian hosts. They even let him stay. I think it was the "Indigo" within these women who "saw" that his intent was not dangerous, and were able to move in quickly, without any force, but with a "maturity of the situation." Don't ever underestimate some of these young people!

If you are a young person reading this, then we have something in common. I still have my youth and my exuberance, but as a memory instead of as a reality. Like any other senior on this planet, I also have been fortunate enough to have lived many decades filled with experiences and remembrances, both profound and simple. But, when young, you don't look forward with the same perspective as you look backward. To the young, life is a beckoning promise – so much time and so much variety looms ahead, with no thought of it ever ending. Now, I am at an age I thought I would never be, yet I am still strangely faced with these same youthful feelings and lots of energy.

Odd as it might seem, I now have the perspective of one who faces unlimited time in a fantastic world of promise. I have yet to scratch the surface of *truth*, and I have all the time I need to do whatever it is I intend to do. This feeling has not always been with me. It has blossomed only in the last three years of my life, enhanced only in the last year, and represents a peaceful and potent revelation that I am indeed an eternal being and that my current life on the planet is but a transitional aspect of something far larger. I've fully embraced the seeming weirdness of being the original spiritual channel for Kryon exclusively, without apology to a skeptical world.

Check out the two photos of Kryon Cruise #5 (page 162). Each year we feature a cruise that is interesting from some place on the earth. We've been to Hawaii (a few times), Alaska twice, the Caribbean, and one which left from Europe... Venice! From there we sailed and toured portions of the Mediterranean. Venice was about the most romantic place we have ever been! By the time you read this, we may have also done Kryon Cruise #8, which is scheduled to sail from Barcelona Spain. These cruises are fun and feature about 100 Kryon attendees. We eat together, have special lectures and guests, and (of course) a few Kryon channellings along the way. We also always include our music maestro, Robert Coxon!

The photo of us in Paris in 2002 has a secret behind it (page 82). In it, you see 2,500 people in full meditation, with Jan Tober (unseen) leading it. It was almost completely dark in the auditorium. I snuck out on stage with my tripod, in full sight of everyone (if they could see in the dark) and took this time exposure. Then I went back. Nobody saw me! I have fun with my photography.

Too Many Books!

This is my 11th Kryon book, and I seem to again be writing multiple books at once! It's not the first time this has happened, and somehow I do better with these deadlines hovering around me to "do another one" as my readers often encourage me to do. It's funny – all you readers can finish these books far faster than I can write them! Slow down, I say. Stop the speed-reading courses and limit yourself to a page a month... or... read each book about 20 times! Anything to slow down your desire for another one right away. (smile)

The second book I'm working on is another with Jan Tober regarding the Indigo Children. It will be the third on this subject since we introduced the term *Indigo Children* to the earth back in 1999. Since you are currently reading these words, it's obvious that I have at least finished this Kryon book, and probably the other one as well.

Still another one will be the most esoteric one of all, on the 12 interdimensional layers of DNA, their many meanings and complexities. It will be a smaller book, and one that is illustrated with wonderful color graphics by our Israeli host and graphic artist, Ilan Dubro-Cohen.

Current Times

There has never been a time like this one in my channelling career. Most of the things Kryon said would happen have. The remaining one is the final battle he speaks of often, between old and new energy. Metaphorically this isn't one battle, but a series of years where we take on the old energy consciousness of an older civilization and time, and decide how to create The New Jerusalem, which Kryon has defined many times as both physical and spiritual. Physically it is a Jerusalem that can be shared with non-Jews. Spiritually, it means *peace on Earth.*

The meaning of apocalypse comes from Greek and means *lifting the veil*, which is the title of this book. The reference to understanding the apocalypse is therefore what my work is about – getting folks to see the real meaning and dismiss the specter of massive world destruction to instead see a revelation of illumination. Here is something else you might not realize: Do you see 11:11 on the clocks? Eleven in numerology is a master number and means Illumination. So the 11:11 is a balanced Illumination, which is the energy potential of our time.

Are you afraid? You are not alone. The last year or so of Kryon channelling has been about this very thing, and through many subjects, he targets fear and depression and helps us to understand that we are not only a part of what is going on here, but it is no accident that we are here. Does this make you wonder what your purpose is? Well, read on, for you can't escape that very message from channelling to channelling as Kryon tells us what is really happening in these "end times." It's the end of an old kind of Earth and the beginning of a new one.

If you are also afraid of 2012, then keep reading, for I have something to show you that was given to me only months ago (as I write this) in Mexico. It's a year that is a marker from an old energy to a new one, and the ancients have predicted a new civilization with a changed consciousness that Gaia will enhance with energy already in place.

New to Channelling?

OK, let's get this over with: Each Kryon book starts with something I have to say to those new to all of this, about just how weird this all might appears to be, channelling Kryon and all. Appears to be? OK, it's weird.

If you grew up with a standard perception of what your culture gives you as the *way things work spiritually,* then what I do appears weird and strange, if not downright Satanic, based on what others have told you who are ensconced in their mythological religions of our culture. If, however, you are willing to consider that God might be bigger than the ancient box you were taught to worship within, then there is a chance this material might be expansive to you. You don't have to surrender anything but an old concept, and it might even make sense to you, eventually.

I don't have an evangelistic work. In other words, I don't have a doctrine for you to accept, and I don't really wish you to dump your old ways and see mine as great. What I really want is somehow for the channelled messages to open a door within you, expanding what you might think of yourself, and for you to examine some information of what most of the masters on the planet tried to teach us. Do this, and it might expand the horizons of the reality of your spirituality.

This does not diminish anything about what you might think about the glory or splendor of your perception of God. In fact, you might even begin to see how God's plan is far more elegant and rich than you thought... with fewer restrictions and far more spiritual logic in what might really be happening, instead of just simply believing in the mythology of the ages.

A Kryon Cult?

Even since I mentioned it in the last book, the energy behind stopping Kryon in certain countries continues. There are many who don't want you to read this book. They say that Kryon must be a cult. If you wish to stay in a very old box, filled with fear based on what you have been told by others, then so be it. Don't read this. (The photo taken in France on page 142 is where video cameras were sneaked into the meeting and later edited and reassembled. This was done to create fear-based messages for those who want to capture our attendees' attention and funds for themselves.)

I'm not evangelistic, and perhaps you are not who this book was written for. But at least read this so you know: Within the Kryon work, there is nothing to join, no membership required, no money asked for and nobody to worship. Go to my English Website and observe: We don't take the e-mail names of visitors for any lists, you'll find lots of free channellings and audio downloads, and there is no setup to allow contributions. We don't ask for money! Our site is there for you to simply absorb any information you may wish to read and go inside and ask yourself if any of it is real. There is no vast Kryon organization, no team of Kryon teachers, no doctrine and no building with "Kryonites" scurrying around planning ways of taking your money.

I'm not here to tear anyone's faith away. I just want to explore the idea that God might be bigger than we all were told. What if everything you felt about God could be enhanced with further truth, not taken away? But if channelling is not for you, then put the book down. After all this time, I have nothing to prove, but I'm joyful about what I've found that has filled my life with empowerment and light. That's what you might feel in my presentation... my passion for the changes in me, and the many who have taken these works seriously.

What I Teach

I teach, through the Kryon messages, that we all have a piece of divinity inside, and that it is ready to be found. In fact, it's waiting to be found! I also believe the greatest masters on the planet taught us this. Check out the October 25 issue of *Time* magazine in 2004. The cover features something called "The God Gene." Many biochemists now feel that we actually have a biological gene that intuitively prods us to "search for our creator." All the fuss lately about creationism versus evolution has been created not by fundamentalist Christianity, but by astronomers and physicists who are forced to embrace a way-out theory called "The Anthropic Principle." Forced, I say, because of the fact that, against all odds, the Universe shows clear and undeniable proof of intelligent design.

Don't believe me? Go look up *Time* magazine from November 29, 2004. The science section article is called, *"Cosmic Conundrum-the universe seems uncannily suited to the existence of life. Could that really be an accident?"* The information is becoming more bizarre all the time, as science, through scientific investigation, is beginning to prove the existence of God. Discovery magazine also carried this new concept back in 2003 in its February issue. Stand back, for it's only going to get clearer as time goes on and our instruments get more refined. Is it possible that science will prove "intelligent design?" I believe it already has. It is against religious teaching? Only if you wish to leave God out of science and creation.

For Those Brought Up Like Me

The U.S.A. was founded on Christian principles. Although we embrace all religions and give laws to back up our intent, many of the men and women who landed here originally were "protesting" both the Church of England and the Catholic Church and wanted free worship in the new lands. So the fundamental founding religion of America is Christianity in all its forms. If you are Jewish and reading this, forgive the many references to Christ in this introduction. Later on in this book, you might be interested to read the profound channellings that occurred in Tel Aviv and Jerusalem. But I wish to address the "culture of my land" since I was born in the U.S.A. Since I also know this book will end up in the Hebrew language, I say "Shalom" to my Jewish brothers and sisters. Just skip the next few paragraphs if you wish. I know that "Christ talk" is often not what you want to hear.

My message is that there is far more here than meets the eye, and that the love of God is richer than you have been told, more profound than any religion has ever taught, and that you are part of it in a powerful way and always have been. Now, within the last 60 years or so, humanity has also found original manuscripts of many of the disciples of Christ [Nag Hamaddi, Egypt – 1945; "The Lost Gospels," *Time* magazine, December 22, 2003] They have been validated as the real thing*, and give tremendous insight as to what Christ really had to say during those times, and what might have really happened regarding the interaction between some of these disciples. They are a treasure trove of history, being discovered so recently, untouched for so long and in very good shape. The con-

*52 manuscripts were found in Nag Hammadi, Egypt, in the late 1940s verified as Coptic translations of earlier Greek manuscripts. Coptic is a language of part of Egypt – in this case, "Coptic" refers to the written language of the early Egyptian Christian Church.

troversy in all this is that they differ greatly from the much older scriptures that have been canonized and passed down through the ages, which most Christians cling to as their bible and their sacred resource.

Most of the writings of the Holy Bible were only allowed to be seen by the common man only recently in our history. They actually went unseen for more than 1,000 years, existing for centuries as documents only for the eyes of those who had the power to interpret them. They were carefully kept by religious leaders who were also the heads of governments, something even today I see as very dangerous, and which is happening in some places with a younger, alternate, but very powerful belief system.

If you are a Christian, wouldn't you really love to see the originals? Which writings do you think are closer to what was actually written – the ones that had passed through countless hands by those who had the ability and power to copy and translate them over and over with the bias of their particular group, or the untouched ones that have been only recently opened and translated? Don't ask your priest or minister, for they are going to give you the church answer, which reflects what they were taught. This question seems to be either moot in the church or filled with energy, as these recently discovered papers are seen as blasphemy or heresy. The reason? They vary so greatly from the canonized ones you have in your Bible. Ask yourself. Investigate it yourself. Pray before you do! Ask for guidance and truth.

There is a new book that I recommend called *How the Bible Became the Bible* by Donald L. O'Dell. It's for non-scholars like most of us, and is a history of how the Holy Bible came to be what it is. Do you dare read it? It's just history, but it may very well bring the reality of the actual past in conflict with what you were taught. Then you might have to decide to believe history or mythology (stories handed down from the past)… what a choice!

Everything we are discovering creates a giant question mark regarding *the old time religion* and what we were told about what God expects from us. What if we are here to find out *what's inside us* spiritually? That's exactly what the disciple Thomas has to say in the unabridged texts of this disciple of Jesus as presented within a book called *Beyond Belief – The Secret Gospel of Thomas* by Elaine Pagels. She reveals not only Thomas' writings, but also some of the dynamics between the disciple John and the disciple Thomas, and the energy between them that actually created the mythological term "the doubting Thomas." It's not what you think, or what you were told.

Thomas writes about what Jesus said on countless occasions, and it's profound to read it. When you are only used to seeing the words "Jesus said" in Holy Scripture, it's exciting to see new words and teachings quoted directly from someone else who was also there with him and heard his words. They are fresh with discovery and they tell a great, encouraging and uplifting story by this believer who walked with the Jewish master, Christ. It's worthy of taking a look, and very different from the writings of some of the other disciples in the older texts. Who is right? You be the judge. But be ready to have an open mind.

An Update on my Unusual Life

[OK, Jews can continue reading here.]

I'm a 30-year engineer, who, so the perception goes, has either turned into a Satan follower or someone who got unbalanced enough to be firmly embedded into the lunatic fringe groups. These groups regularly clone Humans in their spare time – time left over from their busy schedules communicating with the many spaceships that are constantly bringing the "cloaked" Humans to our planet, or are spraying substances into the atmosphere to control the minds of all earthlings. Boy, do I have a busy schedule! Between visiting the extraterrestrials planning the takeover of Earth, conspiring at the United Nations with the Illuminati, and fitting in meetings with French cults in order to kill their children, I'm really tired! (I'm being facetious here, of course.)

Sorry if I offended any of you with these last statements, but every one of them has been associated with me, even though the Kryon teachings don't echo this in any way within 18 years of writings, and never have. I'm also not interested in fulfilling any self-proclaimed prophesies by the many cult busters who, for whatever reason, have me in their sights. As the plan goes, they make me a villain by saying anything they want, then discredit me, and then become a hero for the revelation. In the process, they collect followers and lots of money with their own books and seminars.

Many know that this is mainly happening in Europe. In most cases, the *cult busters* are not anything but old energy cults themselves, trying to keep from having any light shined on them or trying to morph into something new before they get exposed themselves. Unfortunately, this process is alive and well and they count on the fact that I don't speak their language, and I'm not there that often to clearly show it isn't so. The tragedy of all this is that many Humans will be pulled out of their power, receiving fear messages that keep them from any kind of spiritual advancement or independent thinking.

Their efforts are all about power and control and money... Human attributes that have been with us for a very long time. Their success has only been marginal, attracting many who are weak, but causing confusion for many others. Despite their efforts, I continue to produce books in their language, continue to be invited to the United Nations, and continue to attract crowds more than 1,000 wherever the Kryon work around the globe takes me.

Channelling is bringing the word of Spirit (or God) to the planet through a Human. This is the way all spiritual information has been transmitted since God started talking to humanity. No matter what you believe within your scriptures, be it Jewish, Muslim, Christian, Buddhist, Hindu or anything else, you will notice that it is the Human who brings you the words, not God directly. It has required an obvious interaction between the intuitive spirit of a Human Being and whatever energy you call God. In other words, Humans wrote all the scriptures on Earth. No matter how sacred you try to make the writings, it's still a Human translating God's word or energy. In my opinion, that's channelling.

I'm not a modern-day prophet. I'm just one guy and my work is not that big. My messages are not meant to create another religion. (Please don't let it!) When I'm gone, someone else will take my place with updated, channelled information within an energy that isn't here yet. The Kryon books will be seen as a "beginning primer" to the earth changes that began in 1987 with the Harmonic Convergence. Hopefully, the next generation of channellers will be far clearer and better accepted than what some of us went through. But meanwhile, I'm the "weird guy of the day" and proud of it.

The Indigo Children: Subject Under Fire

Slightly more than two years has passed since Kryon Book Ten. In this time, much has taken place in the Kryon work and around many others as well. But here is one thing you might like to know about, since I'm speaking to many who understand fully about the Indigo Children.

Many of you know about our book published by Hay House called *The Indigo Children*. It was written by Jan Tober and myself in 1999. In the book, we told of something we believed was happening regarding the kids of the planet. It's a clear evolution of Human consciousness we are seeing and, yes, it was also later validated by Kryon [Kryon Book Six]. We brought in many facilitators and credentialed persons to help us with this premise, as presented in the book. We wanted to show that it was really happening, and that parents and teachers might wish to take a look.

But the Indigo book was not a channelled book, and we involved many professional individuals who also saw this in the mainstream of child development and weighed in on the phenomena, including our good friend Doreen Virtue. We reported that a woman named Nancy Tappe had a brain disorder called "synesthesia" and had developed a system for "seeing" different types of people because she saw color around them which correlated, oddly enough, with personality types. She had written a book about it all called *Understanding Your Life Through Color* (now out of print). For years, she held profound, exciting workshops that clearly exposed her talent, and she used her disorder as a benefit for us all.

Synesthesia is real, and can be described as a cross wiring of the brain where perceptions are greatly affected. [http://web.mit.edu/synesthesia/www] Nancy used to tell us that when she ate certain food types (peas, for instance), she "tasted triangles." This was her description of what it was like to have this altered perception. But the positive thing she received due to this unusual perception was the ability to see color around a person. As much as we wanted to tell folks that it was a spiritual aura she was seeing, it wasn't. It might be an interdimensional electromagnetic field around a person, but we don't know that either. Spiritual auras follow a color system, too, with well-known hue attributes that world-class psychics have known and accepted for years. This didn't fit into that system at all, and was obviously very distinctly created from her own altered and documented perception. In other words, Nancy was not seeing something psychically, but physically, enhanced by her disorder.

In the 1990s, experiments by a Russian scientist named Vladimir Poponin clearly showed that DNA has a previously unknown field around it. In addition, this field has now been shown to force light into structured patterns in controlled experiments, indicating that it somehow is an intelligent field, perhaps a quantum one. This field could be related to what Nancy is seeing, but again, we don't really know. But there is mounting scientific evidence that there is something to see and measure around Human Beings, both in 3D and in a quantum state, and it has nothing whatsoever to do with the New Age.

So Nancy's unusual sight should be classified as not that of a psychic woman, but rather of one who had a brain malfunction that had given her enhanced perception. She could see "life colors."

Some years ago, she began seeing a new kind of Human color with her synesthesia... a color she had never seen before in her life. This was an Indigo color and, of course, was surrounding only the newcomers to the planet, the children. She had, therefore, named them "The Indigo Children." Further studies began to show that they also had personality types that were unusual, and that's the basis for the Indigo Children books that Jan and I wrote. It also fits right into the Kryon channelling of 1989 that indicated a new consciousness is coming to the planet.

In the past years, she has not seen any other new children colors. Many categories of these children of new consciousness have been noted, however, but we firmly believe they are all *Indigo* as defined by the attributes of Nancy's unusual brain perception. So an *Indigo Child* is, therefore, a child of new consciousness on the planet, and would include all the names you might be hearing and the myriad of books that are being written about the different kinds of new kids. If this were not so, then Nancy would be seeing other colors as well. She isn't. So that's the first thing I wanted to clarify.

There are many of you who read Kryon who are familiar with all of this, so that is why I'm spending time on it here. I wanted to give you a heads-up on something that is happening that you should be aware of.

Since 1999, it has been wonderful to observe how many on the planet are seeing what we have been talking about regarding these children. Even more shocking is the fact that since 1999, *The Indigo Children* book has sold almost half a million copies, and was translated into at least 20 other languages. Indeed, it has been noticed! With it, of course, came scathing criticism that we were nuts. (But then, what else is new?)

Next, many books began to spring up that were really well written and helpful to parents and teachers alike. You can see some of them at our Indigo Children Website [www.indigochild.com]. Then came the movie, *Indigo*, and then a documentary, *Indigo Evolution* (neither of which we were involved with). With all of this attention, money began to be spent promoting these new endeavors and suddenly the Indigo subject was in the mainstream media. Now, add to this those who have jumped on the bandwagon for profit-only (who have no real interest in the subject or our kids), and you have a circus.

The New York Times featured an article, as well as *USA Today*. These were mainly promotional articles (submitted by agencies who want the publicity), but they had to cover the issue of what the kids were all about. In addition, the Indigo subject appeared on *CNN* and *Good Morning America!* We also got tapes from many local TV stations that did their own reports, including Houston, Texas, and a Fox station in our own town of San Diego.

Even on an episode of CSI, one of the characters in the show had an "Indigo Child" (honest, CSI!). Naturally, it turned out to be a difficult child and one that somehow was written to fit right into the mystery plot of some murdered person, of course. (sigh)

You would think with all this attention on the Indigo Child subject, we would be ecstatic, but instead, we were horrified! Somehow along the way, the entire Indigo subject has turned into some kind of New Age media free-for-all. The kids were being toted as "all psychic" or kids who were going to save the world, and all of them had dark blue auras! Yikes! What had happened? Not only was this blatantly incorrect, but it placed this very real phenomena firmly into the woo-woo category, robbing needed credibility to a subject that needs to be studied seriously in order to help our kids!

Thousands of educators and parents want to have good, solid information about what to do next. Day care workers all over America are validating that our children are changing. Medical professionals are finally starting to come around to at least take a look at why ADD, a social disorder, is looking like an epidemic. Wonderful Websites with great resources are beginning to appear [www.childrenofthenewearth.com]. Yet right in the midst of it all, the whole subject is being hijacked right into the weird realm of *super psychic kids who know their past lives, have different DNA than you and I, and have odd looking auras.* The press is having a great deal of fun with it and the reports, no matter from what prestigious publication or TV station, are mostly tongue-in-cheek. They are disrespectful, misunderstood and overly dramatic.

This is the reason Jan and I wish to do still another Indigo book, an endeavor to try to center all the nonsense and get back to practical solutions to our changing children. We hope it's not too late, and that the trend is reversible. We wanted you to understand it, too, and let those know around you, especially if you have friends who may need help for their kids. It isn't what you are being told by the media. Hopefully, our new Indigo book will be filled with information, resources and references by the pros to get this back on the correct footing using integrity and truth and not what has recently been generated by those who want to "make a buck" with the Indigo subject.

South of the U.S.A. Border

Since the last book, the Kryon team has traveled to Mexico and Argentina. Both trips created great learning for me personally and were delightful in their scope of new experiences. I have lived in San Diego all my life, where almost 20 percent of the population speaks Spanish, so the language is familiar to me and the culture is, too. My favorite food is Mexican, and I really love these people! My exposure to Mexicans in San Diego was always a positive one, and I got to see up close their family ethics and their gentle ways. I was really ready for these trips, but especially the one to Mexico.

What I wish to do is to tell you about a personal experience that meant a great deal to me, given to me by two professional men in Mexico – an M.D. and an engineer. These were experiences I didn't expect, and through their time and graciousness, I again was educated about things that are on the cutting edge of discovery and understanding.

Dr. Luis Oscoy is a medical doctor who has created a beautiful spa called Hostal de la Luz (which means "Inn of the Light") in Amatlan de Quetzalcoatl, a village south of Mexico City. Not only is it a high-energy and enlightened place to be, but while we were there it was blessed by a representative of the Dalai Lama, who had come to dedicate the facility as the first *zone of peace* in Mexico. The *Hostal de la Luz* had fulfilled all the requirements set out by the Dalai Lama for inclusion of a blessing in this manner, complete with an ashram and a labyrinth. You can see this spa and parts of the ceremony in 2006 in the scrapbook area of my Website at [www.kryon.com/mexico].

Dr. Luis (as I call him) introduced me to Jorge Alberto Báez Guerrero, an engineer who is deeply involved in the interpretation of Aztec and Mayan calendar research. *Deeply involved* is putting it mildly… it is his passion, and he had some startling discoveries to share with me.

Jorge had used both his vast personal knowledge and enlightened intuition to realize something that most had missed. Even though Aztec and other writings have survived in codices and the walls of the ancient sites for hundreds of years, and the amount of information about them and the Mayans is vast, Jorge cut through it all to discover something we all should understand. I wish I could simply point you to his book, *Energia Vital en Movimiento* (Vital Energy in Movement), but at this writing it is only in Spanish. The title of the first edition is deceiving, for it seems very academic. But he has now released the second edition and called it *Vital Energy in Movement (The Secret of 2012).* That's more like it! I want to honor Jorge and Dr. Luis here, in that they are both involved in this, with Dr. Luis being a believer and supporter of Jorge's work… thus the invitation he had given to me for this experience. I thank them both.

Jorge is working against the grain of the traditional Mexican scholars who follow a "party line" of information. It was odd to me that such a thing could be. I always thought that archeologists were like scientists, and when a breakthrough was unveiled, they would all be excited and take a look. How wrong I was! I often forget how politics plays with the truth. In the case of parts of Mexico, it is a situation of academic survival. I hope I don't offend anyone, but I speak of what I saw.

If you are an archeologist in Mexico, you are probably working for the government in some way, and if you stray too much from the accepted information about the indigenous ways and accepted interpretations, you don't last long. What went on in the temples and observatories is very sacred and closely held information and the government wants to hold it pure and close to the vest, as they say.

Here stands Jorge, however, with spectacular information about how all these things fit together in a well thought-out system, yet they kind of accept and ignore him at the same time.

I saw how Jorge was treated at the ancient site of DNA in the state of Morelos, located 38 kilometers (24 miles) southwest of Cuernavaca, Mexico. I was quite excited, for Dr. Luis and Jorge had made arrangements for myself and a few of the team to go to a place that few ever see, one of the ancient solar observatories of the indigenous at the temple ruins. This was one of three vertical observatories there where light would stream in from above, be focused by a system of ancient design, and create patterns on a slab placed at a predetermined height in the observatory. The ancients would observe the movements of the sun and moon as the light scribed patterns on this slab through the year. It allowed them to understand more about the earth and the moon, even allowing them to estimate its size, not to mention having specific information about the equinoxes, solstices and eclipses. We were on our way to enter this sacred place and see it in person!

Before we went on this adventure, Jorge and Luis gave us a one-hour PowerPoint presentation on what the true discoveries were. Jorge has assembled a complex calendar using this ancient information. But instead of a calendar of days, months and years, it was a calendar of energy! When I saw it and held it, I called it a "calculator." For, intuitively, Kryon was giving me information about what it was really for. In addition, Jorge included information about our DNA, relating it to the changes in the earth energy. He associated the different polarities with amino acids in the DNA chain, saying that the active polarity is being left behind with the old consciousness in order to give place to the passive polarity that is being activated with the magnetic changes we are going through. (Magnetic changes!) He explains the mechanism within the DNA that generated light in the DNA itself that actually strengthens our energy field.

Jorge showed that the Mayans and Aztecs (and others) knew about the various shifts in Earth energy and had plotted them accurately. They are Earth energy consciousness shifts, not just calendar shifts. Taking it to a new level of explanation, he showed the phases of the shifts and how long each had taken (more than 1000 years each). They had names, colors and were clearly indicated by those ancients who had plotted them. Although they used the observatories for tracking the movements of the sun and moon, they had also developed a method for tracking and predicting the phases of energy that the earth had gone through and would go through in the future. This is why Kryon told me it was a calculator – for, used correctly, one could calculate what was coming.

What the calculator shows is that clearly, in this age, we are headed for a major shift. This custom circular energy calendar shows that the ancients indicated we are closing an old energy consciousness on the planet and opening another. The date for all this? 2012. Here it was – a full explanation of what the Mayans really told us about 2012, and the energy around it, complete with explanations and history, and even a physical phase calculator based on their observations. They had predicted the end of an old time and the beginning of a new time.

When you see it laid out this way, it is obvious... really obvious. Jorge had used his intuition and intellect to see through what the information seemed to show, and draw logical conclusions on what it really said. His circular calculator showed how their phases of energy in the past lined up with world events, our own history, and what we are now facing. The exciting part was that everything he was showing was *Kryon 101* [basic Kryon information for 18 years]. He must have gotten tired of me interrupting his presentation, and through an interpreter saying, *"That's what Kryon told us!"* Later, I realized that Jorge wasn't even a Kryon reader. (I'll try to be more subdued the next time this happens, but I was very excited to find validation of the Kryon messages written on the walls, so to speak, of the temple, and then have Jorge speak of the magnetics in the DNA!). Jorge's work is quite exciting to me.

Basically, the Mayans and Aztecs are telling us that a new energy is coming in 2012, and that it will be a high one. Typically, as with any major energy shift, those who have become used to the old energy will not last. We are moving into the energy of what they called "a new sun" (in this case, the sixth sun). Each phase of civilization has a sun color within their system, and our new color is going to be yellow, moving from violet. (Remember, this is part of a spiritual notation system and not an actual color of the sun.)

For years, Jorge had been allowed into the observatory by those in charge of the historical site, which by now simply looked like a cave deep underground. He had spread out his papers and had plotted the movements of the sun and moon, just as the ancients had. So he wasn't just reading what archeologists had given him, but he was using their own tools! It was impressive, and now I had a feeling of comfort knowing that what I was teaching through my channelling was also given by the ancients in a very clear form.

It's not clear to me what those academics around Jorge believed, since they could not really say. But they greeted him with smiles and respect, and allowed him access to their "inner sanctum." I think it says a lot about what they really felt for him.

Dr. Luis was also involved and had some clout in getting us into this place. I had the feeing that Jorge and Dr. Luis were familiar figures at the museum and temple grounds. Dr. Luis is well known in that part of Mexico for his humanitarian work, as well as his professional medical standing. I think it helped all of us that day, for he had really opened the door for us.

Before I tell you more about the actual visit into the observatory, let me tell you something fun that happened, and that represents the *controlled ignorance* of what the officials there wish you to believe. Again, the party line is important to the politicians, but I still do not see why they do not allow the new information to be presented. In fact, the very idea that there was a sophisticated observatory is also suppressed.

Above ground, at the top of each vertical observatory, is a customized round opening. This is where the light enters, and it's critical to the whole system. If they had complex glass lenses back then, this would be where one of them would reside. The other would be midway in the shaft, allowing the image of the sun or moon to be focused into a small light at the bottom (on the table-high slab) so they could scribe the precise movements of those celestial bodies. In this Aztec/Toltec temple, they had something similar for the optics and Jorge actually described them as "shutters," but they were simply different sized holes and perhaps some diffusion screens made with the materials that they had back then. But they were able to construct these shutters in a way that would indeed focus the image to a degree of sharpness where they could use it to plot the light in precise ways. They had to control the light; otherwise, it would just be a distorted blob of light on the elevated slab.

Picture a telescope, if you wish, with the glass removed on both ends. It would just be a tube and would do very little without the lenses. But remember about optics: you can focus the sun on a wall by using only a pinpoint hole in a dark piece of paper, if you do it right. Many artists found they could do this with a pinpoint hole, and paint over the projected image on a wall, creating art realism as yet not seen in their time. In other words, there are many optical ways of focusing light that don't require sophisticated, manufactured glass lenses.

The hole at the top of the observatory was precisely aligned for the movements of the sun and moon. In addition, it had a system of alignment (perhaps grooves) for a missing and specialized top round lens piece that could be placed at precise angles that enhanced astronomic viewing (just like the marks on some telescopes of today). These ancients knew a great deal about where the sun would be at various times of year, so the top piece could be rotated around and slipped into specific small holes or markings that existed for that purpose. There were probably several top pieces with different viewing options for different times of the year.

Now it gets fun. These top pieces of the observatories were lost long ago. Jorge told us that if they found those pieces, it would go a long way to prove that the observatories were far more sophisticated than the historical site let on. It would show that those doing the observations knew far more than they are given credit for.

We entered the temple grounds by first going into the area where the overall grounds map was kept, the gift shop, restrooms and a museum where some artifacts resided behind glass. This is where the tourists begin their journey and where guides often meet them and take them on a paid tour. I also saw again that the on-site guides knew Jorge and treated him with respect. They delivered their speeches according to what their job descriptions told them, but stood there as Jorge gave the *rest of the story*. Most of them didn't even blink. It was as though they all knew he was right.

We entered the area where a few well-preserved artifacts were displayed in glass enclosures, complete with explanations in Spanish of what they were. Everything was in Spanish, or course, but I never gave it a second though. We are always blessed with interpreters around us in any country Kryon visits, and this time we had professional translator Leslie Pascoe, the one who was the official world-class interpreter for the Kryon conferences in Spanish (Mexico, Argentina and Chile), and the one who is helping me remember all this and edit this very article!

Jorge walked over to one of the cases and stopped in front of it. He said, *"Do you recognize this?"* In front of us, under glass, was one of the top observatory pieces! It had been found! It was very well preserved, and you could clearly see the holes and markings where it fit perfectly into the observatory top hole! In addition, there was an angle marking on it that Jorge explained corresponded to other well-known, Earth-based degrees of viewing now used in astronomy. It was so obvious that this was a valuable missing piece to the observatory that we would be visiting soon.

I was elated until Jorge invited us to read the explanation of what the historical site said it was, as indicated in Spanish on the museum card beneath it. Leslie translated that it was a "sweat lodge artifact." What? We all burst out laughing! Jorge just looked at us, as if to say, *"What can I say?"* They had mislabeled this very valuable observatory piece. Hey, at least they kept it! I was beginning to realize that much of what you and I have been told about these ancients is not the whole story, and has been withheld. Sadly, those who are responsible may have even forgotten themselves why the deception would be needed, and have passed from power long ago.

In my opinion, this has left a group of archeologists who are now simply grounds keepers who keep their hard-to-get jobs by keeping quiet and not doing their life's passion. I was reminded that Jorge is a lone scholar, who doesn't work for the government or any branch of it. He is free to teach the truth as he has researched it. Still, at some level, it's a dangerous position to take.

We visited two other "horizontal" observatories that faced each other about 45 meters apart. Both were positioned on top of large plateaus with lots of steps up to each. Jorge showed us how they worked, with the sun scribing patterns of light on the back wall as it rose and set during the year. Again, the process was obvious for what their purpose was, but not according to the official guides who indicated they were used for a ceremony of some kind, perhaps even Human sacrifices. Perhaps they were, but they were built as observatories.

We also visited the very famous pyramid of Quetzalcoatl on the top of a mesa where the glyphs are present over four faces of a pyramid. After the official guide explained what it said, Jorge revealed the rest of the story... that it really represented the phases of energy, rising and falling, which the ages had gone through. As he taught, it was obvious he was right. It wasn't just one guy's opinion either, since the glyphs supported the idea historically in what he was telling us, and you could see it in stone... yet it was not in the official guide's handbook. How could such a thing be missed?

It was time for the main event, and we filed into the side of the mountain to get into the entrance to the observatory. Wow, was it dark! There were seven of us in the group and I was last (on purpose, with my camera so I could photograph the others). We finally navigated to the main room, directly under the hole where the light would stream in. Without the ancient observatory lenses in place, the light coming in wasn't focused and simply showed a column of light creating a hexagon on the ground, which was the size of the hole. It wasn't very bright, either, and we had to sit in the dark for a while to let our eyes get used to it.

To some, this would have been a "ho-hum" visit – a dark, cold cave with a light from above. To me, it was as if I were with the ancients! It was very exciting to be in a place that few go, and one that I could write to you about later. I tried to take a few shots with the camera (no flash), but I didn't have a tripod with me and these would be time exposure shots. It was tough, but I got one of Luis standing in the middle of the light. I liked it. Although he didn't say so, I think this highly educated doctor feels he was part of what happened in that place in ancient times. Certainly he was emotionally moved to be there, and he had visited it many, many times before. I was very pleased to be allowed into this place and to be called "amigo" by these fine, educated men.

If you wish to contact Jorge for more information about his book, or you are a publisher who may wish to publish it in any language (including Spanish), his contact e-mail is <jorge@kryon.com>.

Enter the Orbs

This may seem like a huge departure from the given subject, but now I wish to reveal one of the other things that both Dr. Luis and Jorge have documented... the presence of ORBS – always there, always photographable – within this cave.

Orbs are small balls of light that appear on film and digital cameras at odd times. If you magnify them on the photos, they are multi-colored and seem to include complex patterns of some kind... always a bit fuzzy. They are not created by "lens flare" (a common camera phenomena created by bright light showing lens manufacturing phenomena) and do not have symmetry that would indicate they are glass abortions. (In other words, they do not "line up" in a symmetry that would occur if they were part of internal reflections from a man-made, manufactured glass lens anomaly.) They are real, unexplainable and appear with regularity on many photos.

I'm not going to discuss much about the reality of orbs, what they represent, or how they are generated, since there is a great deal of this on the Internet already. I personally have seen three photographic books on the subject, but what I have not seen is any real research. I have spoken to some metaphysical photographers who actually teach photography at a university. They defend a point you might not agree with, but they are also men of science and they still feel it's somehow "in the camera" or photos of dust. This is a fair and expected appraisal, but without any real research, we really don't know. I have never seen tests of the kind where you can take photos of orbs in controlled situations. Suddenly, we had one of those situations and I was going to take advantage of it.

The previous day on the PowerPoint presentation, we had seen photos of many orbs in the observatory, and within a cave adjacent to it (just as dark). I saw a photo of Jorge meditating on some steps in the cave with lots of orbs around him… more orbs than you have ever seen in any one photograph. I guarantee it! Want to see? Go to [www.kryon.com/orbs] to view it yourself. Both Jorge and Dr. Luis told me that the orbs were always there, and that each time photographs were taken in the cave, they showed up. Here we were in that cave with three cameras! Let's do some basic orb experiments, I say! So we did.

Luis and I sat down on the steps of the cave in total darkness. This is important, since many who doubt the orbs feel that they are only created from residual light inside the camera, sometimes coming in from the back viewing area. So right away we eliminated the problem of stray daylight. (In all fairness, however, the very light of the flash could be contributing to stray light.) I've never seen orbs as photographed in total darkness. They have always been in situations where there was light coming from many places. So I felt we almost had a scientific darkroom to examine the event. No stray light… three cameras representing two kinds of digital, and a time set aside to try and analyze the orbs!

Cameras are something I know about. I spent all my youth in my father's graphic arts shop (Carroll Graphics in San Diego) and photography has become my hobby. In my dad's shop, there were cameras so large a Human could get inside them, and I spent many years working summers and learning all about optics and how all these things worked. I also have a scientific mind, so I was ready to examine anything that might be a factor in the appearance of the orbs.

One of my suspicions was that the appearance of orbs through photography might be *camera specific.* In other words, the logical question might be, *"Do some cameras photograph orbs better than others? And if so, why? What does that say about the orbs or what they might be?"* I was ready for any answer, although all those around me were convinced that orbs were interdimensional energy that "show up" only on electronic flash photography (which, due to their high photonic frequency, allows the orbs to be captured), and are not predictable.

Our cameras that day were of two types. Two of the cameras were *pocket digitals.* These are the kind in the $200 to $400 range, where you can see the subject in the small video viewer as you photograph them. My camera was a high quality Digital Nikon SLR. It had a professional zoom lens from 18mm to 70mm. Each camera was using its own built-in flash, but my flash was more powerful than the others (more light).

I have never seen orbs in photos done with available light or time exposures. They seem only to show up in electronic flash photography. This would indicate to me that the light from the flash process has something to do with the illumination of whatever they are, or somehow is catching them at a juncture in physical time that non-flash photos cannot. Each camera was set (default) at 1/60th of a second, which is the typical default flash setting for most cameras. For the record, orbs have been caught with both digital and film cameras.

If we were really doing it scientifically correctly, this "lab experiment" would have had us do flash, non-flash and different exposure timings and shutter speeds. We didn't have that ability, or the time. But what we did have I feel is significant, and I offer it up for anyone doing more research on the subject.

Luis and I sat down on the top step of the cave with our team about 20 feet away from us. We were elevated slightly. We began to meditate, and the cameras were instructed to shoot at intervals of several minutes each. We stayed on the steps for about 10 minutes while the cameras flashed away. The operators of the cameras did not synchronize their shooting. In other words, it was random. In addition, we were all very still so as not to stir up dust.

The results were fun and created more questions than they answered. What I report here is from what we saw in examining the exposures afterwards. First, there were no orbs caught by any cameras within the first few moments. That was interesting, since if orbs were dust, you would have expected our climb up the steps to have released a flurry. After a few minutes, the orbs began to show up. By the seven-minute mark, there were lots of them and they stayed to the very end. Naturally, as meditators (and weird guys) our explanation is that the orbs represent the energy we were *calling in* to our area, and that they increased with the high energy we were creating spiritually. Skeptics would say that we had great shots of dust in a very dusty place. But two things don't ring true to that. First, our movements should have created dust, not our stillness. We received counterintuitive results if orbs are dust. Second, then why did the "dust" not show up on the better, more powerful flash camera?

There is also another explanation that must be considered, and that is that whatever they are, they are heat sensitive, and as we warmed the area with almost 100 degrees a body, they came from wherever it was they were to our warmer area. Who knows?

The two small digital cameras produced plenty of orbs. What they had in common was that the amount of orbs was consistent, in that there were few at the beginning and lots at the end. But they were never identical. This is also interesting, for it shows that whatever is being photographed, even side by side, is unique to the exact moment. A rough comparison showed that the orbs were not in the same place from camera to camera.

The next attribute is disappointing to me, since it foretells of a coming problem. My professional camera never was able to photograph one orb! No matter when it was triggered, it never captured an orb. When the others were seeing lots of them, mine saw none. Why? I can only guess. But remember, it's a different type of camera, has lots of glass in the lens (the others don't), and perhaps a brighter flash. The reason it's disappointing to me is because cameras are becoming more sophisticated and being offered with bigger lenses all the time. There is a theory that the simplicity of these "lesser" digital cameras, combined with a very thin, one-glass element lens, lets these orbs show. But when you add the sophistication of more glass and multi-element zoom lenses, they don't. So whatever is actually showing itself to the camera may go away as cameras are improved. I hope not! Keep your cheap digitals!

I have created a page on the Internet that is only referenced from this book. It is [www.kryon.com/orbs]. First, it shows me at the United Nations on March 31, 2006. We didn't know until later that a giant orb appeared next to me. We enhanced it and you can see what some of these things look like up close. Next, I show Jorge sitting on the steps of the cave in the first moments of a meditation. After that, I show an unbelievable photograph of the orbs around him after a few minutes as he continues to meditate (as I stated above… more than you have ever seen!). Also on this page is a photo of the top piece of the observatory, which was labeled "sweat lodge artifact" (yeah, sure). And finally, you get to see some other photos of the observatory shaft, plus one of Luis I took without a tripod in the dark.

So what are orbs? The jury is out. All I know from that day is that Luis and Jorge are right... the orbs were there in mass… easy to photograph and always in that place. The greater our meditative energy, the more the orbs seemed to appear. One settled on my throat and stayed there while many grouped around Luis. Seeing the photos later was quite startling, realizing that perhaps we are getting a glimpse of interdimensional energy that is only captured because a flash from a camera somehow forces part of it momentarily into 3D? The camera is different than the Human eye because it only opens for a 60th of a second, then snaps shut again. It also synchronizes itself with a very bright light. Our eyes don't do that. I don't have the answers, but I'm happy to present this simple experiment to those who may take this further.

Into the Breach

I normally don't talk about my personal life much, outside of the Kryon work. It's almost a violation of the situation here, where you are reading a Kryon book and have to plow through the author talking about himself. I try to include only things that I feel might be interesting to a Kryon reader. However, I'm going to suspend that rule because of something that happened in 2004 and 2005 that is directly related to Kryon, and something that you can actually see within this book.

Kryon (with my permission) often places me into situations that test how I will react. I don't like it any more than you do when we realize that we have had something unpleasant happen that has made us eventually stronger. There is phrase from Christian scripture (Proverbs 27:17) that reads, "Iron sharpens iron," and this is what I mean. I've known for a long time that I can't travel the world with a message like mine and not experience some of the most dramatic parts of life, just like everyone else. I'm not immune to any of life's issues, and I use what I teach to work with them. But normally, I don't publish them or tell you how I faired.

At the end of 2004, coming off of the Austria tour, I knew I was in trouble. I was on my way home in the airplane and realized that my chest was not right. It was hurting. I couldn't breathe well without it hurting, I wasn't hungry, and I was in physical distress. I shared it only with those who needed to know, and understood the signs. I needed to go see a heart doctor as soon as possible.

Nothing wakes you up like facing your own mortality. Although I have a young brain and attitude, my body must still plow through the stages in life that all of us face. One of those stages is when you truly understand and realize that you are not going to last forever. That sounds funny, but if you had asked me when I was 30, I would have had a very different attitude about my longevity. Back then, it was something in the very distant future, if at all. Those were the days!

Heart disease kills more Americans than anything else out there; 28 percent of deaths each year in the U.S.A. are heart related. This even beats cancer or traffic accidents. It's the number one reason for death in the U.S.A., and it's "U.S.A. specific." That is, you won't find it in Europe or Latin America or the Middle East to anywhere near the degree as in the U.S.A. It's an American issue and it's almost an epidemic. Don't tell our enemies. If they only knew, terrorism would cease, and all they would have to do is promote fast food franchises, then wait long enough while all us North Americans would commence to swell up like balloons and die at very young ages if we continue like this.

We all know why, but can't change it easily. Our food is bad... real bad. The nicely packaged things you see in the supermarket are almost universally bad for your body, even the canned products. This isn't news to many of you who study this issue. It has to do with the fact that almost nothing is fresh, and the emphasis is on taste and keeping it longer rather than nutrition. The result is that our food slowly clogs our veins and the "stuff" of American know-how and popularity is slowly killing us.

Studies clearly show this, and in Europe, even the heavy-set Italians, who have survived on pasta all their lives, die with open, unclogged veins. Ours (Americans) are beginning to clog by our mid-30s, according to the studies. I remember when I sat in a restaurant one morning in Munich and my host, Hanna, saw me taking all my pills (up to 20). They are all supplements, anti-oxidants, homocystine boosters, vitamins and minerals, etc. She laughed and said, "How American of you!" I almost lost it, laughing so hard. She was absolutely right!

We Americans are nutritionally hobbled! Europeans don't even really need many of these things that are actually keeping some of the rest of us alive. Their entire food structure is vastly different than ours. If you have gone to Europe and sampled the food, you know exactly what I'm talking about. Fresh, fresh, fresh! Almost nothing is frozen, and there's no chemistry added ever (unless, of course, you are eating at a popular fast food restaurant with a giant "M" out front). It seems our major influence and export to Europe is *unhealthy food!*

Almost everything is organic by nature. Chances are it came from a garden the day before and the first time it got the dirt washed off was in the restaurant sink right before they served it. Also, most meals last hours to cook and consume and are served with wine… a natural blood detoxifier (I take grape seed extract for that).

I visited the doctor, knowing that I would have to face up to my years of bad eating as an engineer gulping down fast food from a local chain blocks from the studio. I ate a 10-minute lunch day after day for all those years so I could get back to my clients. I did this for almost 20 years. Intuitively, I knew I was not in good shape in the heart department. But I was unprepared for the news of how bad.

The MRI wasn't a fun thing. You know, it's really not an invasive physical test. It's true that they have an IV in your arm so they can make your heart race faster with a "stress chemical," but it's not like you're being operated on or anything. It's just "looking" at your body, and there is no pain. However, I found the test to be psychologically invasive. My brain kept telling me they were sliding me into a coffin! Yikes! There isn't much room to wiggle around in that tube; your arms are tied down, and the top of the tube almost touches your nose. It's actually smaller than a coffin, come to think of it! I really had to call on my angels that day. I lasted for more than an hour in that thing peacefully. (Thank you, angels.)My good friend and Kryon team member, Dr. Todd Ovokaitys , was allowed into the tech room with the heart specialist who was looking at the scans as they arrived on the screen. At the same time, the images were being recorded onto a CD, so future analysis could take place. I was so glad Todd was there for a number of reasons, and one of them is for validation (for what's coming up). It's good to have a medical expert as a friend during these times.

I'm going to spare you all the details of the results, since I don't want to give energy to that situation. But it wasn't good. Included was a number of internal issues, as well as enlargement of my heart. There was also a visible "scar" in the back of the heart, indicating that I must have had at least one heart attack recently. What? I didn't remember anything like that and had never gone to a doctor with chest pain. But there it was… proof of it all. My blood pressure wasn't good either. Years of my heart trying to pump through ever constricting veins and arteries had taken its toll. All this was recorded on the CD, which Todd was able to get a copy of for me.

I went on a protocol of active, intravenous chelation under the care of a wonderful, enlightened Southern California doctor. I used a combination of methods that took advantage of what we all know today, and not just what the allopathic folks wanted. Although my heart was weak and damaged, at least I was going to clear out my veins and give it a lot less stress for the rest of my life.

Funny… I have lots of energy. I always wondered why it was that my heart would be a weak link, yet my energy never wavered. I'm the guy who leaps out of the bed in the morning singing songs, instantly awake and bubbly, and a huge irritation to my wife, Patti, who can't believe that someone let Peewee Herman into the bedroom before the sun was all the way up. I have had to "cheer down" a number of times in the morning when I realized it wasn't really helping things much.

So there was a dichotomy going on, where I was not "feeling" what the MRI said was really happening. A "meeting" with my cells helped, but I continued to get an internal answer about my heart that was confusing. My cellular structure wasn't in denial, but it kept "winking" at me. That was odd and I didn't know what it meant. Now I do.

To make this story more compact, I'll jump to the end of 2005. I was scheduled to have a minor hernia operation. Because of my heart issues, I obtained heart specialist who wanted to perform a full check-up on me. So one year later (December 2005), I went in again for tests. This time I did entirely different kinds of tests, including treadmill stress tests, profusion studies and a heart echo sound. This doctor also had the original MRI CD that showed the first test a year earlier.

I'll never forget the meeting with him. After all the tests were done, I arrived the next week into that small medical office room where doctors hum and haw and try to make bad news better. I was not worried and expected good news due to my year of work on myself, but these "get the results" meetings can be stressful. I didn't expect what happened next.

He hummed and hawed all right, but in a different way. He was trying to somehow justify what the MRI of one year ago had indicated against the tests he held in his hand. He said, *"Lee, sometimes our systems are not always as good as we wish them to be. After all, they are only machines..."* I was kind of in a fog. I didn't understand what he was telling me or where he was going. This is a very fine heart doctor whom I trust. He is the top guy in town and I was listening the best I could, but what was he trying to tell me?

What he finally said was that the new tests showed very little was wrong with my heart! In addition, the scar was gone, too. The scar was gone? He reminded me that scars don't heal... they are forever. So the fact that it was not visible in 2005, but very visible in 2004, had to be a malfunction of the MRI somehow. I smiled. I knew better. I had experienced a miracle and was a very happy guy.

What I want to tell you, as a Kryon reader, that is most profound, is that I now know when it happened, and you can share the moment with me this book.

In the last year or so, we have been experiencing healings in our meetings. Sometimes they are physical, often they are spiritual and mental, but the incidence is increasing. During those times, Kryon calls them out, and tells us what is happening in the room. I have become used to it in some ways, but it's always emotional to me to think that someone would leave different than they came.

In this book, there is a channelling done in Sedona, Arizona, toward the end of 2005. I was editing it in October 2006 and getting it ready for the transcription to be published here for you to read, when I read page 118. I stopped. There, in my own words, channelling Kryon, was my own healing! Kryon spoke of a heart being healed, and how that person had no idea of it. It was me! How could I not know? When you get to that page, take a look at other things that are said around it, about potentials and things unseen. I just wanted to share with you and celebrate with you a process that is very real, with validation and 3D proof, and it happened to me. I was actually healed in one of my own channellings, and never knew it until the tests months later.

Now, as you read it, you will know the rest of the story, and can celebrate the miracle along with me.

About This Book

Every channelling presented here is also on the Kryon Website [www.kryon.com]. Two years ago, we wondered if this would diminish the sales or even the desirability of this book. We were surprised to find out that it did not! Many who had read the various channellings on the Website wanted the book anyway, just to have it printed out and in a convenient package with my comments. But mostly we realized that English is only one of 23 languages that will be represented here, and there are few Websites in any language but English. Therefore, the majority of readers (who are non-English) will never have seen any of this information.

In addition, we did something different this time regarding these additional languages. We have given them the text of this book before we published it in English. Therefore, Kryon Book 11 was finished way before it was published in North America in English, which is an unusual move for us. But we wanted to allow the publishing release to be more coordinated... more like a worldwide release than the way it has been in the past. This may help explain to the English speakers as to why the book came out when it did.

Typical of many channellings given over three years, you will see some subjects repeated or revisited. This is typical of any profound teaching, where the core issues are sometimes given more than one time for emphasis.

Enjoy this book. Like all the other books, it is a compilation of my favorite live channels from many different places. Unlike the other books, these channellings have all taken place within a growing fear of what might happen to us as the war rages on, terrorists have their way in the world, and the news outlets pounce upon the bad news and ignore the good. Kryon addresses it all, and gives us hope for the future. You will see many references to the Jews and to Israel and Palestine in my channelling – more than ever before as we approach the end of an age. I have even included three channellings given directly in Israel for the Jews specifically, but all of us in general.

Some have called me "biased" and slanted toward the Jews in these times. My reply is that when Kryon indicated 18 years ago that the main issue of these times would be the very right for the Jews to exist, I knew that this would be my focus. The challenge is therefore with Israel, whatever that means to you. It doesn't mean I've taken sides in a multi-sided, complex issue. It means that I've decided to concentrate where Kryon said to. Yes, I'm biased. I'm biased toward peace on Earth, non-violent solutions, and allowing many cultures and religions to exist side-by-side in peace. That's my vision.

My main question for all of you is this: Are you are going to follow the soothsayers down an old energy path of fear and hate, or strike the light of the Lighthouse you are, and begin to shine it upon an Earth that needs you more than it ever has in Human history?

Blessings to all of you!

Lee Carroll

" 'Kryon, when are you going to give us some new information? Every time we hear you, it's all about the same things. Different words, different parables, different metaphors, different stories, but always the same information.'

I'll make a deal with you, Human Being: When you fully implement what I've been giving you for 16 years, I'll move on to something new. My message is about mastery. And when the masters stand and create the New Jerusalem, I will move on to the next phase. And when that happens, I'll celebrate all of you even more than I do now."

From the Writer

A Message to Lightworkers
in The U.S.A.

Lee Carroll

Online Blog

A Message to Lightworkers in the U.S.A.

by Lee Carroll

The definition of a BLOG is an online diary, a personal, chronological log of thoughts published on a Website. For those who wonder how this name ever came to be, it was shortened from "Web log," a log of comments on a Website. Typically updated daily, blogs often reflect the personality of the author. They have become very popular for political commentary over the past years, and have even impacted and competed with the main editorial pages of many newspapers and TV newscasts. As I have said in the past, the Internet is changing our lives every day.

It was July 25 when I started getting the e-mails. The border between Lebanon and Israel had flared up. Rockets were being fired into Haifa, exactly where I was a few months earlier, and the Jews were responding typically as they have many times... with overwhelming force. They did this, as they have before, because they understand that just on the other side of an imaginary line, there are those who have been training and stocking weapons to eliminate them some day.

No matter what side of the fence you are on with this issue, I admit I'm biased – not toward Israel, but toward the peace process. Those who openly proclaim that the answer to this issue is to "kill them all" are not part of the peace process, but rather part of the problem. The Jews play a very important part in the future of all our lives, according to Kryon, and these things should be studied and examined if you are really going to understand it all and have any wisdom about it.

With this in mind, I believe you owe it to yourself to find out about the last 50 years in Israel, and what happened when the UN gave them their land, and the back and forth disputes and wars that have raged ever since. The Jews have made many mistakes, and some of those have created suffering and sadness. But they are not alone in the mistake department. Civilizations grow, as did ours in the U.S., and this very new, 50-year-old country known as Israel continues to change their minds and develop more wisdom on how to give back disputed lands that were the spoils of wars never declared, all while keeping safety for their citizens at the forefront. Many are convinced they can have a peace process, and many are not. Their volatile government demonstrates this every time they meet.

When you study the past 50 years and the "who did what to whom," the quagmire of the situation becomes clearer. Then, when it all erupts suddenly, as it did recently, you are not surprised or fearful. In fact, many of us actually thought to ourselves, "It's here... what we knew was coming."

The e-mails I got were awful. They told me that the world situation proved to them that Kryon was a hoax, and that war and disaster were obviously upon us... that my cheerful, hopeful attitude was a sham, and that it could no longer be believed. This was the reaction of many – to kill the messenger of good and positive news when the going got tough. Much to my disappointment, fear had grabbed the writers of these e-mails and taken its toll on their logic and faith almost overnight.

Darkness doesn't do that to me anymore because I know how to carry my own light. It doesn't spring up and scare me, either, since I know where it is at all times. It's behind me in the back seat, irritating me through life, but I won't let darkness have me anymore. This is what I teach from Kryon, too, and so when those e-mails came, I was saddened to see such a wave of fear overtake people who should have known better! Instead, they simply gave up when the storm arrived!

So I blogged. It was the first time I allowed my bias to show and my disappointment to be written for all to see. I share it with you in these pages, even if you are reading this years from when it happened. I believe in the potential for peace on Earth and will until my last breath. Kryon tells us that's it's well within our grasp and that it's demanded if we are going to move easily into the 2012 energy of a gentler time. So, here's my blog as published that day.

A Message from Lee Carroll - July 25, 2006

It's an important time in history right now, and those who are watching the international situation absolutely know that it marks a turning point. If you are a Kryon reader, you may recognize that this was predicted 18 years ago in Book One, and was discussed after that in most of the continuing books in the series as well.

Kryon spoke of a "battle to come" that will be the fight between the old and new energy of the planet. In subsequent books, Kryon even mentioned that it would be the definition of "civilization." He called us warriors of the Light, and named us "Lightworkers."

Almost all of the channellings for the last few years have been about this, and about the fact that we should be prepared by changing the vibration of ourselves first, and that this would change the vibration of the planet. He has told us, "Real lighthouses are never built in safe places," and that we are needed right now to balance ourselves to the degree that our light can make a difference. The storm approaches, and we are the front metaphysical line to meet it.

... and now it begins.

My disappointment in all this comes from a small group of New Age people who are making themselves vocal to me, plus the overall reaction of many Christians.

I have received a number of e-mails laden with fear, blasting me and my work, and telling me that there simply can be no way out of this mess, and that peace on Earth is impossible. They go on by saying that the "joy of God" I profess is not possible in our lives, cannot be had, and that hatred and fear are the way of the earth. They have given up.

My reaction to this: "How about a little fire, scarecrow?" In other words, now that the meal is about to be cooked, they somehow are afraid of the kitchen! Obviously, there are many who wish to float through this and light candles and hold crystals and close their eyes and "pray it away." It's not going away unless Lightworkers do their part, and that's work... personal involvement in self-improvement, and work for the planet. If you are paralyzed in fear, then you haven't really "heard" the Kryon message. If you are paralyzed in fear, you become part of the problem of Earth, not the solution.

The Kryon message has always been clear and strong: (1) Create a strong vibration within yourself as practice against what is coming. (2) Learn to put fear behind you, because it will disable you if you don't. (3) Send your light to those places on the earth that need it, and do it often and in groups. (4) Know that you have help from God, and that you are never alone. (5) Peace on Earth is possible in your time, but you will fight the battle with fear first, and with each other second, until you create "the bridge of swords," something that is used both for real battles and ceremonies. (6) Many will have to leave the planet before the battle is over [Kryon Book One].

Lots of metaphors, but how can you miss the fact that there will be a struggle? Part of it now begins and I wish to ask, what are you doing? Are you shaking in fear, or are you on the way up the staircase of the lighthouse to strike your light? Are you complaining that peace on Earth is a myth, or are you watching it begin to happen, through the balancing of humanity and their choices? Do you understand the struggle of light and dark, and what happens to those steeped in darkness when the lights are turned on? Kryon has told us that they will "fight to the death" to have the darkness back. Sounds like a battle to me. This is what happens on an Earth that is vibrating higher, and where the light is beginning to make a difference.

Many Christians are rubbing their hands together in glee... sorry for the death and destruction they see on TV, but expecting the rapture to come any minute. They have completely ignored the fact that Hal Lindsay's book is now fiction [*The Late Great Planet Earth*]. Even *Time* magazine said, in an editorial about his predictions, that they had "passed their 'sell-by' date." In other words, the Armageddon that is so anticipated cannot happen as scripture told us it would. The players are missing, and the timing is simply wrong. What they are seeing is the beginning of a solution, and doesn't have anything to do with the second coming.

Proof? Read these words in 20 years and tell me if the rapture happened. It didn't, and won't. We changed that collectively at the Harmonic Convergence in 1987. We are collectively charged with creating the New Jerusalem and I believe that's what will happen.

In Jerusalem in 2005, Kryon told an audience that their solutions may actually eventually come from their enemies! What could that mean? I don't know. Long ago, Israel realized that they would have to make concessions to those who feel their land was displaced... right or wrong. It has been a unilateral, national policy that has been growing for more than six years and through three prime ministers. In the year 2000, Prime Minister Barak actually offered the Palestinians a shared sovereignty over Jerusalem itself – but it was not accepted. I say this only to point out that the issues between the Jews and their immediate neighbors are no longer the big issue, and compromise is on the table and ready for action.

The big issue is the right of the nation of Israel to exist. Kryon told us that this was the core, metaphysically, for the "chosen people" of Earth. Even now, they continue to be a target of complete elimination. They have been enslaved by the Egyptians, the Romans and the

Nazis, and now verbalized yet again in modern times by Iran. [Kryon has explained why this is in many channellings since the Jews are the "pure karmic" group of the planet and hold the power of the Akash. Anyone who eliminates them will gain this position.] This may sound odd, too esoteric and unprovable, but what other group on the planet has had these attributes for 4,000 years? Show me and I'll reconsider my statement.

The Potential

This flare-up in the Middle East will create many issues. First, they WILL stop fighting eventually [sorry, Christians]. After that, many will finally realize that in order for the earth to do anything at all about peace, Israel will have to be allowed to exist. Those who don't think so will slowly be identified as the actual problem. This has been the "big issue" all along, and Kryon indicated it when he said, "As go the Jews, goes the earth," 18 years ago. The passion of Kryon has always asked us to put our efforts into Jerusalem, and not anywhere else, and "everything else will follow" [meaning the solutions for peace].

Potential: Out of this, the United Nations will get a new leader who will be more effective in putting some "teeth" into the terrorist resolutions that have been unanimously passed by the delegates of that world organization. If this had been done earlier, the battle you see today would not be happening. The UN has a place in all this, and can eventually be a major player in the resolution, the way the creators of that institution had envisioned many years ago.

This battle we are seeing right now has the potential to bring understanding of the actual situation to the world, and to begin to help sort out the real issues for those who have been sitting on the fence.

Who likes war? I don't. But if you thought that all this "foreign stuff" would slowly go away with time as you sit serenely in the U.S.A. with peace and plenty around you, then you haven't understood anything Kryon has said. Kryon told us that the very reason you are in this great land is to allow "the strength of the Lightworker, who is not in survival mode, to shine greatly." In other words, it's your responsibility to send light to Palestine [as Kryon calls the whole Israel/Palestinian area] in ways that nobody else can. Did you ever think of that?

Those in other countries often ask me, "Why do you in the U.S.A. have so much metaphysics... so much information, and so many channellers?" I'll tell you: It's not an accident. It's a mandate that this is where the work must come from to help those who are in survival mode... the ones you can see nightly in the rubble on TV. We are the ones who have most of the answers! Now, let's manifest Light so that others in darker areas can "see" the treasures that have heretofore been in the dark – like wisdom, solution and appropriate action.

If you are offended by this blog, I'm sorry. It's not my intention to offend anyone. Even my Christian friends [of whom I still have two], understand where I stand. I wish they didn't hang their hats on problems in the Middle East and gear up the "rapture wagon" every time there is a conflict. They are so strong at praying, and we need them to concentrate on sending light, too... the Christ light. It would help so much. Instead, they are concentrated on "getting out of here." They are going to be disappointed.

So if you are prone to sending me an e-mail telling me how my positive attitude and joyful continence are badly timed, don't bother. I'm busy climbing the Lighthouse stairs.

Lee Carroll

The Seven Great Human Illusions of God

Channelled in Edmonton, Alberta
Canada
July 2006

Chapter One

The Seven Great Human Illusions of God

Edmonton, Alberta, Canada – July 2006

Chapter One

Well, there's probably something here to offend just about everyone, as I often say. This is about the way we see God. Between giving you concepts that are far, far different than you were taught, and being seemingly disrespectful with metaphors, this is certain to get some folks going.

The truth is that God is so far beyond anything Human that to compare God consciousness with Human Beings is absurd. Having God communicate with us on the same level is like asking your dog to go out and check the circuit breaker. Yet we continue to believe God thinks like we do, looks like us, and that Heaven is just like Earth, only with no problems. I won't even go into the 72 virgins thing… that's really over the top. Get used to it. Earth was created for humans, and the Universe was created for God.

Greetings, dear ones, I am Kryon of Magnetic Service. It's a precious time here, tonight. I want my partner settled down, because the emotion of this moment might be too much for him, for there will be a message. But beyond that, there's something waiting to happen that may seem miraculous to some of you. There are those here who will leave differently than they came and all of the preparation of the day is centered on this moment.

So the message is secondary to the healing that is going to occur tonight. Perhaps you're the one. But more than one has the potential. Reader, it's no accident you also walked into our room, for everything we are saying in the "now" refers to you, also. There are those hearing and reading who need a healing of the heart, and I don't mean physically. I know who's here in this room or listeners and readers. I know who you are. You know me and the duality separates us so completely in your life that you cannot see your sister as she sits here. Partners, we are, in this test called Earth. I see you coming and I see you leaving. And I see the duality that separates us… especially those who say, *"This cannot be happening."* The energy is impacting into this place and your allowance of it is strong and the entourage feels it as they pour in here and stand among you.

There are those here who need, and will receive, a complete healing of heart. That's why you came and you don't have to tell us the circumstances around anything in your life, because we've walked it with you, every day of it. We've been there for every single step of the way. We know where it hurts. We know why it hurts, and you're going to stand from this place and feel the peace of Spirit and recognize the mastery in your veins. I'll say it again. You'll walk out of this space with a different perspective. Strong. Peaceful. Wise. Understanding. Then you may see certain individuals differently than you ever saw them before. I guarantee it. You'll see them as enablers, enabling you to move from where you are – and you know who I'm talking to, don't you?

Then there's the one who actually came for the physical healing. Oh, dear one, do you think that's really impossible? You don't have to wait until the end, you know, you can have it right now. What is your reality and your truth about these things? Let me tell you about DNA. There are those who'd say, *"Well, we ought to be able to see evolution in DNA."* You're right. If you could really *see* DNA, you could! But you only see one-twelfth of it. You don't even see that much, because even in the one layer you study, you don't know what's going on. There has been a profound change in

Human DNA over the years, even in the last 10, but not in the 3D chemistry. Instead it's in the seemingly random characters of the pointers to the non-protein encoded parts. What changes, therefore, is the relationship of the 3D layer to the other 11 layers that I have given you. Interactive, they are, and as you make decisions, they change and they shift.

What do you think happens to the *ascension layer* and the *communication layer* when you open that door of pure intent? [Speaking of the DNA interdimensional layers] I'll tell you – they change colors. That's what some of you are going to do tonight – change colors for good. And then, indeed, there will be what we call the seeds planted that can be used any time you want to, for illumination and information. There is energy here in this place that will help those in just a few weeks. There are entities here... all invisible. Some of them are going to make themselves known to certain individuals who are in the room. Some of you will smell them. Don't be surprised if their fragrance smells like the roses or the violets, the land, the flowers. Sometimes some of you will be aware of an aroma you didn't expect, that of those you loved and lost and you'll know they're here. And they are! You see, that's what happens when you give permission to do this [place yourself into meditation in front of Kryon]. You put yourself in a quantum state for just a little while, when we can talk about these things of the planet, and share the love of God for a few moments.

I'm going to give you some no-nonsense information today. It's always loving, but some see it as criticism. Instead, it's truth and exposé. I'll give you information that to some may seem like it's a review. It isn't. It's the only time we've ever put these things together like this for you. You've got to hear it, for you'll need it soon. It's time you moved off of the mythology and into the reality of your mastery. The earth calls, and times are approaching in which you will need to know the difference between God and the Human stories of God.

This particular channelling is long overdue, but now you've reached a place where there can be even more plain talk. I'm going to give you seven attributes and we're going to identify them as "The Seven Great Human Illusions of God." It's hard to know where to start, so in honor of the interdimensional, I'll start with seven. [Laughter] The seventh one is the sacred one, you know? After it, then I'll back up and start with number one... just to make you feel linear. [More laughter] This seventh, which would normally be the end, is instead the beginning and will represent the overall view of God... the greatest Human illusion of all.

The Overview of God

Humans only have one model of consciousness to compare anything to. One model – themselves. So Humans considering God naturally feel that God must have Human attributes. Many of you don't even know what I'm talking about. You see, when you are at the top of the evolved ladder of consciousness and creation, there is only you to evaluate anything to. Your knowledge has always limited your imagination, for everything you think about references the great Human "self." In addition, scripture seems to indicate that you were "made in His image," so now you also have what you feel is credibility that, indeed, God has Human form, and that since there is nothing higher that you can see, it must be the highest in the Universe.

I'm going to give you a cute little metaphor to ponder. Imagine for a moment that Earth was made up of all dogs. No humans, just dogs. And imagine that dogs had your intelligence. Evolution had somehow gone differently, and intelligent dogs now ran the world, just like you do now. They also have their problems, just like you do now. And dogs, just like you, have their own spiritual thoughts on what God must be like, and naturally they have religion. They pray and ponder, and have intellectual ideas, just like you.

Now, if I could take you to this metaphoric place where all of these intelligent dogs lived in their civilization, let me tell you what their religion would look like. First of all, God would be a dog! [Laughter] And each breed of dog would have a photo of God represented as their own breed, of course. All of the angels would be dogs with wings, and one of the things they would do would be to constantly smell each other! [Laughter] How far do you want me to go with this? You know what's coming next, don't you? Society's proof that God is a dog is that the very name of their kind, spelled backwards, is God! Shall I continue? And you know, even though it's funny, that I'm right.

Do you understand? It's the only consciousness they have. It's the only thing they know. The way they are is what God becomes in their mind. They cannot think past the highest consciousness they understand, which is themselves. Humans do that, and they place upon God all of the attributes of humanity. Some of the basic things that you think are intuitive in the Universe are not! It's just *you* thinking that everything is like *you*. Human attributes only belong where you exist. Oh, you might say they belong also to the dimension you're in, including some of the planets that are in your dimension, and you'd be right. But they don't apply to God. The very word *Universe* to you means *what you can see with your telescopes.* And again, we say, that's very 3D of you! The word *Universe* to us means God! There is so much more than Humans in the real Universe.

"What about 'made in his image,'" you might ask. *"Doesn't this indicate that we must look like God?"* Step out of your own enclosure

for a moment and think about it. If you had the power to bestow your "image" on a group of ants in a far away place, would you suddenly look like an ant? No. Instead, you bestow upon them the light you carry and your spiritual intellect. Your interdimensional divine "image" is not what you see in the mirror, but far beyond that. It's an interdimensional image that can easily fit into an ant, if you understand about such things. Now come back and realize that everything we have been teaching all day long [during the lecture series] shouts that God is *in you.* It doesn't mean that God looks like a Human. The image of God is within the mastery that is in the Human DNA.

So, attribute number seven, therefore, is the propensity for Human Beings to see God in Human form, but it goes way beyond that... way beyond that. You see God as doing what Humans do, enjoying what Humans enjoy, fearing like Humans, going through drama like Humans, and also having all the Human evolutionary residuals. Did you every realize that? Read on.

War

Number One. You want to assign war to God. Did you know that? All your mythology has it. These particular gods went to war with these other gods, etc. Many have said, *"There must have been wars in Heaven, in order to have only one God – the one who won over the others! After all, just look at humanity: To have one peace, we have to regularly slaughter each other. Since we are like God, and in his image, this must be universal."* Now, of course, in your modern religion, you say that you have no mythology. That's not so. What you think is sacred and true is very much mythology, but you don't think of it that way. Your story of Heaven and Hell is something that came right from duality and the Human mind. Can you imagine a battlefield with a bunch of dead angels? We can't! And where do angels go when they die? [Laughter] Many will say, *"Scripture says that there was war between the angels."* And we say, "Scripture says?" Did God write that or did a Human? Humans put upon God all their own traits to make things make sense to them.

The first myth is that there was a giant struggle on our side of the veil, which created war. That's a description of duality, dear Human, not God. You are looking in the mirror and placing your own limits on an energy that encompasses the *all of everything*, and the creation of everything. But you have inserted it in your religion anyway, so you would feel somehow close to the way everything works and relate to it better.

There was no such thing as a war between angels and there never will be. You see, that story reeks with Human struggle. Intuitive and at the cellular level, it is, and so you build it into every expression of being, even placing it on the highest of the high. There are stories in your mythology of how God got to be God, as though we had to climb some mountain of victory and war in order to become what we are. That would be like all the dogs deciding that God must have dug under many fences and warded off legions of fleas to become God.

No, dear Human Beings, there were no wars – no wars between angels, or even near angels. The love of God is stable and it is pure. It always was and it always will be and you know that inside. It's who you are when you're not here and the system that is here on this side of the veil had no war. There would be those who will argue with this immediately, *"Well, that's not what I was told."* And I will say to you in all love, "Told by whom… God? Or a Human?" Use your divine intuition. Does it really make sense, or does it simply appeal to that Human part that loves a good story? Even the greatest spiritual men used the metaphor of only what they understood to interpret the grandest of the creation stories that you needed to hear. Not everything is what you think it means. That was number one.

Good and Evil

The one that is so difficult for you to understand and is so sad for us is where you say there has to be *black and white everywhere*. There's got to be good and evil. *"Kryon, you mean there isn't good and evil on the other side of the veil?"* And I will tell you, just like there was no duality or war, there is no struggle on our side of the veil.

Listen: Your mythology says that evil is not your own, and that you have it because there was "trouble in heaven." One of the angels, it seems, just couldn't get it right and fell from grace. His name was Lucifer and he, of course, is responsible for trying to get your soul and making you do bad things. It is the devil that creates the difficulties on Earth, the mythology goes, and it is the test of Earth to defeat this bad angel. And dear ones, I just gave you your most modern religious doctrine, not the ones practiced hundreds of years ago. As odd as it sounds, this mythology continues and continues.

Good and evil. This concept belongs to Human Beings because it is so much a part of the test of your own duality and existence. Oh, it belongs to others in the Universe, too, but not God. *"Wait a minute, Kryon, do you mean there's no light and dark on the other side of the veil?"* That's exactly what I'm telling you, at least not the way you see it. There is no light and dark on our side of the veil that creates struggle and imbalance. The light and dark on our side of the veil is simply energy that moves around. Some need to argue and say, *"Well, there has to be! It's part of everything."* It isn't. It's only part of *your* everything. And I will tell you it is just as absurd as the angels smelling each other. That's not God.

The duality represents free choice. That's the duality set-up of Humanism within planet Earth, and has nothing whatsoever to do with what you call God. There is no evil angel who wants your soul. We told you over and over that the darkest of the dark is the power of the Human Being, who's decided that the dark is what they wish to create. We have said it before, that you are masters at energy and you can go to the light or go to the dark and make either of them powerful. The ones who chose light have an edge, however, because they are then using the "image of God" in their lives. They can create the lightest of the light, the ascension status, and represent the one who has chosen the pathway of sacredness and unity.

Many Humans laugh at this and say, *"Well, Kryon, or whoever you are, I don't agree with you, for you have not seen what I and others have seen. We've seen demon possession."* No, you haven't. You've seen the energy of Human dark possession, posing as the darkest and most fearful thing you can imagine, which is demons. Fear will do that to you, and many will see the same thing and report many truths instead of seeing the real energy. In the case of the occult, it is the Human who is fully in control of all the darkness, conjuring up the worst of the worst for you to wallow in and believe in. That's all about the Human. How does it feel to be so deceived? And when you are, you say, *"It was the devil."* No. It's the Human who has taken power to a very deep and low level. Look at your history, or what's going on in some dark places on the planet. You won't find the devil there. Instead, you will find evil within the free choice of Humans who are making it work for them. This is what the duality test is all about right now on Earth.

And so, dear Human Beings, I am telling you yet again that free choice is the key. I'll also say to you that my very existence in this room is because there is more light than dark on this planet, believe it or not. It is the reason you are here at all. It is the reason you did not have your Armageddon, and won't. It is the reason for the 11:11 energy [the Harmonic Convergence]. Celebrate the fact that this planet is beginning to illuminate. There are more of those holding the light than not. There are thousands who want to hold the light, they just don't know how, yet they are awakening inside. This awakening is not yet representative of the leaders of the planet or of your governments. I'm talking about the people of Earth, not what you see on the news, which is all about a whole different generation.

There is an awakening going on. Indeed, leadership will change and show that awakening. It's about illumination. We'll say it again. Light is active and dark is passive. If you have a dark room and light appears it in, it illuminates the whole room, does it not? Darkness goes away and can't continue in the light. If, instead, you have a light room and darkness walks in, nothing happens at all. What does that tell you about your light and abilities? Do not be afraid of those who are dark. You carry an energy that is very strong, yet you don't even have to think about it – ever!

There are so many who fear those who are dark, who fear the dark energy they carry, and they say, *"Well, I have to protect myself."* No, you don't! You are your own protection. Just shine your light with the love of God. That's your protection. They can't touch you. They can't touch you! This battle I told you about 18 years ago is here and you're fighting it. And it is, indeed, a battle between a dark and a light energy on Earth and it's called civilization. Duality is the reason there is a battle at all, and you're in the heart of it and many of you know it. It doesn't feel very comfortable to you either.

I tell you that there are angels in this room. All of you, when you're not here, are angelic beings. We have said that over and over. We've heard the arguments from the intellectuals in your midst who would say, *"Aha, how can a Humanized angel ever become so dark that they seem like the devil?"* And we remind you yet again that this is what you made up to explain for yourselves when you had an angel fall from grace named Lucifer. It is the metaphor of a Human Being who falls from their mastery with choice. So much of your mythology is about *you*! Yet you say it's about God. It is not. That was number two.

Timing

Number three. Timing. You apply Human 3D timing to the timing of God. *"Dear God,"* you say, *"I've got to pay the rent in three days and I don't have the money. Would you help me with this, please?"* The Human brain says, *"Nothing will happen in three days. That's way too short of a time."* And then it doesn't! Yet again, you scramble, don't you? Blessed is the Human Being who understands that if they've already made up their minds what can and cannot be done, then they have sealed it, have they not? Your mastery in your own veins is the catalyst for the miracles you're asking for, and if you don't believe them, they won't happen. Blessed is the Human who understands that God's timing is where *forever equals a minute.*

It's almost like God can stop everything and have universal committee meetings about your rent for 100 years. Your three days is *our* forever. That's how we see it. This is how it works. This is how synchronicity works, and the complexity would astonish you. When you seem to meet those you're *supposed to meet* in places you didn't expect to meet anybody, you can't then think you were there by accident. Did that happen today to anyone here? [Kryon smile, since it did] You put Human timing on God, and you make up your mind what cannot be accomplished because there is simply no *time to do it*. Now, maybe it's time to revise that? The next time you ask for impossible timing, I want you to understand some other things about timing. You may go past the point at which you say your prayer needed to be answered. In other words, you gave up and disengaged the prayer.

You see, the solution didn't happen, and the prayer didn't get answered, at least not the way you envisioned. You were asking for your rent to be paid, but Spirit was in the process of giving you abundance for the rest of your life! But you just disengaged the whole idea. What you're asking for when you are asking for the rent to be paid is not what the words mean. I will tell you what your soul is asking for – it's saying, *"Dear Spirit, I don't want to worry about this anymore."* That's what you're asking for and we know it and the angels around you know it. *"Dear Spirit, I want sustenance so I don't have to worry about this every month."* That's the definition of abundance, isn't it? The definition of abundance is not money in the bank. But it is so that your needs are met day by day. The abundance of Spirit will always be there. It may come at what you think is the last minute from the storehouse of God, or it may come in the abundance of peace around how you feel, even if you didn't make it! Ever think of that? That's abundance. I know who's here. I know what your fears are – so many of them are based on these assumptions and illusions of humanity and God. Throw away that clock when it comes to God and expect the miracles that are there for you! That was number three.

Reward and Punishment

Number four is reward and punishment. We have said it before, and we'll talk about it again. *"There has to be reward and punishment in Heaven,"* they say. *"After all, it's fair and it's correct... just like God. If you're good, you get a reward. If you're bad, you get punished."* Well, it's not that way on my side of the veil, dear ones. You won't find that in Heaven. You won't find that in any angelic realm, either. There is no reward and punishment. It's an entire different *culture*. It's divine culture and it doesn't work in duality like yours. Yet you put reward and punishment right on God, don't you? If you're good, you go to Heaven. If you're bad, you don't. One has you spending time in eternity with the Heavenly Father – what an image! The other has you spending time with the fallen angel, Lucifer. What a vision! It's not like that, of course. First of all, in an interdimensional place that has no time, what would "time in Heaven" be like? Do you see how this fits so nicely with your version of punishment and reward? An eternity in Hell might be three minutes to me!

We've told you again and again that this is simply not the way it works with God. Yet there are those intellectuals who would say, *"Well, there has to be a system like that. How would you control anything?"* And we say to you, that's *your* system. That's *your* duality, so control it. That's not what God's system is, however. We don't need to control angels or Humans on my side of the veil. *"You mean to tell me, Kryon, that a Human can come into this planet and become the most evil Human that ever exists and kill millions of people in genocide and then when he gets to the other side of the veil, there's no punishment?"* And I'll say it again. That's exactly right. Because you don't understand the test. You are free to do whatever you choose while you're here in duality. Don't assume, however, that on the other side of the veil that system is extended. It's only for you, here.

Again, we say that this was clearly given to you even in the scriptures you have in the parable of the Prodigal Son. That parable represented the father, who is God, sending two sons into the world, which is sending two angels to be Humans on Earth. One does everything right, one does everything wrong; one does everything good, one does everything bad – very black and white for you. Yet your scriptures tell you that when they come back across the veil, they get the same party! What does that tell you? Let me review it. It means that the test of Earth is not carried back to where you came from. You don't carry the test back here, either.

It's about the test of the planet and it's about Human duality. It's why you're here and what you do with the planet while you're here. It doesn't mean it's what's on the other side of the veil. Oh, if I could disengage this in your mind. The perceptions of humanity are that you must somehow please God with your goodness. I want to tell you, angels, you've already pleased God because you're here! It's the reason there's going to be healings here today because you're sitting here – because you are waking up to who you are and you are finding the divinity inside. You've already pleased God! You don't have to think about being fearful or worry about what you might do to displease God because of some kind of a super reward and punishment system on the other side of the veil. There isn't one. It's hard enough while you're here, isn't it? If you ever knew how much you were loved, you would never think for a moment there'd be punishment on the other side of the veil, even for the darkest among you. Yet your major religions are all based around this feature. A billion of you feel that you arrived "dirty," already broken and carrying the burden of humanity's darkest deeds. Then, if you join and perform certain rituals and beliefs, you can overcome this horrible fate. In the process, those who never find out about how it works go to Hell! Therefore, God loves you so much that the majority of you will burn in Hell. Does this make any spiritual sense to you? It's time to understand how Human this concept is.

If you are going to accomplish something and please anyone, then please the divinity that you came with. Seek peace on Earth and see yourself as an instrument of the divine intelligence that created you. Claim the angel inside; stand up and claim that you are ready to be the Lighthouse you came to be in a trying and difficult time. It's time to drop all the energy of divine punishment and reward, for it harbors feelings of defeat, depression, an unfulfilled life, openness to control by others, and a fearful countenance... some religion, huh? You need a religion? Then seek one that amplifies the power of the Human spirit and teaches that you are a divine piece of the God Universe. Blessed are those who gather together and celebrate the power of the love of God within the Human Being, and all that can be accomplished for the planet.

Work and Accomplishment

We have yet another story of Wo for you. Now Wo is not a male or a female, as we have said before. Wo is a wo-man. So Wo can be either gender in your mind, but we'll call him a "he" because my partner is a he. You realize that in your languages everything is gendered, don't you? English, the language that my partner speaks, is the least-gendered language on the planet. Almost all of the other languages spoken on Earth must have every object be masculine or feminine. You're consumed with it. It's not that way on the other side of the veil, dear Human Beings. There's no gender on my side of the veil. Get used to it!

This is number five and it's about Wo, who asked for ascension status. He sat before Spirit and indicated that he wanted ascension status. *"I have pure intent,"* he said. *"May I begin the process?"* And God saw the purity and said, *"YES!"* The angels were excited.

Then Wo, on his own, examined what to do next. He stood from that meeting and said, *"I've got it! Now, what I will do is work hard in order to climb this ascension mountain, because I know that an ascension energy is the goal and I'm going to climb this mountain to get there. I know what to do. I've got these steps over here, and I'm going to do this and this, for it is the way of it. I'm on my way to ascension."*

So Wo started climbing the mountain, and climb he did, for three years. He went here and he went there; he attended classes; he read books; he fasted; he prayed; he meditated; and he followed the many steps that he felt were leading him to the top. Oh, he slipped a few times, bruised his elbow, hurt his toe. [Kryon smile] But he got right up and started again. *"I can do this,"* Wo would mutter to himself. *"I know I can get to the top since Spirit said I could have ascension. I'll get to the top!"* And he did.

There he stood, at the top of the mountain, and claimed his ascension status and it was beautiful. *"Oh, I feel peaceful. I know this is the beginning of a better life,"* he said, *"and I know I have a lot to learn, but this is the first step and I've worked hard to get to it and it took years!"*

Wo was congratulating himself when he happened to look over on the back side of the mountain and he gasped in horror! There was a ski lift! A real ski lift! And there were people like him on that ski lift. They were all coming up the mountain one at a time. The total time from the top of the mountain to the bottom of the mountain was three minutes! They were experiencing ascension status!

Wo cried, *"It's not fair. It's not fair."*

He went into meditation and said, *"Dear Spirit, it's not fair. Why is it this way? I've spent all that time and all that hard work getting up the mountain. Why didn't you tell me about the ski lift?"*

And Spirit says, *"Wo, you never asked, did you? You took a Human assumption to the maximum and never once examined anything else. You felt you had figured it out, had to work for it, and so you did. It was your choice to make the climb difficult."*

Human Being, let me tell you where the *ski lift* is. Each one of you carries in your DNA the profundity of lifetimes of sacred experience. Shamans, you know who you are in the room. Have you ever wondered, regarding your past lives, who you've been and what you've done? I'll tell you: Those who spend time in a room like this have *been there and done that* [massive experience with hard work on Earth] and carry with them in their Akashic Record all of the mastery and the Shamanship and experience they'll ever need to go into this ascension status.

Do you understand? The "work" is cumulative, and you've already done most of it by the time you ever have the conscious thought to ask to work on yourself spiritually. You don't have to work and you don't have to climb that mountain and it won't take years. Just go to the Akash and open that jar that carries the sacredness in it of your experiences on this planet, and put it upon yourself and walk out as a Shaman. You can do it now if you wish! So for Wo, we say that if he had only looked at the divine instead of the Human way of doing things, he would not have spent three years climbing a mountain that he didn't have to climb.

How many of you feel that you've got to work for it? *"Kryon, I'm not sure I like your message,"* you say. *"We don't have to work for some of these things?"* No, that's not what I said. I'm telling you that you already did! You want to do it again? You want to go through it again? Why use Human logic with a spiritual attribute? Reach in and take your divinity and pull it out of your own experience... one that surpasses almost anything you could dream of. That is, unless you buy into the Human idea that in order to progress spiritually, you have to suffer a bit? Does that sound like God's logic or the ideas of men? Some of you will feel wiser tomorrow because you have given intent for your mastery today.

"Kryon, what is mastery?" I'll tell you what it is, Human Being. It's when you walk around and you're not afraid of life. It's when you're peaceful when others are not. The situations that would cause drama in others do not in you. It's when the world around you is in chaos yet you walk into it and you don't feel chaos. Instead, at some level you feel the wisdom of the ages. You absolutely know it doesn't have to affect you, and it doesn't have to touch you. It's when somebody yells at you and calls you a name and your first reaction is to wonder if they're right! That's mastery. A Human's first reaction is to fight back. A master's first reaction is to check themselves for integrity. Blessed is the Human Being who's asked for that this

night for you're going to start to see a change in your life, and the earth will be a better place because of what you've done.

Love

The last one is number six, since we already covered seven. Remember? I love doing things in circles, since you think in a straight line and it makes you have to adjust. It's good practice.

You think you know about love, don't you? There are many kinds of love. There is Human to Human – the beauty of a simple partnership between Humans. There's nothing like it. It's designed perfectly so that you would enjoy it in its most intimate sacredness. Yet it is painted by some religions as evil, carnal, even though it is one of the most sacred things you do to create precious life between two Human Beings who are in love.

We told you that before. That's just one kind of love. Oh, there's the love of the mother for her children. That's profound, is it not? For the mothers are all ready to give their lives for their children in a heartbeat. Sacrificial, it is; beautiful, it is; but that's not the love of God. I cannot tell you what the love of God is like. I could press it upon you and I could give it to you and I can fill you with it. You would feel the compassion of the ages and would weep... but not because it's heavy. It's a release.

Did you know you're eternal? Do you know that there are answers to every issue you have? Did you know you could leave this room differently than you came? That's the love of God talking to you. Every cell of your body cries for this because when you're not here, you are a piece of this process... a piece of God, you are. That's why every DNA strand has the name of God in Hebrew stamped upon it. Do you think that was an error? [The work of Gregg Braden and *The God Code*]

The love of God is beyond your comprehension. It's what brought you to this room. It's part of the synchronicity that is here, and it's that love of God that your DNA layer nine will respond to and layer six wants to be part of. [Speaking of the new DNA identification that Kryon is teaching] It's beyond anything you can even reach for, since your Human mind cannot grasp it. It is interdimensional and beyond comprehension, and has to simply be trusted. Can you do that? Faith is trusting in the unseen, and it's needed to even begin to imagine the concept of love from the Universal core… an energy that is home to you.

Dear Lightworkers, we are together tonight to help create peace on Earth. We will start the seeds of light that will, indeed, spread from this place and make a difference within the planet. There are so many who feel this is foolish – that visualization and conceptualization can never stop the fighting. They are stuck in 3D and will be the ones to hide when the storm comes. You are in training to instead hold your light tall. We have the young and we have the seniors here. Yet you all have one thing in common on the other side of the veil – there is no age. All of you are ancient and eternal. And I sing your name in light and I will continue to, over and over. Each of you has arrived on purpose to this planet, where you can make the biggest difference you have ever been able to make in all your earthly expressions. If you'll vibrate higher, you're going to have a light that will shine brighter, and that is what will change Human minds and the very dirt of the earth.

The entourage stirs here. It's about time I leave. I'm about ready to say the words, but the entourage is telling me something else. The ones who wanted the healing of the heart have it. They feel it. They know it. And the ones who came for the physical healing – there isn't one, but three. That's what happened here in this room tonight. Perhaps they'll share it with you when it's time and you can leave this place and know it's real.

Blessed are you who leave differently than you came. And that is why you come to a place like this – to sit in the energy of *home*. The entourage pulls away, back through the crack in the veil that they came through. This experience is called channelling. We don't call it that. We don't call it that at all. When it's time to do this, we gather our forces and we ring the bell. And we say, "They're letting us in again! It's time for the reunion." Then we come to see you, and love you yet again with a compassion that goes way beyond anything you've ever experienced. And so it is you've come.

And so it is that when you leave this room, you take a piece of me with you. You didn't expect that, did you? But then, that's always the way it has been. Until I see you again.

And so it is.

Kryon Around The World

Paris,France - 2002

Salzburg, Austria - 2004

How Are You Doing?

Channelled in Newport Beach, California
December 2005

Photos at: www.kryon.com/newport05

Chapter Two

How Are You Doing?
Newport Beach, California
Chapter Two

This channelling was presented at the end of 2005. Much was happening, although we did not yet have the kind of war in the Middle East that presented itself in mid-2006. Still, this kind of channelling is what Kryon is known for... uplifting in the midst of trial. Newport Beach is the "home room" in California for the Kryon work. It was the first place we did a full Kryon seminar, and it continues through all these years. It is held each Christmas season at the beginning of December.

Greetings, dear ones, I am Kryon of Magnetic Service. This is a sweet place, made sweet by the family before me.

Could God really be talking? [Speaking of the message being given] God speaks every time you have a beautiful thought, did you know that? How divine are you? The answer is that there is more divinity in your DNA than not, but you don't know that. All of those invisible layers of DNA that my partner speaks of will have more explanation as time goes on. You deserve to know the whole story, even if it is very esoteric.

Let us speak of your angelic-self – of the mastery inside. There are so many who would question this very premise. They would wish to ask the question, *"If that were so, then why are we even here? What's the deal?"* they would say. *"Kryon, you say we're more angelic than we are Human, yet we have a duality that hides it all. We come and we go and there's so much sorrow – so much pain. This doesn't make sense. We are angelic beings? If so, then what are we doing here?"*

So many Humans stand before me and often say, *"Why me? What can I do to change this dark place? What's it all for?"* It's time to use your intuition. We again ask you, "Are you eternal?" Examine this question and you'll know the answer. Indeed, you are, and you know it intuitively. Look inside. When you've breathed your last breath on this planet, do you think that's all there is? Does it make sense that you would have such a spiritual passion and then suddenly cease to exist in a blink of an eye?

Can you not feel who stands around you now? When physicists tell you about multi-dimensionality, where distance and time are irrelevant, then what is that all that about? What does it mean? Could it be that physics is becoming math-based philosophy? And the answer is that there is much divinity surging through your cellular structure, yet it is hidden until discovered – activated through self-discovery.

Yaw-ee is in the audience! [Speaking of Dr. Todd Ovokaitys, an M.D. researcher who often travels with the Kryon team] Do you know what he's really discovered? He's discovered how to "tickle" the DNA enough to awaken the angelic energy in a certain area. Then it does the work by itself! Did you ever wonder how true spiritual healing is accomplished? Do you ever wonder about the process when you start to engage your own self-healing? Many of you work so hard at it. Some of you screw up your face and you try so hard! You repeat phrases and make interesting gestures. You say, *"I'm going to heal myself, so what words do I use? What energies do I use? What emotions are needed? What shall I do?"* You have no idea.

Go back to basics and just be quiet... know who you are. All you have to do is open the door, and discover that you and God are one

– a divine partnership. Let the angel that you are, who is responding to 11 other layers of DNA, heal just the one that needs it, the one you can see [the Human genome]. It's not that hard. Yet you make it harder than it is. *"It's so profound,"* you often say, *"that it must be accompanied by ritual, worship... perhaps even some sacrifice?"*

Let me tell you something, dear Human: You already made the sacrifice by coming here. Did you think of that? The ritual? It's birth! The mantra? It's I AM THAT I AM. What we are saying is that it's time you discovered who you are and how these things work. There are those who have come for a healing tonight and they didn't even know it as they came in. So we're going to say this: Why don't you give permission to say to yourself, *"It's well with my soul"?*

What condition are you in? What is your situation right now? Do you like it? Some will say, *"No, Kryon, I don't like it. I came here tonight to get out of it. That's why I'm here. I'm going to find some way of getting out of it."* I'll give you the way: Just stand before Spirit and say, *"It is well with my soul."* This is you telling Spirit that all that is within your body is divine and that regardless of your fear and your pain and your suffering, you're saying it's OK. Because you know who you are. And so do we, angel!

Many have said, *"Kryon, it is the holiday season. It is time where we sing about peace on Earth, and good will toward men. But right now, we don't have either! And we are tired; we are afraid. It doesn't look like any of the things that we want and have been visualizing are happening."* Indeed, I wish to address that. Before you leave this room, you'll know how Spirit sees how you're doing and you can compare it to the Human view.

Let me first remind you of the lineage of what has happened on the planet due to your energy. To do this, you've got to go back with me to the year 1987. I remind you of the Harmonic Convergence. It was a beautiful time, the year 1987, and a time specifically targeted where, at a higher level, your Higher-Selves would be asked, "Do you want to go forward with the energy that you have developed for the last 1,000 years, or do you wish to change it and move into another energy entirely? Do you wish a new dispensation, defined as a new energy layer over the planet [a new future]?" All of you said, at a higher level, *"We want to move forward."*

Some might say, *"Well, this is very interesting, but it cannot be proven and we don't know anything about this since it happened at an etheric level."* So we'll say, let what followed after that be your proof, for this is the core of what everything is truly about at the moment. In 1992, many of you celebrated this 1987 energy as the 11:11 energy. All these 11s! You chose the numbers, remember. [Kryon smiles] Now, many of you even see this on your clocks, don't you? [the 11:11 numbers] It's more than coincidence, isn't it? Why would this be? It's a celebration of this new dispensation!

Every time you see that configuration on your clock, dear Human Being, I want you to say, *"Thank you, Spirit."* It is a reminder of who you are, Human Being, and why you are here. If there was ever a reminder of your goal on the planet, it is when you look at the clock *accidentally* and it reads 11:11. Did you ever notice that you didn't look at the clock accidentally and see 11:12 or 11:10? That's because that angel who taps you on the shoulder waits until 11:11 and then says, *"Look now!"* [Laughter] How does that feel to you? It's way out of the chance of reality, isn't it, that you would see it so often?

Eleven, in numerological terms, means "illumination and appropriate spiritual action." This is a master number. [Master numbers are two identical numbers together such as 11, 22, 33, etc.] Not coincidentally, it is also two "ones" next to each other. The number one means "new beginnings." The energy around 11:11 is therefore a master number that means, "the beginning of appropriate illumination on the planet," yet some of you have missed that entirely.

Some of you believe it's the end times and that it's awful. Well, it isn't either one! Oh, I want to take you back again to the wind of birth. You were there. I was there. It was right before you committed to your actual biological Human birth. What a place this is… so awesome a commitment, so beautiful a time. I was there, angel! I saw your face, your energy; I saw the resolve, the commitment… more than commitment. I saw the colors of your passion and desire regarding this planet. I saw you express your love for Gaia! Then you teetered on the edge of being thrust into the planet's energy… accepting humanism and the canal of birth. You knew what was ahead. Think of what you had to go through to arrive at this day – this hour, when this message is being given to you. I was there!

And I want to again remind you that most of you were born during a time of old energy and the year 1987 [meaning before 1987]. And if that's you, that means that you knew full well that when you came into the earth, the energy you would be presented with would be old and stagnant and about to end in 1999 to 2001. All the prophecies said so. All of your scriptures pointed to the Armageddon, to the various things that would end life as you knew it. If you read the scriptures, they told you that the issues would start in Israel… and they did… right on schedule. And I've said this to you before. Why? Why would you come at that time, knowing this? And I'll tell you why. Because you knew that you could change it! And you wonder why you're here? How could you wonder?

Of all of the lifetimes you have ever lived on this planet, this is the one that will make the difference. This is the one you prayed for… to discover who you are and make a difference. And some of you will say, *"It's too late. I have a broken body. I am not up to par to do these things. I'm too old, or I'm too ignorant."* So, do you wish to complain about it or change it? Maybe that's why you sit in the chair right now, Lightworker? Did you see what my partner [Lee] presented today about the scientist who discovered that your DNA actually has a field around it that changes matter? And that when the matter changes, it stays changed? Did you see that? That's power! And you wonder what you're doing here? Start connecting the dots, as my partner says.

Connecting the Dots

Did any of you notice the other numerological events? Did you put it together that the nine is important? It means "completion," you know? You put the nines and the 11s together and they start adding up to things that maybe you didn't realize. The Soviet Union was responsible for part of the prophecy that would bring about the end of the planet. They and the U.S.A. and China all together had a scenario, a game to play, you might say, all centered around the trouble with Israel. And this game goes with names like Warsaw Pact and NATO. It was going to be the war to end wars, and the prophets all saw it. But did you notice that none of that happened? Even with all the prophesy? Because one year after the Harmonic Convergence, the Soviet Union fell over! This monster political system, one of the greatest powers on the planet, just evaporated! And I say to you, go find that in your scripture! You won't. Because in 1987, you turned a corner and changed the reality of this planet metaphysically and physically, and no prophet saw it coming. And again, who is it that did this? It was you.

All manner of things have happened since 1987. Did any of you put together the numerology for the symbol of the division between East and West? A famous wall had to crumble, what you called the Berlin Wall. The date that it was pulled over by both sides was November 9, 1989. The day was 11:9! And if you add 11 plus 9 plus 1989, you'll get 11! It's everywhere, you know? It is the "number of the age." And, believe it or not, it will lead to peace on Earth if you can get out of your disbelief and discover why you are here.

Who would have thought, dear American Human Being, that when you suffered through the horror of what you now call the 9/11 experience, that it would be a focus point of your new energy? And, my dear Human, who among you had the courage to see it and say, *"It is well with my soul"?* Did you dare? We're going to talk more about this.

You're on a track that you have put together, that's going to change the fabric of civilization and everything around it. Some months ago, my partner took me to what you call the United Nations. I spoke and I said these words to them, "What you call the 9/11, which was not in any prophecy, will change two full generations of life on Earth. America was the only country that could do anything about it because they are all powerful, and there is no opposition. This was the plan. " We told them that they may not like the politics of it, and indeed, who here wants death and war? But sometimes these kinds of things are what Spirit uses to create massive change on the planet. There's only one country on Earth who has the ability to stick a big stick in the middle of the Middle East and stir it vigorously, and that's you, and you did. [Speaking to the Americans again]

Oh, we've answered so many questions about the wars and about politics! However, history will show that this one thing alone changed everything, in order to lead up to the energy of 2012. If it had not been for your reaction to 9/11 [the Iraq war], there would have been portions of this planet that would have stayed in the old energy for another 1,000 years! And that's not what you chose when you came here. You are responsible for all these things, even if you don't agree with them, and don't feel you had anything to do with them.

Now, how do you think you're doing? Have you seen your news lately? It doesn't look good, does it? Many have asked the following:

"Kryon, why is there so much more hate today than there was when I was born?"

"Kryon, why is it that we seem to be headed for the abyss and blackness?"

Some of you went through a golden age called the '50s. It was nothing like the energy of today. It was the end of war, and you'd seen enough so you celebrated peace and prosperity. You say, *"There was none of this hate back then."* Well, let me tell you something: It was all there, but there was just no illumination to show it. Suddenly, you get a generation of Lightworkers that strike their light and it exposes the unthinkable, the things that have always been there, but hiding. We also told you before that what you changed was the light quotient on the planet. [The amount of light-to-dark ratio] You didn't create any more hate. It was always there. Instead, you created a situation that demanded a solution for humanity. And that solution is called peace on Earth.

Did you ever think about that? How are you doing? Some would answer, *"We're not doing well, Kryon. We sing about peace on Earth and good will to men. But how can we sing the tunes when we don't have either one? It's getting worse, not better."* That's what we hear from humanity. Now I'm going to give you the rest of the story.

First of all, here is something we said earlier: You have no idea what's going on. There are things "percolating underneath the news" that you will never hear about because it is not going to be reported. *"Where have the heroes gone?"* you might ask. *"And when will we receive them?"* My answer is, soon enough. Can you celebrate the unseen? Can you know that underneath all of the turmoil and all of the hatred you see, there is something else going on that might very well bring about situations that you can't even dream of?

Perhaps the dream is wisdom that goes beyond what anyone has ever seen their lifetime? We told you there would be a battle and there is! Is this news to you? We told you that there would be a battle between the old and the new, and here it is. But many of you are crying, *"Woe is me."* Yet we told you that it's all part of the 11 energy. We told you there would be weather changes. Have you seen any? [Laughter] It can't be a shock. It cannot be a surprise. We told you there would be severe weather; we told you that some of the places that grow your crops wouldn't be able to grow them anymore, and that was 17 years ago.

"Kryon, why would such a thing accompany spiritual growth and lead to peace on Earth? It doesn't seem related." We have been asked this before, and we still say that this is the way God has always done it. Don't you understand that your consciousness affects Gaia? The earth is in shift because of what you have decided for your future. You cannot have a consciousness shift of this quality on the planet and not affect the elements that are here. One cannot be without the other, but you separate them in your perception.

"Well, Kryon, we don't like it." You're not expected to like it because you have a heart that's built to be compassionate. Some of you have said, *"We don't understand the reasons for the terrible hurricane, Katrina. We don't understand the earthquakes that have happened recently."* You won't understand the ones coming up next, either. It's all part of the reaction from Gaia. Some of you have said, *"And what purpose can it serve to have that many souls leave overnight?"* Last year at this time during the holiday season, the earth shifted underneath the ocean in a greater way than in any time in your lifetime. The result created a tsunami. So great was this shift for the planet, that the actual rotation of this planet changed its speed. Did you see this, perhaps, as a spiritual event? Or did you look at the horror and the sorrow and fear, and wonder where God was in all this?

Human Beings have compassion. They're built that way. What possible good could it do to have this horrible event? Your news has said that up to 200,000 individuals lost their lives at that juncture. I will tell you that is incorrect. It's 283,000. That's the real number. But many are crying out and asking *"Why?"* Let me remind you of some questions we have asked before. Do you think death is the end? Is it the horror of horrors? Is it the sorrow beyond sorrows? Or is it a Human transition that the planet needs and plans for? Is it well with your soul over these things?

Oh, you can cry your heart out and you can be as compassionate as you wish. I'm not asking about that. I'm not asking if your heart hurts, because we know the answer to that. I want to know about your soul, angel. Can you get above it all and say, *"This is part of spiritual shift"?* Can you say, *"I would have given what they gave"?* Can you say that, Lightworker? Every single one of those Human Beings had the tsunami potential when they came into the planet. At the wind of birth, I looked in their eyes and I said, "This is what you might do for the planet. There is a potential that you might come and go quickly and be part of an event that history will talk about forever." And they all said, *"We're ready! Let's go and do it!"*

We ask you this, last time: Do you understand what their spiritual sacrifice did for this planet? It created a compassion wave that this earth has never seen before. A compassion wave! What you learned today about Human emotion and DNA [in the seminar] will coordinate with this. I tell you that this compassion energy went into the planet and it stayed there. Did you ever think of that? Did you ever think that something so awful as what you call the tsunami could have been a giant catalyst for peace on Earth? Well, it was, and it is! It's all part of the nine and the 11 energy that you agreed upon. How does that sit with you, dear Human Being? Is it well with your soul? Well, maybe not your heart, but what about your soul? Can you get above it and understand the bigger picture? And again, we say that if you could talk to these now, they're fine! They made the transition and are well. We've said this before. You've got thousands of smiling faces on the other side of the veil. So many of them, by the way, have already returned. Did you know that? So many of them! That is how fast the energy is shifting.

What about the polarization we spoke of? Are you shocked that your politics has changed so greatly? Are you shocked when you watch television and there's so much polarization between opinions – so much yelling, so much hate? Well, do you remember that we told you that this exact thing would happen? Why would that be, you might ask. What is serving the purpose of this? Why would it occur this way... this polarity division? All humanity will be involved before it's over, and at some level everyone will have to make a choice. You cannot have "fence-sitters" any longer. Even those who sit back and say, *"I don't care one way or the other,"* will eventually change, too. Everyone will care when they see the profundity of what is happening. It's about the future of humanity and it's too important to "sit it out."

That's what peace on Earth is about. How are you doing? I'll tell you, Human Beings. You are closer to this goal than you've ever been. It may get worse before it gets better in your perception, in your reality. But if you see that, I challenge you in this holiday season. Can you stand up and say, *"It is well with my soul"?* If you can, that's courage. That's what the soldiers do in battle. They armor themselves. Frightened they are, going to meet the enemy... and we told you there'd be a battle between the old energy and the new energy. We told you that you are the warriors of this new energy and that you carry the light. Some of you are afraid now and some of you are in this battle and some of you don't understand it at all.

The overview? You're winning and you don't even know it. We've had Lightworkers say, *"Take me out of this!"* They only see what 4D shows them. Can you get above it? Can you take on the mantle of the masters who are all here and have returned for this event? I'll ask you some questions that may help your perception. What do you think 1987 and the 11:11 was really about? Did you have any idea that all of the masters on this planet who had shown you their mastery in the various cultures and had said they were coming back at a certain time might be connected to the 11:11?

Celebrate the 11:11! It represents *new beginnings.* The masters have returned! All of them – every single one. They are part of this new energy – part of Gaia – part of the compassion of the planet. I'll tell you that this return was one of the major attributes that took place, yet most of you didn't even know it happened.

There has never been a greater time for you to claim the power that you have as a Lightworker. Do you understand? This is a new age of energy. This dispensation you are in is one that will finally decide about civilization itself... where is it going, and what's going to happen. The spiritual rage we told you about – that you're seeing now – was always there. It has been there for 50 years or more. It was there when many of you were small and only saw beautiful things, yet it was there. The earth hasn't really changed that much. The only thing that has changed is that the Lightworkers came along and exposed the hatred. Why do you think we wash your feet? What kind of a situation exists when we send you into a battle, then cover you with a duality so strong that you don't even know why you're in it? It's called the challenge of Earth, and you all agreed to participate. That's why we wash your feet.

It's only when you start opening that ascension channel [speaking of self-discovery], and you get above it all, that you start to be filled with spiritual purpose. That's when you begin to develop another perception of who you are and what you're doing here. Then you'll say, *"Oh, I see!"* Then, when you take your last breath and suddenly you are with us again, one of the first things you will say to me and the others in the entourage is, *"How did we do?"* And I'll tell you what I say to all of those who are asking me that question even now as they make their transitions. I say, "Bless you, for your light was valuable and it's still on the earth and will stay there. You're making it happen!"

How are you doing? You're winning the battle of the light. But you don't know it. Oh, don't despair. You've got to trust me on this one. There are things being developed that you have given permission for, but that have not shown themselves yet.

And the big one? Have you really put it together yet? The big one? What is the distance in years between 1987 and 2012? It's 25 years. It's the children, dear ones. That's what's percolating under the veil of a challenging time. That's what's being developed. A generation of children are slowly coming of age that will change the face of the earth. They began coming in even before 1987, since the potential was always there that you would make this shift. Permission was given for them all to be of the Indigo vibration [which means children of a new consciousness]. Eventually, up to the year 2012 you will no longer see them as odd, since they will be the majority.

Some have called 2012 the end of time, but it is not. It's the end of an old time, and the beginning of a new time. Twenty-five years – a generation, in your language – is the distance between 1987 and 2012. This is designed for the children. So many have been afraid of 2012, yet it is seemingly around the corner. What's going on? What will the children do? Why are they so different? Why did we channel this to you many years ago? We told you that there would be new children that are very different on this planet and who have a consciousness that is so different that it would challenge parenting and schooling worldwide. Why would this be the case? Why would you have allowed it?

The answer is spiritual evolution. You are seeing it before your eyes, yet the "children experts" all deny it. What are these new children here for? I will tell you, dear Human Being. They're here to facilitate peace on Earth. Did you put this together yet? Why would we give you a new kind of spiritual Human Being if you were headed for extinction and termination? How are you doing? Spectacular! That's how you're doing. In the trenches of warfare, it's hard to tell a soldier he is winning, as the bombs are bursting around him. In your case, the bombs that burst around you are your media and your news, and this four-dimensional reality that you stick to and call your own. You can't see the other dimensions, can't see beyond your own, can't see the colors, can't see the grandness, or the hand of the love of God that comes and stirs these things.

We told you that eventually there would be created a *bridge of swords.* How many of you can remember these words, "a bridge of swords," that we spoke of so long ago? I want you to remember this, because we're going to tell you what it represents. *"It sounds like war, Kryon. You said there would be a bridge of swords. You said that the energies would pull apart and the chasm would open and the bridge of swords would be created between the two energies."* Indeed, it sounds like war, doesn't it?

There's that "sword" word again. It's a weapon, isn't it? No. It's a metaphor and I will give you what it means. This was prophecy that we gave to you so many years ago and now we explain it yet again for those of you who need to hear it, so you'll know how you're really doing. The bridge of swords is what we called it. How many of you have attended a union, which you call a wedding, in a situation where warriors get married to their brides? How do they celebrate this union? Their friends take the swords of battle and they cross them in the air. Then these "unioned" individuals walk under the swords, like a bridge above them. Do you understand what

I'm telling you? It's not a war at all, and those swords are not being used in battle. They're being used in celebration of a union between the old and the new... and that is called the New Jerusalem. It's a phrase that means peace on Earth. The bridge of swords is here, and it's being assembled, yet you can't see it and your news media won't report it. Why? Because they don't want to lose your interest! Because it's good news. But eventually you'll see it, too.

So, where is your heart, Lightworker? Is it in despair? Do you like what your country is doing or not? It doesn't matter at the level we are speaking of. What matters instead is this: Can you say at a higher level, *"I understand the appropriateness of all things as we march toward the bridge of swords"?* More and more humanity every day is beginning to join this battle with an energy that is commensurate with this philosophy – and what they want to see is a peaceful civilization on the planet, and they're going to give their energies toward this. This is the bridge of swords.

How are you doing? I would love to wash your feet, right now, even in these closing moments. I want you to go from this place and remember the words given tonight. It is well here! On target, warrior! We have told you so many times in sweet moments like this just how much you mean to us.

You want to know what's going on on Earth? You want to really know what's going on here? I'll tell you. This battle that you are fighting and the energies from it are going to be applied to a much larger situation in the future. When you're not here [when you are on the other side of the veil], you know what that scenario is. It is one of the biggest secrets of the Universe, kept from a Human Being. It's never uttered. The actual name of it is never known by you, yet it is the biggest subject of all of us. It is not in your psyche, your consciousness, not even hidden in your DNA. The information is "protected" from your thoughts. Yet when you come to the other side of the veil, it has a grand name, and that's all you talk about!

What happens on this planet will change something far larger. It's part of a grander plan, and it's something you all set up along with us. It's meaningful. It's spiritual. It's beautiful, and up until 1987, we thought the end of the test would be at hand. You were finished and there would be no more Earth. But none of your biblical prophecy happened, did it? This old prophecy falls on the floor, doesn't it? It's no longer valid. The time has passed for its manifestation, and even the players are missing, politically, that would have created it. And here you are, creating a new future, yet you don't necessarily see what we see.

How many of you can celebrate? Why not celebrate your cellular structure? How many of you can stand and say, *"Not only am I eternal, but I'm here at the right place, at the right time."* Not many of you yet are willing to see this. Some of you say, *"I'm so insignificant. Nobody evens knows me. I haven't written any books, I'm not featured in any magazines. Nobody knows me."* And I will say, dear Human Being, I know you! And the entourage who is here knows you! You are as powerful as anyone who is known. Your light is just as bright as any in the room here. Do not apply Human cultural perceptions and judgments regarding your strength, master. Angel, Human Being, that's why we wash your feet. So much is hidden, yet so much has been accomplished!

We are enamored by the Human Being who would go through this willingly for something that is far larger than themselves, and has to do with love. Peace on Earth? Not only possible, but entirely probable. You are changing the planet in ways that you cannot see, but we can.

Watch for two things. The timing of these I cannot give you, for this is up to you and your free choice. Call this a prophecy if you wish, but it will only happen if you follow the energy of potential that is here as we speak. Watch for two things politically on this planet. (1) Soft revolutions. You can define this term any way you wish. Soft revolutions in two important countries. One is China. One is Iran. And they are going to trigger a change of consciousness – against all odds – an alignment for peace with the rest of you. Watch for it. It's inevitable *if you stay on this track.* (2) Then there's the big one. A change in the Middle East, in Israel, right in Jerusalem. Watch for this. The unexpected.* (3) Eventually, you'll see a younger person arise who we have spoken of before [in Israel], although not soon.

It's happening, but in a way that is hidden for now. Can you celebrate with me, even though you can't yet see it? That's what's really happening. You can't see it on your news, but it's there. Can you say, *"It's well with my soul"?*

Finally, we say to you this night that every single one of you is designed to stay here. You've got mastery in your veins ready to be activated. It has to be free choice, you know? You've got to do it yourself. No healer in the room is going to create intent for you. That's the fairness of the test. Each Human must do it for themselves. So, what is your decision? Will you start this inner search? Will you try to see beyond the 4D perception of what you have been told?

Take this information and apply the mantle of it to your spiritual-selves this night. Let those in the entourage pour in here now, even to a greater extent than before. Let them press upon your shoulders

* This was written right before Ariel Sharon became sick, Hamas won the Palestinian election, and the Israel/Lebanon war of 2006 broke out.

and make themselves known to you. Some of you might be able to see the colors now. [Speaking of Lee's invitation to see the colors around him] Some of you might even smell the existence of the extra entities here. Let the miracles begin. If that's what it's going to take in your life for you to believe it, then let it happen, so that you can get on with what you came for. Let the healings begin, so you may remain here in a healthy body... creating the New Jerusalem. That's what Lightworkers do. That's why you're here, and that is the truth. What we told you many years ago has not changed. Our message remains the same, and it exalts the Human Being.

And so it is.

Kryon Around the World

Jan Tober on stage- Hamburg, Germany - 2002

Bern, Switzerland - 2003

Undefining the Spiritual Path

Channelled in Sedona, Arizona
October 2005

Photos at: www.kryon.com/sedona05

Chapter Three

Undefining the Spiritual Path

Sedona, Arizona

Chapter Three

So, what's with this title? How can we "undefined" anything? That isn't even a real word in English. Shouldn't this have been "*Redefining* the Spiritual Path?" The answer is that with some issues, Kryon wishes we could forget everything we were taught and come at it again with no bias. We can't, since we don't have the ability to "un-know" anything. Therefore, the emphasis is to try to "undo" what we were taught, not redefine it. Then we won't have to deal with multiple definitions, but rather just one... the intuitive one that is the sacred one.

Greetings, dear ones, I AM Kryon of Magnetic Service. I share with you the I AM energy, which is divine, and which so many of you feel is elusive and unattainable, but instead, which surges within the spirit of each Human Being who is here.

Let me tell you, this is a sweet place to be! The Human Being is at the forefront of this experience with their intellect, their emotion, their intelligence and the divinity that defines them as Human as they listen to or read these messages. Let the entourage begin to appear. It's going to flow into this place and begin to fill the cracks between the chairs.

Dear ones, the entourage of Kryon are not what you expect. We have spoken of these things before. It's a divine time. More energy will be displayed to you, and will move through you, than you expect. These are energies you've asked for, for it's a personal entourage; it always is. There is no generic energy that is part of what you call channelling. Each of you is involved, even the doubter... who is always here. Each of you is on a separate path, a path we know well.

So, here is the invitation for the next few moments. Feel this energy. Disconnect from your pre-suppositions; disconnect from what you think can't be happening here. My partner [Lee Carroll] brought you a message earlier, and he echoed within it the ideas of some of the masters of the earth, and even some of the philosophers. They have said, *"What you think, you become."* The power that is yours is wrapped around what you feel your reality represents. If you sit here now, and you say your reality is, *"This cannot be happening,"* then it won't! These will simply be words that fall on the floor.

If, however, your reality is that, *"These things are indeed real,"* and it is possible for an entity from the other side of the veil to come and give you profound messages of love today, then you're in a good place. For these messages from an entity who loves you as much as a brother or sister come flying through this energy, and they're directed at *you*. Even though there is a reader connected to this right now, it's in what you would call the future and you can't feel or see that. There are thousands who will participate in this meeting, and that should make this meeting even grander for those of you who claim the "now" experience.

We see the readers, too. We know what they need, as well. So, reader, this may fall upon your eyes and stir your heart just as much as it may the listener today. Oh, we hope so, for it's a teaching that we need to give you.

The Earth's Weather

As we have in the past, we will say again – the great winds that have torn your country apart for two seasons were predicted and should not be a surprise. We told you more than 16 years ago about the coming weather shifts of significance [Kryon Book One]. They echo a polarity in Human nature. As goes humanity, so goes Gaia. As the polarity between the dark and the light increases, so will the polarity between heat and cold. There will be extra cold and extra hot, and where they meet together are the seemingly dangerous areas. Just as the polarity of spiritual rage has torn many off the fence of their normalcy, so it is that the planet also responds to this energy, exactly as we told you it would [Kryon Book Eight – 2000].

Some have asked, *"What is the appropriateness, dear Kryon, of such things as these great storms?"* In these last weeks and months, there have been two major ones, and I'm going to give you a hint of the energy of one of them. The biggest of this season was given the name of Katrina. You know what it did and the chaos it created. But again, you might ask, *"What is the appropriateness of such a thing?"*

Indeed, all of these storms are appropriate. They all represent a stirring of energy that needs to be stirred. There is no negative targeting of any land or punishment of any Human habitat. There is, instead, a manifestation of the energy you have created as you change the actual vibration of Gaia through your enlightenment process.

As the earth changes, you're going to see more of this. Let me reiterate what we told you so many years ago. In this new energy, there will be intensive weather shifts, and you are in a cycle now that has the potential to last at least five more seasons with the same intensity. You were able to see a hint of it this year when the season began very early with a great deal of activity. The seasons will endure and the intensity will be just as active. Now, it doesn't have to stay that way, for as the earth vibrates faster, you will slowly move out of this cycle. And by the way, dear Human Beings, this is only a potential. You can quicken the cycle by increasing your own vibration and Gaia will respond.

You're not here to suffer or worry and you're not here to be afraid. Sixteen years ago, we gave you the meanings of the *nines* and the *11s*. Eleven is a master number. Master numbers speak of enlightened purpose. When I arrived in 1989 [a *nine* year], I told you that my number was 11. The simple English alphabet numerology of Kryon is 11, which means *appropriate illumination*. The nine is the number of *completion* and when you put them together, such as in 9/11, you get *appropriate illuminated completion*. We have spoken of these things before. Even the greatest tragedies of your time, the ones that had no foretelling in your prophecy, were profound in their energy shifts of your country and of the earth. They were on schedule, and in their own way, appropriate.

Katrina has an interesting numerological aspect, if any of you did the job of testing it. If you were "plugged in," as my partner says, to the energy of what is truly going on in the planet, you will understand the nines and the 11s. I ask you to do the numerology on Katrina and you'll find that is an *11!* And so, we'll say to you yet again that these things are not a mystery or a "surprise to God." Prepare! Nothing should take you by surprise here.

Prepare. You have the technology, you have the wisdom, and now you have the experience. There are simple techniques that can keep a house from flying apart in even the largest of winds... back to basics for this.* There are also very simple techniques for keeping homes from flooding in areas below sea level. It's called "dirt!" While many are sending relief supplies to those in need of reconstruction, you would be better to send dirt! Consider a reconstruction project where all the homes are elevated on a berm row [mound of dirt] at or above sea level. Then, when the levy breaks, and it will, the only things that flood are the streets.

**Kryon has spoken of steel or nylon netting over a home, held in place by pre-installed cement and steel ring pylons around the house, the same techniques as is used with a circus tent. The netting would be very fine mesh and very strong, but lightweight. It's sole purpose would be to keep a strong and long-lasting wind from peeling away the layers of the home, one of the largest reasons why roofs are lost, and also how pressure is allowed to shift between the inside and the outside of a house during a hurricane.*

We also told you that the earth would move. It did, and recently. It was one of the largest movements recorded in your history, and Gaia shuddered at the bottom of the ocean where the plates meet. Although you may feel that the loss of life from the accompanying wave was a Human tragedy, you don't know what you *would have* experienced had the earth moved, with the same energy, in other plates or areas on land. Have you ever considered that? The force of the movement actually changed the timing of the planet's rotation, something that you also should have expected if you have followed what we have been telling you for all these years.

It's going to move again, and in places that are more predictable. The volcanoes we told you to watch are also becoming active again, suddenly and without warning, and often in response to earthquakes. The places to watch are Ethiopia, Russia, New Guinea, India, Ecuador, Japan, El Salvador and Alaska in the U.S.A.

Lightworker, do not be afraid of these things! Don't make your decisions of where to live based on fear. In fact, again we tell you, Lighthouses are built in dangerous areas to shine the light of illumination on the difficulties surrounding the rocks. Lighthouses guide and steer the way in the dark. They are anchored in the rock and do not fear what they were built for. Can you do this without fear?

The Teaching for the Day

Oh, dear Humans, dear ones, let the entourage come into this place in a sweet way. May you feel the energy of those who have come for this sweet message that we're going to give to you. There are those who you've loved and lost who are in this place. They're part of your group, and they always will be. We've explained it many times, and we're not going to explain it again here. There are so many who are a bigger part of the picture who stand next to you.

Did you ever wonder about those who have passed on in your family? What if they could see you now? I want to tell you, they *do* see you now! There are those of you who have wondered, *"Would mother and father be proud of me?"* Why don't you ask them? Because they're here! The picture is far larger than you think. We want to give you some information we've given one time before [the Kryon cruise], but this time it's transcribed. It's about your spiritual path.

Several weeks ago, I asked my partner to change his program and emphasize Human perception. I asked him to spend more time speaking about "getting out of the box of limited Human perceived reality" so that many would begin to understand what reality really is. Now, even your science is beginning to agree that this is needed. There's more to the picture around you than you perceive. The science is not concerned with the spiritual, but the two philosophies collide. Humans never acknowledge they collide, but every time they say, *"We don't know what to make of it,"* or *"There's more here than meets the eye,"* they're speaking of the spiritual complement within reality.

When you speak of the Anthropic Principle [The new realization that, against all odds, the Universe is built for life as we know it], you speak of the love of God! The design in your DNA, and design in the planet Earth, is not an accident! Now, even your scientists are beginning to see this. Here you are, listener, reader, in the right place at the right time, yet some of you would doubt that and say, "*Well, if you really knew about my life, you wouldn't say that.*" Well, brother and sister, I really do know about you, and all I see is your potential and your mastery.

How is it that what you call God/Spirit can be aware of every hair on your head? The answer is interdimensional. There's no *time* where I am. Think of it this way. When Spirit has eternity to look at you and work with you, even in one lifetime, we can take our *time* to do it. That's the way we see it. In other words, one second of your clock is to us an eternity of study and planning and time to love you. This very channelling is forced into a time perspective that is linear, one word after the other. It's a horrible way to communicate! It's slow and it's awkward. We'd love to just take you right now, all of you, and give you everything we were going to say today in one energy packet, and plop it upon you so that you would know it all in an instant.

I could do that if you were dreaming. I can't do it when you're awake. That is why some of the best meditation is done in a half-dream state, for you can be *downloaded*, as you would describe it, far faster in a nonlinear fashion. I remind you of a fun, scientific fact about your dreams. Did you ever have a long, involved dream? You lived it, chapter after chapter as in a book, an adventure that ended abruptly with your alarm clock sounding. Researchers will tell you that your long dream, the one that took you here and there in adventure style, all happened within a split second... as the alarm went off! In other words, in your dream state, time means nothing. That's because you take advantage of the interdimensional parts of your DNA that you don't even acknowledge you have.

If you know how much you are loved, this message is going to be more profound for you. I gave you information not too long ago that told you who you really were. I asked you to see the hidden relationship between myself, as Kryon, and you, whose real name you cannot pronounce. The name that you hear and read today is not your real name. You have an angelic name, indeed, which is unpronounceable since it is sensed as interdimensional light. And the lovely females in the room, are you aware of your warrior backgrounds? Do you know and feel a *maleness* that is there? If you could see the record of the Akash in your own DNA, you would see the joke. You came in this time as female, with an extra piece of early intuition, to get you going faster. But believe me, we still needed the warrior. Even as I look upon you, sister, I will remind you of your battlefield experiences that you wish to deny as you sit there. You are far stronger than you know.

All of you who are on a path of enlightenment face a myriad of puzzles, but I don't want to get into it until we're settled, and we're not settled. [Speaking of the room] I've been stalling. There are still a couple of you who need to feel what's really going on here. Do you doubt this? Just put out your hands and feel it. It's a sanctuary here. This is a precious time. Let time be suspended just for a moment. We can feel the angels around you, and those you've brought in. We wish you to leave differently than you came in. There might even be a healing. This is a good time for healing. [Pause]

Advice to Humans about Their Enlightened Path

I want to tell you about your path. I'm going to give you four attributes of it, three of which we gave once before. This message is about our advice to a Human Being on an enlightened path. For many of you, the advice is going to sound like nonsense, but we have to broach this teaching anyway. Teaching about the enlightened path is a teaching into interdimensionality. It would seem to be a trip into a nonsensical, illogical state, but it is given to consummate a marriage between the Human and the divine. It's interdimensional, and for that reason it won't make sense. This is when we ask you to suspend the intellect for just a moment. Instead, weigh the information with your heart's discernment, and not the logic of the 4D experience you think is your reality.

Your 4D brain will fail you completely until you learn to delve into the parts of it that move past time and distance, into those immeasurable places that seem to dwell only in fantasy. It is these interdimensional parts that are opening up and beginning to meld with the 4D parts, creating the *logic of faith*, and beginning to *trust the unseen* because "it's there and it works." Going beyond 4D logic is the hardest thing a Human can do, and that's why so few awaken, even when faced with such overwhelming proof. Indeed, there is an intelligent force in the Universe, aware of everything that is happening, and it knows *you.*

I bring this to you now because many of you who are reading and listening are ready for it. It's about *you.* I speak to those who consider themselves on a path of enlightenment. First of all, you have to know that this path is never ending. There has been criticism from those 4D Humans who would say, *"Well, in a linear world you have to set your goal. You've got to know where you're going. We live in that world, and you can't ask us to put blinders on!"*

In an interdimensional world, you can't set a goal. You can't set it because without time, you don't have a linear road. If you were traveling around the inside of a giant balloon, where would be your goal, the other side? It never ends. Right away, that makes it difficult for the Human mind to accept. Your eyes are wide open, but you can't see anything that makes sense. What's the answer? Learn how to "see" beyond the limitation of this non-existent road. This involves intuition, intent and learning about what a spiritual map is like [see the next paragraphs]. Meanwhile, you construct your own goals of where you "think" Spirit may be taking you. That's the biggest mistake to begin with. Spirit sees all roads as one. When you decide in advance where you think you are going, many of you will be "stuck" on your own road, not allowing Spirit to change your predisposed ideas of "who you are," and moving you to the road that is your best potential future. Then you'll feel you have been betrayed, or that "nobody is home" upstairs. It's a classic example of Human perception getting in the way of spiritual enlightenment.

In the channelled journey and parable called *The Journey Home* [Kryon Book Five], one of the first lessons of Michael Thomas [the book's hero] was that he received a map that didn't work. At least, this was his perception, since when he looked at the map it only told him the energy of where he actually was, and nothing else. He laughed and called it a "stupid map" for telling him something he thought he already knew.

Part of the attributes of this spiritual map is what I'm going to speak of now, for it applies to your path, all of your paths. The map is a metaphor. It's a map that doesn't seem to work until you actually need it and are at a crossroads of energy. On this path that you have chosen, you want some kind of map. The one you are used to looking at is a 4D map constructed with all of the graphics in place of where you might wish to go. You want to know what to expect as you travel. But an interdimensional spiritual map has none of that, for the where you are going is not known. Your free choice changes the map with every step you take. So right away, what we're telling you is that even God does not know what you're going to do with your path!

Now, that's going to make a lot of Human Beings insecure, is it not? *"If God doesn't know it, how am I supposed to know it?"* But then again, we have told you that your divinity is a part of God, so you are actually a part of the creation energy. Therefore, think of this map as a creator's map. Accept the responsibility of the unknown. Think of yourself as the explorer sending out the scouts a little at a time around your area to find out where it's best to go. We have described this before as pushing on the door and feeling the energy, and using your own discernment energy as you move slowly. The only difference here, between the explorer and you, is that you carry light wherever you are, so whatever you do will be a safe exploration, and one filled with illumination.

We told you it's like purchasing a ticket on a spiritual train, which you call your path, and then being patient until the train gets there. Well, it's graduation time. We're going to change that metaphor to something far more complex. If you want to purchase the ticket, that's fine. That's called intent. But there is no track, and there is no train! Oh, but there's a station! What are you going to do at the station when there's no train and no track? You're going to be laughed at. Well, the track and train are not built yet. *"Who's going to build them?"* You are.

So here's Point One of advice on your path as you move toward what some call ascension status: **Don't make up your mind in advance about where you're going.**

"Oh, great, Kryon," some say. *"Are all of your points going to be this way? Let me see. We're supposed to stand at the station with a non-existent track, no train, and not worry about where we're going or even pretend we're going there."* Yes. That's correct! That's a good beginning. Then you might say, *"Well, how are we supposed to go forward?"* And we say to you, who said you were going forward? Isn't that 4D? How about up? What direction would you call it if you were asking your old cellular structure to vibrate higher? What direction is that, I ask you? How can you stand at the train station if you want it to vibrate faster? There is no *direction* for *higher vibration*. Get out of that box you are in that says, *"I know where I'm going and this is where God's*

going to take me," because you will be shocked to know the truth. The real truth is yet to come. It will be point four in this message.

The most difficult part of your path is the realization that you are not walking a path that has already been established by masters. Masters create their own! As part of the divine plan, you must take responsibility, not by following others or clinging to advice, or even the Kryon teachings. You must, instead, take all of this and mold it into a creation of your own. All the teachings you receive on this planet from those such as me are parts of a recipe in an interdimensional kitchen. Now, go cook a meal that has never been cooked before, using the information you now have about all the ingredients! Your DNA promotes mastery! Do you now understand why, 16 years ago, we told you not to be a follower? Do you understand why, 16 years ago, we told my partner [Lee] not to become a guru? It offends and insults the mastery you have of your own, within your own cellular structure. It also explains why there really can be no real *ascension manual.*

The Second One

Now these are going to sound similar, but Point Two is this: **Don't make any assumptions around your work**.

"Oh, Kryon, it gets even worse! Now we're not supposed to know where we're going and we're not supposed to think about what it might be when we get there." Correct, my 4D friend. Make no assumptions, for the assumptions will get in the way completely of where you might really go. Oh, Lightworker, when you deal with divine energy, it is so much more involved and profound than anything that your Human brain can conjure up. My partner gave you a taste of that today, telling you about the *divine planning session* and just how complex the puzzle becomes as you co-create for yourself.

When you sit in a meeting such as this, some of you are able to reach up and touch, in a metaphoric way, that part of you which is *the group* that is *you* and feel a shower of love, right now. There is so much more going on here! This enlightened path that some of you have decided to take is a path that actually will contribute to the energy of Gaia. It has to do with physics, since that is God, too. It has to do with your own DNA. It has to do with the angel who is inside you. I stood with you at the *wind of birth* when we communicated this, when you decided to come into the earth, and when the prophecies were much different than they are now. Yet, here you sit in a changed place with a potential of *peace on Earth*, and with the ability to send light that actually stays where you send it! [Part of the science that Lee gave earlier in the day was scientific proof that DNA changes energy and it stays changed.]

You speak of contracts as though you come in with some kind of pre-ordained, signed statement where you're going to "do this" and you're going to "do that." You don't understand that when you get to the planet, the contract just says, *"I'm here on Earth, let's begin."* You want to read the contract? It says, *"I'm here on Earth and here are my parents and my starting potential."* That's the contract. It's just a beginning potential, and not an all-encompassing life plan. You think you have a contract to be a healer, or you think that your work is this or that? *"Well, I've even been told it is and I've seen visions of me doing that."* I would like to tell you, dear Human Being, that your visions were part of that dream that only lasted a second and a half, as I mentioned earlier. You don't know what the "rest of it" is. You may have actually had a vision about what you did "before you got here." Did you think of that? You don't know, either, because it's all mixed up. So don't make any assumptions. You are a clean slate. What if your vision is only a statement that you already *are* a healer, and now you are going to go beyond that? If you make a 4D assumption about it, then you spend your life trying to do something you already did!

"How can I go from day to day with a clean slate? There has to be some kind of a goal." OK, don't make your goal "where I'm going." Instead, make your goal "who I AM." Your goal is to "become divine." You might then say, *"I will practice, in the moment, the greatest divinity I can. I will be me, a different me than I was a moment ago, a higher-vibrating me, and in the process the doors will open that should open. In the process, without an earthly map, I'll still be able to get information from my divine map when I stand in the place where I need the information to be given. Turn right, turn left. That's what my map does. It works when I need discernment and intuition. The only assumption that I'll make is that I AM a blessed piece of divinity that creates whatever I need as I go. This will lead me to the perfect place."*

The Third One

Point Three sounds like the others: **Don't put a timeline on any of it.**

I've heard so many of you say, *"Well, here's the plan. We're going to do this and do that, and by then this will happen, and here's how many years, etc., etc."* It's useless, you know. It's constricting. It's a prison of your own making. When you start putting a time frame on any of these things, you've put yourself into a cosmic 4D time prison. What if the plans for you, dear Human Being, were grander than any time frame you could imagine? What if you push on a door tomorrow and there's a miracle there? Are you going to stick to the old timeline and say, *"Excuse me, Mr. Miracle, you're just a little early. Can you come back when I thought you were going to arrive?"* This is humorous, is it not? But so many of you do this!

Some of you, when presented with the miracle, will say, *"Uh oh, I can't do that because it doesn't fit my timeline! I'm not ready or prepared."* My partner wanted this particular channel to be titled, "How Humanity Avoids Miracles." But I wouldn't let him.

"Dear Kryon, I have waited a long time for this process to occur. I've been very patient, but nothing is happening in my life." Really. Really? What about the repair in your heart? [Pause]

I'm talking to somebody right here. *"What do you mean?"* you might say. I'm talking about what *didn't* happen, dear Human Being, when you started that path. I'm talking about the repair inside of your heart that you needed to keep holding your light... so that you wouldn't perish at the time an old potential said you would. I'm speaking about the repair you knew nothing about. I'm talking about something physical. I'm talking about what went on inside you one night to patch it, and you didn't have any idea about it, and may still not know until some day through x-rays or sonograms they are going to ask you about what they see. And you'll say, *"I didn't have an operation."* Yes, you did – a beautiful one, a divine one! One you did yourself with your own intent.

I'm speaking of things that are going on inside you that you have no perception of. What about the vibrations that you get every day? What about how you're being "amped" up? Nothing is happening to you? Everything is happening to you! But you measure "happening" by your own standards, from a list on the wall of your own 4D mind. Why don't you open your perception and feel this as it goes on in your body?

Enlightenment itself is a grand, healing energy that literally lifts you out of one place and begins to take you to another. So much around you begins to shift and change. I invite you to drop the drama in your life. Perhaps that's what the goal has always been? What if that was the goal, all along, to get you to a place where you could send light? What about that? What if there's nothing more than that? What if you're supposed to be a Lighthouse, and for the rest of your life all that's going to happen is your light is going to get brighter so you can affect Gaia. Is that acceptable to you? Is creating *peace on Earth* acceptable to you? Or will you sit around feeling you failed because it didn't match the 4D list on the wall of your mind? It's your choice.

The Last One

Point Four, the last one: **Your DNA is far, far more complex than you think.** I have given you up to 10 meanings of the layers of DNA and we'll give you the last two soon. The last three are a combined energy [10-11-12]. I shouldn't even be numbering them, but I do it for you, for your 4D perception. Within all of these energies I have given about DNA, there is still something grand that is well hidden. If you start looking at the DNA layer names and what they mean, you will see something. There is *mastery* there.

What happens when a Human Being goes on a path that actually shifts their DNA? I will tell you. They seem to become someone else! Well, not exactly someone else. Let's say they become, to you, someone else. This is because your perception of "who you are" is limited by 4D life experience. When you begin to activate the DNA, out comes all of the attributes that ever existed in any past life you had. Were you ever an artist? You're not, this time around, but what happened to the talent? The talent is still in there! *"You mean by activating my DNA, I could actually become an artist?"* Yes, that's what I mean as, indeed, you were one before, old soul.

It's truly time to say this, and I'm going to say it in a way that all of you are going to understand. There is an enhanced Human Being inside each of you that most of you will never know, but which some of you will discover if you really pay attention to what we're saying right now. Some of you listening and reading have the seeds of the master. Some of the most profound healing energy on the planet is in this room or reading these words. Will you ever believe it? Some may say, *"I'm too old."* And I'm going to say to you, *"There you go again, counting the years!"* Or you'll say, *"I don't have enough energy,"* and then I'll say, *"There you go again, measuring energy in 4D."*

Do you not understand, Human Being, that your lifespan can be increased, and that your energy can be altered, and that your DNA and your health can be improved dramatically? All of these things are within your own bodily functions, ready to go, ready to be instructed by the "boss." But the big one is "who you've been," *Lemurian*. How would you like to have the beginning of the development of that extra dimensional perception that we have spoken of? It's there for the asking. Some call it intuition, some call it advanced intuition, and some of you are even able to see the colors and know what I'm talking about.

I want to take you back 30 years. I want to take you back to when my partner was, what he calls, young. He was 31. He was finished with his "goals" timeline. He was in the profession he wanted, was accomplishing everything he desired, had the professional family he thought he was going to stay with, and he was happy. Now, let's interview him. My partner hates this part of the channel, for its personal.

Thirty years ago the man who sits in front of you now, who is channelling, was a hermit. He did everything he could to close himself into a room and have no interaction with any other person. He was a wonderful hermit engineer. When he dealt with equipment only, he never had to deal with the drama of humanity. He didn't have to socialize with anyone, and he didn't have to hear their opinions. It worked for him. And so now I'm going to interview him as the hermit engineer and I want you to listen to the questions and answers.

"Tell me, my partner, at what point did you receive the ability to talk to people about spiritual things, as a good public speaker, on stages in front of thousands at a time, without getting nervous?" And his answer would be, *"What are you talking about? I'm not a public speaker. I've never been a public speaker. I don't know what you mean. The thought of it frightens me. That will never be me. What are you talking about?"*

"At what point in time did you understand you could write? How many books and articles did you do in school? What courses did you take?" And he'll say, *"What do you mean? I don't write anything. I'm an engineer. I do sound and video, technical things. I don't have to write anything. I'm not an author at all, and I don't have that ability."* Are you starting to get the point? Where did all this come from? I want him to be the example.

Although he was happy, he was in a reality prison of his own making. Yet when he started his path, slowly the abilities that were always there began to change "who he was." Inside, we invited him not to be nervous in front of the large crowds and he wasn't; to write all of the books, and he did. With what training and with what talent did he do this? We say to you that all the talents he needed were there hiding in his DNA, ready to become the new "him." It was automatic, and there was no training, because it was there already. And he is embarrassed that we speak this way for it seems we are aggrandizing him, but instead what we're doing is talking about the love of God and how, in each of you, there is this same exact attribute. You can become something more than you think you are!

"Dear Spirit, I know I've been asked to do this and I've been asked to do that and I feel intuitively that I should go and start this, but I don't have that ability!" Oh yes, you do! It would never have occurred to you otherwise! Look at the example we have given. Spirit would not

push you in a direction that is inappropriate for your abilities. Have you been asked to write children's books? Have you? I know who's *here*. Then do it! Let it flow out on the page using the love of God as your guide. I know who's here! This is magnificent information from this brother/sister Kryon, is it not?

Now, there's an entourage here and we described it to you a minute ago. Are they proud of you? Oh, yes. But there's other energy here as well. It's one some of you have begun to feel. It's not impatience, but do you feel that anyway? There is a push from Spirit. It says, "Now you know, so get on with it."

Now that you've seen the weather change, be in the safe places. Use your divine wisdom, guidance and your discernment to bolster the things that need bolstering. Don't be surprised when Gaia again visits you in what you might think is an outrageous way. How many of you dare to sing with the wind? Do the numerology on the names. See these things as appropriate cleansing and scrubbing of the planet in places that need it, and that all is part of the great shift. The biggest attribute inside your DNA is that of a fearless warrior, Lightworker. It's time to claim it. And if you do that, you'll also be on the way to healing the body that you came with.

It all goes together in a package that we call enlightenment. We would never tell you these things if they were not so. These are the truths of the hour. Magnificent information, for magnificent beings who sit before me, and read these words.

And so it is.

Back to Basics

Channelled in Harrisburg, Pennsylvania
June 2005

Chapter Four

Back to Basics
Harrisburg, Pennsylvania
Chapter Four

Note: The core of this channelling was also received in the cities that Lee visited right after he went to Harrisburg, including Grand Rapids, Michigan, and Dallas, Texas. Each channelling was unique to the group, but this is a transcription of the first time this channelling was given, and it holds that energy.

Greetings, dears ones, I am Kryon of Magnetic Service. You have no concept of the energies that you would call appreciation, a Human emotion that we don't have. We have something far grander. Think of the highest love you can – whatever that means to you – something that would make your heart leap out of your chest in appreciation and grandness. Now double it, triple it, and you'll have what we call the emotions of the angels.

This is how we feel for humanity, especially the ones who would take the time to come and hear or read a message such as this. It prompts us to wash your feet. It prompts us to give you signs that we're here, and that will happen tonight. For there are some here that are ripe for healing. It's not always the ones you think, either. Healing encompasses many things. There is the healing of the soul, relationships and the body. Isn't it time to settle down? Some of you know what I mean. Isn't it time to stop the inner voices? Some of you know what I mean. Isn't it time to heal that body? Some of you know what I mean... and this would be a good time to do it.

Let the entourage come into this place in fullness, for this is a place that they've visited many times before. [Speaking of the church where the channelling is being held] Prayer is common here. Meditation is common here. Raising your voices in song is common here. Raising your heart in joy is common here. And so it's a good place, as my partner says, and it's warmed up for you.

Indeed, we look upon you and we say that it's no accident that any of you are here. Even those who came from long distances, we say that this is a message for you. But we're not going to start the message just yet, because we're not in place yet. Blessed is the Human Being who knows what's happening right now. There are energies pouring into this place because you've asked for them and you've given permission for them. It goes beyond your logic. Blessed is the Human Being who regularly suspends the 3D logic and lets God work in his life. Blessed is the Human Being who knows who God is, for when you let Spirit work in your life, it means you're connected to the other side of the veil and you let you work with you.

We've told you many times before that you're not who you think you are. Eternal, you are. Each one of you always was and always will be. It sounds like the definition of Spirit, doesn't it? All of you have challenges and lessons that have been developed from lives in the past, and there's a majority of Human Beings in this room pretending that this is the only life they have, yet these are the ones who actually seeded the earth and once called themselves Lemurians. That's who's here. And that's not uncommon, for those are the ones who would awaken first on this planet of free choice. You've come through a trial and you're in a difficult time right now where the lights are being turned on very slowly, where consciousness is changing and you're seeing it first in the children. You're doing your very best to echo what you're seeing and stay tuned with the changes afoot. And even in your spirituality, you're challenged, are you not? We're here as support for that.

Being Connected

There are a few points you should hear again about being connected – things we've told you before, but which should be revisited. The reality is this: There's a pipeline to you, directly from Spirit. The only thing that keeps you from using it is your belief. Once you start to reach up and turn that metaphoric knob, it tunes to the vibration of the pipeline and you turn the spigot. Then your connection is complete.

This connection isn't with some higher source. But that's the way you see it. You want to see the pipe as coming from above, and it doesn't. It comes from *within*. It's a divine, interdimensional connection from within. And when you're able to tap that source is when you'll understand about light. That's when you'll begin to receive peace where there has been no peace. That's when you'll get a personality shift and everybody will want to be with you. You won't become strange; you'll become balanced. There's a big difference.

Oh, those who are in that status who sit here and read this and know of what I speak... there's nothing like it when the love of family visits you and sits upon your lap. There's more than meets the eye going on here and some of you are feeling it and you want to know why. It's more than just this entourage being here; it's more than just washing your feet... it's the presence of those you've loved and lost. And they're here, too.

This is because all of you are eternal, and you deny it! You may not be able to talk to them in 3D, but you can certainly feel their love. And you might hear it in your heart when they say, *"All is well. We are in support of you."* Before this meeting is over, we're going to have you pray for each other, to send interdimensional divine energy to each other in a beautiful way.

Counter-Intuitive Human Behavior

One more time we're going to expose several Human attributes that are very interesting. If anything, these Human attributes should show you very clearly that this life you call Human is actually something that isn't what you're used to. Remember, you are angels – divine ones. It's true, but you don't believe it and you can't see it. Let me tell you, when you're not sequestered by this duality, you're used to a far larger picture than this. But there's that duality, a veil that hides the truth of who you are, who you were, and the real, true way of it.

It hides you from seeing the masterhood that's in your DNA, waiting to be exposed. It hides all the other things that we've talked about that are divine. That's what the duality does. But in the things I'm going to expose, you'll see the joke. You're uncomfortable because you're not used to being Human! Did you ever think of that? You've spent a lot more time as a divine ball of energy, which you call angelic, than you have on this planet as a Human. Even the Lemurians, who have been here ever since the earth started, have spent more time as angels than they have as Earthlings. That's because you had no beginning. You're a part of absolute timelessness and are "alive" in a circle of existence that isn't linear and has no beginning or end. So how are you doing in this Human body? Let's look.

Need to Know

Let's start with the first one. It's an odd thing indeed for a sacred being of the Universe. *Human Beings have a passionate need to know about energies that have not yet arrived.* Here you are, walking along on a path, and you see a fork in the road. You can actually see the fork and you can even see a little bit of where the split roads lead, so you're not anxious about what they are, but you don't know which one of them to take. So the Human Being will often sit down in consternation and worry about what's coming! Which direction should I turn – right or left? This is your linearity showing itself and the discomfort that you have with it.

Again, the reason you sit down is because in Human life, you've got a mystery. The best way I can explain it is again the train. You're on a linear train. The train car is you and the track is your linearity. You go in your linear fashion from your past to your present to your future, and you experience the energies of them one at a time as they invade your track. Therefore, you're always wondering about the next energy, because the train is always in motion passing through these seemingly new events.

Now let me take you to the other side of the veil and tell you what you're really used to. Picture the train there. There's no track at all. All the energies that are on the track in front and back of your 3D train are now overlapping in the middle, right on the actual train itself. So you might say that you can experience all of them at the same time, and there's no mystery. That's what you're used to as a creature of the Universe, and it's called "The Now."

You can rotate your train car to face the energy you wish to talk to, one at a time, if you choose to be linear. But all the energies of the past, present and future are overlapping in the middle of your train car and you're sensing all of them at the same time. There's no mystery about any of them, since they're all there, all the time.

So on the other side of the veil you have no problem with this, but when you become a Human, things present themselves in a linear fashion and it's confusing. Therefore you exhibit a passionate need to know about energies that haven't arrived yet. That's counter-intuitive! Why would you care about an energy that hasn't arrived yet? The fork in the road, even when seen clearly, is a mystery to you.

Blessed is the Human Being who understands patience. This is the Human who stands up instead of worrying. He proceeds to the fork in the road knowing that it's the only place where decisions can be made. He sings a tune while he goes there and he's peaceful in his heart until he gets to the fork. Then he stands in the energy of choice. Then and only then does he get the message from Spirit.

This is the energy of the moment, and the message may be an intuitive: "Turn left!" That's the connection! That's the pipeline in action. The Human Beings without the connection have no intuition about these things. Even as they stand in the fork, the energy of choice, they're still worried. They say, *"I'll try this, I'll try that. I wish there was somebody who could tell me."* Well, there is, and it's called the *Connection With Spirit.* It's called turning on that faucet from the pipe of the Higher-Self, the source that has the wisdom and the truth of who *you* are.

We've given lesson after lesson of how this is accomplished. Humans plead, *"Dear Spirit, you talk about doing this and doing that. How do we get there? How can I find this connection?"* And I'll tell you this – it comes with pure intent. God knows who you are. God knows what you're about. When you start to process with pure intent that says, *"I want to know more about this,"* you'll get the help you need. Pure intent is different than passive intent. Passive intent is, *"I'll try this, I'll try that, and if none of these work, I'll try something else."* That's your perception of a mind that's already made up: *"It's not going to work."* Pure intent says, *"Dear Spirit, I know it will work because I'm part of it."*

Do you see the difference? When you trust someone else to do something very important for you, you worry. When you do it yourself, it's right in front of you, and you don't worry. So when you "own" your divinity, you're actually doing the work of God, yourself!

Fear of the Future

Number two will sound a lot like number one: *Unreasonable fear of the future.* Again, you're not used to this. Angels don't have this! In order to be a Human Being, you're on a linear track, one energy at a time. What are you going to do? Where are you going to go? Many are afraid. You really don't know what's going to happen, and positive personal experience from the past doesn't seem to help you at all. It's counter-intuitive to everything that's happened. For instance, yesterday, when you were planning on coming to this meeting, this energy you're sitting in now was the future. So you might say you're sitting in the future! I say to you, how do you like it so far? [Laughter]

What did you fear yesterday? It's simply counter-intuitive to everything you are. It's because you're not used to it. Human Beings have spent most of the eons even before the Universe existed in an overlapping situation of energies that were always in the now. No matter how many times you've been Human, you're still disturbed by this linear train. You don't know what's coming and you can't see it. Yet you want to know about it because that's the way it normally is for you. You get to see all the potentials of everything at once.

And so here is a message to the dear one who says, *"I'm ready to go and I can go anywhere."* We say this to you: You're in your sweet spot and you don't have to worry about where you're going. Because when the energy arrives, it'll push you and pull you around because at some level you're connected to your own divinity – something that knows the big picture. You have pure intent and the set-up is complete and it's taken lifetimes to get here. We told you to be patient and you have been. And so now is the time to celebrate your inactivity and wait for the energies to come... and they will.

Being in the right spot at the right time starts with pure intent. Yet there would be those who would say, *"I'm wasting my time. I'm marking time. I'm not doing anything. I don't know what to do."* And we say again to you, why don't you just sing a song and let it happen? Spirit knows you're there and sees your light, and it'll bring to you the energies of what you've asked for. It has in the past and it will in the future because you're in the right place.

How many times have we used the very Human historical event of the Israelites walking in the desert for 40 years? Well, we do it again. Remember this history? They had to be going in a circle because the desert isn't that big. They knew it, too. So they were visiting places that they had visited before, through leadership that was actually taking them in a giant circle over the years. In addition, they were fed every day from the sky. Some have said this is a metaphor. It's not. There is physical science behind the food from the sky. These tribes were fed every day for all those years, visiting places that were familiar to them, because they were walking in a circle. Yet every single day they worried about tomorrow! There were even movements within the group to break away and make contingency plans just in case tomorrow didn't bring them what they expected. *"What if it doesn't happen?"* they would ponder. They had committee meetings and planning sessions in secret. *"What if it doesn't happen tomorrow? Where are we going to go and what are we going to do if the food doesn't come?"* Then tomorrow would come and the food would arrive and they'd be fine for a few more days... until the Human part took over again.

Just think – physical proof every day for a generation or more. There were those born who didn't know anything else but that. As children, they thought it's just the way the world works! Yet the Human mind would take over and the "what ifs" would prevail and create anxiety. And these were *the chosen ones of the time.* Historically, they were the ones who needed to be taken care of. Well, let me tell you who the chosen ones of *this* time are – I'm looking at them, and they're reading this page! These are the Humans who can shine their divine light and work on their own vibrations and DNA and actually change the planet! That's why you're here, dear one.

There are those who have perished just recently on this planet who are here now looking at you. And they're saying, *"What we did was a set-up for you."* They sit beside you now and they're saying, *"Make your life worth it, for you're within the crucible of history, the crux, the pivotal point, the anchor for the New Jerusalem. You're poised to create the new Promised Land!"* It's the message I give wherever I go. You don't know how important it is. You don't know how important your thoughts are, for they generate energy, you know?

Disbelief in the Actual Source

Here's number three: Against all odds, you don't really believe in the source! Now, that's really counter-intuitive, since it resides in you. But it's invisible. Here's what I mean about "the source" – I'm talking about in the essence that flows through this metaphoric pipeline. It's the connection. Even though you can see the results, you really don't believe in the source. As proof, look around you. Humanity is locked in a struggle all about who God is, what God wants, and who is right and who is wrong about this invisible force. Many are so fed up with it all that they've resigned their consciousness to even believing it's there at all. They shout *"Enough already!"*

Let me give you an example of something that's interesting to us on the other side of the veil. It shows how powerful the duality is, and how counter-intuitive this is within yourself. In your culture, when you go into your food preparation areas, there's a spigot there... a small device on the wall. And because you've lived long enough in your culture, you know that if you turn it, you have almost unlimited water. It's a resource that comes through a pipe, but your visual sense doesn't see the pipe, it only sees this tiny little faucet. Yet that tiny little faucet will supply you with water all your life, because it's hooked up to a very large source. So you don't even think about it anymore. It always works.

When you turn on the light switch, you don't see the electrical generators that are out there giving you the electricity to put light in your home. You think nothing of it. You go to the switch and expect it to provide unlimited power. It's a very small thing, that switch. But once you know what it is and how it works in your reality, you get unlimited power. Think about it: It's all invisible, those resources behind the small devices, yet your 3D knowledge lets you trust them, since you "know how they work."

Now, take a fantasy trip with me. Let's say that there's a Human Being who's never seen a faucet. OK, he's come from another Human planet. He wants to know how your kitchen works. And you say, *"Well, this is a small thing on the wall and when you turn it, you'll get water so you can fill up buckets and buckets and buckets. It just keeps coming and keeps coming and always will."* Then you let him turn on the water and sure enough, it flows out into the bucket and he's astonished. He looks at it and he's excited about it and he plays in the water. To himself, he wonders, *"What kind of a miracle is this that such a small object manifests such an abundance of needed mater. This is a process that I don't understand."* Then you turn the faucet off and you go away.

In several hours you come back and there he is, sitting and staring at the faucet, obviously anxious and wringing his hands. *"What's happening?"* you might say. *"I'm thirsty,"* he replies.

"Well, why don't you just turn the faucet and get a drink?"

"Because I'm not sure it will work again. And if it doesn't, I'll be very disappointed and I'll go thirsty, too."

What would you think of that creature? Would you shake your head and walk away? Would you think, *"Boy, what issues he must have on his planet!"* Well, dear one, welcome to Earth! [Laughter] Because that's how you treat the spigot of God! Afraid to turn it on, are you? Afraid that it might not work? Has something happened in your life before that shows it works, yet you're still afraid to use it since you don't think it'll work again? Is it just too odd, these spiritual things? Indeed it's counter-intuitive to everything we've shown you and what many have actually experienced. That's duality at its best!

There's no judgment of this, dear one. Blessed is the Human Being who plows through the duality to what we call *The Missing Bridge,* which is a story within the Kryon teaching regarding the parable of the man who had to cross the chasm of belief in a car. When he knew the bridge was out, he proceeded anyway because he knew he was supposed to cross. Unbeknownst to him, there was a new bridge that he only saw as he rounded the corner at full speed. He crossed it, because somehow he knew it would be there.

This is what we teach. And we'll tell you this: For some of you, this duality never gets any better. In other words, every single time you come to that bridge of belief, you'll be challenged with doubt. So if you're one of these, we say blessed are you, for you're experiencing the duality and moving through it anyway. That's the test of the planet. That's the challenge. There's nothing wrong with you if you find yourself tested daily from the duality you agreed to.

Oh, we know who's here and who's reading! We know what your needs are and your doubts. And so we say to you, in your spiritual kitchen there's unlimited power and sustenance. What you don't know is that it comes from the family that has your name and energy all over it. When you open that pipe, in will come wisdom beyond what you think, helping to show you what to do next. For on the other side of the veil, the other part of you is still there! Your Higher-Self is that part. That's where the peace comes from. That's where the power comes from.

Fear of Being Alone

Number four: As we've said before, Humans fear being alone and the loss of love. Imagine what it would be like to be placed somewhere in the future. So far that you know absolutely no one and you haven't got a friend on Earth. No one knows your name. There's no sustenance. There's no help, for there isn't a Human Being on the planet who even knows you exist. There's no one to love you or care about you, and there you sit.

I want to challenge you to go there with me, because I'll give you the real story. Countless entities called family are circling you all the time. They know what's going on in your life; they know of your challenges, of your joys and of your fears. They're countless! Some of you have tried to enumerate them, give them names and shapes, and some of you even put Human skin and wings on them and draw them and call them angels. They're bigger than that. Because there's an attribute we have talked about before where the divine pipe is always open, but you can't see it. You're linear and wish to count them. Let me ask you this. When you open the faucet in the shower, how many waters come out? Do you understand?

This fear is counter-intuitive to what you know. You absolutely *know* better! You want to practice it? You want to get over this fear of being alone? Go some place where you're as alone as you can be. And we challenge you to feel as alone as you can, then say these words, *"Family, are you there? In the name of Spirit, I call you into my life, into this alone space, and I wish to feel you on my hands,"* and you will feel them! My partner can feel them now – tingling sensations.

[Lee holds out his hands.] For some of you right now, we challenge you to feel it on your shoulders. That's what that feeling has been all along. You wonder what that is? That's the love of God! That's the family. You're never alone.

It's counter-intuitive to all angelic things that you had before you got here. But the duality makes you think you're alone, and your mirror proves it to you, but only in 3D. I'll show you how good the duality is. When Jesus the Jew was being crucified in the front of the city, He needed the energy that had been with Him from birth – the master energy that He'd had all along – the pipeline. He called upon it and He got nothing. Then He cried out, *"Where have you gone? Have you forsaken Me? What's going on?"* This Man was going through yet another shift of vibration, going to the next level. And in that place there was a momentary lull, and his own dark night of the soul. It shocked him and startled him that the connection was missing. That's exactly what we wish you to be able to claim – a connection so common that it would be like turning the light switch and having nothing happen. You'd be shocked! That's how beautiful and dependable the connection is.

Drama

Number five is the intrinsic, built-in need for drama in some Humans. Now, you might say, *"I'm a Lightworker, I don't need drama."* Well, there are various degrees of drama, and all of you feature it to some degree. It's just that the ones who call themselves Lightworkers limit it to what we would call *controlled drama.* These are the things that happen on your terms, for you, which are fine with you, but not to others. It's still a bit of drama.

Human Beings often need to create activities of energy around them that keep them distracted from their spiritual quest. Some of them are so successful at it, they'll distract themselves all their lives. Some of them are really good at it and you know who they are. There are as many who do as who don't feature drama, and it makes life very interesting, does it not?

Many of you have gotten past it and are trying to eliminate drama in your lives and are realizing that you can control your own situation, but you're still besieged by those around you who create drama. And you can't stop them, since they're always there! Some of you have even asked, *"What do I do about the Human Being who thrives on this?"* Well, let me tell you about that Human Being. That Human Being is probably a Lightworker who this time around will do anything they can *not* to look at their spirituality. It's part of a defense mechanism and it's intuitive for them. And so they create drama and they're very good at it. Through their lives they've learned to argue, debate, and confront, and they like it. This drama is their friend. I think you know who I'm talking about.

Everyone has got someone they know who is like this. So if you're the Lightworker who's trying to escape this, I'll give you the words of a wise philosopher – a Human Being: "Never wrestle with a pig. First, you'll get dirty, and second, the pig likes it." [Laughter] You have a choice to wrestle or not. And so if you're one of those who is trying to get the drama out of your life, I say to you: simply disengage. *"But it's not that easy,"* you might say. *"What do we do with the energies that are thrown at us from these kind of people and the situations that occur around us, the anger, the hatred, the distrust, the envy, all these things?"*

Here's a concept you probably haven't thought of before. Remember that pipeline, that metaphor we talk about, which is pouring information and divine wisdom to you? Why don't you now think of it in reverse? It's a divine vacuum cleaner! It'll take those energies and suck them right out of your energy. Do you have things around you that you'd like to have vacuumed away? You don't have to do a thing except connect to the hose.

My partner [Lee] goes many places on the earth and there are those in drama who would disbelieve him and his work. There was a time when it laid upon his heart in a heavy way when they accosted him with their biases and their own ideas of God. There were times when he was anxious and would wring his hands because there was so much unbelief and he was thought to be a fool. Many left him as friends and others have tried to stop his work completely. But when he started his divine connection and he made it pure, he found the spiritual vacuum cleaner really worked! For every time he was around this drama, it was taken away for him and he stopped feeling the anxiety and the hurt of his heart.

He started to see the antagonists in a different light and he loved them. They're Humans; they're Lightworkers just like you, but they simply don't wish to go the route you have. In their own way, they're working their own problems for their own divinity. So he sees their anxiousness and anger and sends them energy to allow them more peace. You could do that, you know. Think of it in reverse. It's not how to ward off those with drama. It's how to love them so completely that they have nothing to say. Do you understand?

Nobody's Watching the Store

There are still those who think that *no one's watching the store.* Now, this is a metaphor that means you feel that God is only there when you call. Other than that, you're on your own until meditation time. Counter-intuitive to everything you know, you think that you're only connected when you meditate. You don't understand yet. The connection, the pipe, is a 24-hour event. You're connected when you dream, when you bathe, when you drive. It's a sustenance that's part of your life process.

Still, there are those Humans who say, "*Boy, wait until I tell God what happened today. Spirit's not going to believe this one! I had this challenge, then I thought I was going to be able to do this and I couldn't, and then I got this phone call that made it even worse because of what you-know-who said about me, and now I really don't know what to do. Everything's changed since my last meditation. I can hardly wait until five o'clock when I'm going to go into meditation and get this off my chest. I'm going to find out what to do.*"

Some feel like they're in a vacuum and God has no idea what's going on in their lives. That's not the way of it. Every single challenge should be met at the moment from the source. There isn't anything that you'll have in your life that's unknown by God. Family stands next to you. When you get that phone call, when you open a letter, when you hear from a friend, it's all seen by your "connection." Through good news and bad, through challenges and joy, that family is there directly through the pipeline, and it's there to deliver the wisdom you're going to need to conquer duality.

Change

Number seven, the last one, is *change*. Need we say more? Humans don't like change. Well, let me give you something to think about. What about a change where you heal your body? Is that OK? What about a change where you become peaceful when you're having trouble with peace? What about a change where you have the answer and the solutions to the unsolvable? What about a change on Earth where the Palestinians and the Israelis have a meeting point where they can agree on something and begin a process that actually works? It's only a matter of keeping the energy on this planet the way it is now and accelerating the light and vibrations until those things can happen. And you are the accelerators – all of you! And you fear change? That's like the cook in the kitchen fearing that a meal might be produced! It's not even logical.

There's a precious soul in this room who has come for healing and you know who it is. How strong are you today, Lightworker? Do you believe anything that's been happening in this room? Can you feel the entities around you? Now would be a good time. I want you to take your energies and I want you to hold this man in love. I want you to see him for the long life. All together. Practice it now. Create a bubble of green energy so that he can be balanced enough to talk to his cellular structure and eliminate the cancer in his body. We wouldn't ask you to do this if it weren't possible. You can control your immune system, you can control the disease. You want to play a part in his future, why don't you do that now? [Silence]

And as you do this, there's an entourage of trillions who see your pure intent and they're doing it with you. It's all up to him, but you're the balancing catalyst for these kinds of things on this planet, for the New Jerusalem on this planet, for your own cellular structure. If you want to make a difference on the planet, take care of yourself. Start a process of connecting and becoming more angelic and remembering what it's about. Don't fear the future; walk into the crossroads. Prepare for a journey without ever knowing where you're going, dear one, and feel confident that when you're supposed to travel, the ship will arrive.

And so it is on this night we have given you seven attributes of humanity – things that angels have trouble with, as they exist as Humans. It's called duality. If you ever wonder why you sometimes fear the things we have mentioned, just say to yourselves, *"Oh yes, I remember,"* because things are not like this on the other side of the veil. You'll never get used to them because you're divine.

I was there when you were born. I was there when you leaned into the wind of birth. The last interview on the other side of the veil before you came in asked you, *"Do you mean it? Do you really want to? Are you ready to do it again?"* And you said, *"Yes."* And here you are hearing and reading.

And so it is that we say to you blessed is the Human who understands the connection, who strives for it, in the degrees that it can be attained, because they will be the masters of the future. Ordinary. Meek. Masters of the planet, all.

And so it is.

Kryon Around the World

Dr. Todd Ovokaitys on stage
Segovia, Spain - 2004
A very crowded hotel venu
1300 where 800 were scheduled!

Guest channeller Rona Herman on stage
Pont A Mousson, France - 2004
The Abbaye de Prémontrés

Current Events

Channelled in Washington, D.C.
April 2005

Chapter Five

Current Events
Washington, D.C.
Chapter Five

Normally we don't publish information on current events since it tends to "date" the channellings and isn't very interesting or useful by the time it get edited and published in a book, often more than a year later. In this case, however, a very profound channelling was given in Washington, D.C., with respect to recent events, but containing deeper messages that will always be "current."

Greetings, dear ones, I am Kryon of Magnetic Service. There's a grand entourage that pours into this room, which meets your entourage – the one you don't think you have.

The process of channelling speaks of the love of God, who cares about humanity. Humanity is a piece and a part of the consciousness of God. There is God in you, and you are known, dear one, by God. Your real names are known, and I know them all. Remember, I was with you, as it was my job to be, when you leaned into the "wind of birth"... before you came and before you agreed to do what you're doing now.

The first thing you might decide to heal is drama in your life. You know what I'm talking about, don't you? Do you think it's a mystery who's here with us or reading? Maybe you had to hear today in order to know that we know who you are. Do you go to sleep peacefully, awakening not with the realization that you're back in the struggle, but with a fresh breath, a release that says, *"Oh, I love this planet. I'm happy to be here, happy to be the age I am, working where I'm working and doing what I'm doing"?*

The more peaceful you become, the more years will be added to your life. This balances your immune system. Did you know that? You don't have to concentrate on the T cells. Instead, concentrate on getting the drama out of your life, on claiming that which is yours – mastery over your own countenance! The T cells will take care of themselves in reflection of your peace of mind. It goes together.

Human Beings love to compartmentalize everything. You've designed a dimensionality that's so restricted; it affects all the thoughts around you. You have some very, very difficult decisions to make as you build this new track [speaking of the new "track" of reality that the Human train is on], and the decisions, if they're to be solid, must be "out of the box" that you like to think within. You must tear down the walls of the paradigm that you grew up in – an older energy, which will no longer give you good answers.

Humans ask ethical questions and they expect a yes or no answer, as if it was that simple or generic to all humanity. They ask profound questions regarding your current events and they want black or white answers, as though things were that simple. They don't see the big picture. They only see a small spot, but they want decisions around the spot – never understanding that there's so much more around them that's so grand!

Some are already asking, *"What are you talking about, Kryon?"* Today I'm going to give you a lineage of your current events. Now, we haven't done this before where we actually time stamp the events within your linearity, but we're going to do it today. It's due to what has just happened on this planet in several areas and what's continuing to happen in this new energy.

Recently, humanity has had some questions put before it that need to be discussed. Some of them are difficult, and some are interesting. Some of them you're not going to understand and some of the discussion you're not going to like. I can tell you that because my partner doesn't. He's just like you.

The Ethics of Life

You, as a Human Being, are designed to appreciate and love life. But you put it in a box. You think you live once. You say, *"Life is precious; make it count; keep it going at all costs; make it work."* And the underlying thought is that because you only go around one time, all the purpose is wrapped up in one lifetime. Well, I'm going to give you something to think about, something that happened just recently that 10s of millions of people all over Earth who have the western news media know of.

It was all about one woman's life, and you know whom I'm talking about. I'm talking about Terri [Terri Schiavo]. And I'm going to talk about Terri because, you know, she's here [speaking of the real Terri]! And I'm going to give you a perspective about Terri that perhaps you hadn't thought about before, and as I do it, she's going to watch.

It's very metaphysical, you know? This perspective is one from my side of the veil. Terri leaned into the wind of birth many years ago, just as you did. I was there, too. There were potentials lying in front of her – a track that she could take if she wished. There was no predestination, only predispositions of energy that laid before her: the parents she would have (which she had selected), the man she might meet or marry, the accident waiting to happen. All of these things were in her "potential track," and she could have chosen not to go there.

But like so many of you, she looked at it and examined it. These were the times we spoke to her and said, "Dear one, you're going into another Human lifetime that has a potential that's awesome

– grander than most Humans on the planet will ever experience. You'll get to present something to 10s of millions of people. You'll make them think about life. You'll change the legal system of your country. You'll awaken peoples' awareness to situations that need to be addressed with respect to morality, integrity and even intuition. Will you do it?"

And I remember what she said. The grand angel who stood before me, who you now call Terri, smiled broadly and said, *"I'm ready for that."* And some of you cry in your sorrow and say, *"Why is this Human dead? How could such a thing be tolerated? Why would such a thing happen? Life is so precious."* And I ask you this, as Terri looks on in her joy, would you take this away from her? Would you take that away from humanity, what she showed and did that resulted directly in her passing?

Start thinking of these things, perhaps differently. We've told you before that there are even those Human Beings who come in with a predisposition of suicide! What a horrible thought, you might say. *"Kryon, could that even be appropriate?"* And we say this: More than appropriate, it's by design! *"But why should that be?"* you might say. *"What a horrible, dishonorable death."* And if that's your reaction, you're placing the whole grand picture in your own little Human box.

When you start examining it spiritually, without Human bias, you start to see that around a suicide there's this energy that develops. It's all about the family. Is there shame? Is there drama? Does it kick the family in the pants so that perhaps they might study things they never did – or perhaps they might even look within themselves for spirituality? Blessed is the one that comes in with these tasks [like suicide]. There are so many of them who do. For these are the grease of personal change within families, and provide a gift that is grand!

You see, Spirit looks at these things differently. The curtain goes up, it goes down. You come and you go and there are profound lessons, some of which are taught harshly by those who teach them through their own deaths.

"Well, what is it, Kryon? Don't dodge the question with a diversion to suicide, for this isn't what Terri did. Is it proper or is it improper to have somebody in this vegetative state put to death by others around her?" Our answer: Exactly which Human are you talking about? You want a blanket answer, don't you? For six and half billion souls and paths, you want one answer for all. Well, you won't get one. For Terri, the answer is a solid yes. It was as it should have been. She came in with this grand opportunity to change the world, and she did it while everyone watched.

There is appropriateness in all things and sometimes you create for yourselves what seems to be inappropriate. Yet later you understand what the gift was within the challenge. Celebrate Terri, and don't think of this as a shameful thing that Humans did to her. Think of it instead as a book that was written for you to look at, one which pushes you to a place to ask, *"What should we do about this now, personally? What should our legislatures do about this, if anything? How can we approach these things more humanely and with more honor? Is our culture addressing this issue? Are we addressing this issue personally?"* Let's put these questions where they belong. It's not about "right to life"; it's about the appropriateness of "this life." Each case is individual, and some are profoundly given for the planet and for those around the individual.

Oh, as all of you came into this planet and leaned into the wind of birth separately, each was unique. Each of you has a different story, a different goal, but all have the same purpose: the elevation of the vibration of the planet. Sometimes it happens to many of you at the same time. We'll get to that before we finish.

Animals and Reincarnation

On a lighter note, we interrupt the life and death discussion of Humans to talk about animals. There are the questions not asked, but lying there, of which you are more than curious. *"Dear Kryon,"* it has been asked, *"do animals reincarnate?"*

Again, the Human Being looks at *animals* as one word that covers trillions of entities on the planet. You believe that all of them either do or don't reincarnate, and you want one answer for them all. What if I was from another planet and communicated to you this question: *"What color are animals? I want one answer, please."* You'd laugh, and wonder what kind of singular consciousness I might have in my reality to ask such a thing.

So I say to you regarding your reincarnation question: Which ones? *"You mean there's a difference, Kryon?"* Oh, yes! We've already gone over the purpose of animals on the planet. We've told you many things about animals. We've told you that some of them are actually designed to be eaten, and they come for this very purpose. We've indicated to you what's wrong with the way you're treating them, and that you don't honor them in their death, or even as you extract their resources while they're alive. And that, my dear friends, is the reason there's disease in the meat. When you start honoring these animals in their death so that they can create the food that's needed for you, then you'll see the disease disappear.

This is a factor that has yet to be named in your language or your culture – the idea that there's an energy that the Human creates even in the appropriate slaughter of animals for food, the results of which change these animals and the health of the Human who consumes them. Why is it that the indigenous knew about it and you don't? It's an energy that addresses the consciousness of Gaia and the animal kingdom. It addresses the way animals are honored in death.

Animals don't all reincarnate, but some do – *if it's appropriate for the Humans around them.* Most of the animals on the planet don't reincarnate, but there are a select group and individuals who do, and even a "rule of thumb" that you can apply to those who do and those who don't. When I tell you about the ones who do, you're going to understand a little bit more about the process of who *you* are. Blessed is the Human Being who walks this planet in lesson: Everything revolves around you! It may not look like it, but it does. Gaia knows who you are when you walk on the dirt! You have a light that you can strike [create] and carry with you that will change the very elements around you. Matter will respond to what you do because *you* are the angels disguised as Human Beings.

Some of you have selected various animals on Earth to be your partners or friends, and you call them pets. Even some of the ones to be slaughtered, if they have a Human who loves them, are pets... if only for a while. These are the ones who reincarnate.

"Why should such a thing be, Kryon? How does that work? Do they have souls? What's the 'rule' you speak of?" In a way, they do have souls, but not as your souls are structured – not with the lessons your souls carry or the multiple aspects you have. They're not angels, but they're support entities to those who are. [Humans] When they reincarnate, the reason is in honor of the Human Being, you see? Animals, in general, don't last that long on the planet. You might have this beautiful partner, this love essence that you have with an animal pet-friend. Then that animal-friend disappears in death, for again, they don't live that long. The rule of incarnations is, therefore, "If the Human needs it, it happens." So there is a scenario created within the system that helps Humans temper the loss of this love, and we'll give it to you.

When your precious animal-friend dies, go look for another one right away. Don't wait. Don't wait! I'll tell you why. Immediately go looking in places where animal babies are. Make no presuppositions about the kind of animal or the gender. Don't necessarily try to match the one you lost. Instead, go to the places where you intuitively believe the young animals are, and look into their eyes. One of them will be the one... because it – and the *Universe* – knows intuitively where you're going to look!

This is the system that honors you. Many know this and have said, *"I know this is so because when I found this other animal to be my partner and my pet, it started doing the same things that my former animal did – it even responded the same way to me."* It's a beautiful system in honor of you. It's an acknowledgment of a broken heart, you see? So you can pick up where you left off.

Some may now ask, *"What size animal are we talking about, Kryon? Is there a limit?"* We say, there you go again. [Kryon smile] What size do you want? An elephant or a mouse? It doesn't make a difference. If they're loved by you and part of your karmic energy, they'll reincarnate. However, it might be prudent of you to intuitively look for the size of animal that meets your living needs. God doesn't give you an elephant when your mouse dies. [Laughter]

The Last and Next Pope

[Note that this was channelled right after the death of John Paul II, and before the conclave of Catholic Cardinals had selected the next pope.]

"Kryon, we just lost what appears to be a great religious leader, Pope John Paul II. What are the ramifications of this?" My partner eluded earlier to the man called Karol who became the pope [spoken of earlier within the seminar]. He discussed what his goals were and what he did on this planet that really had nothing to do with his religion. Oh, perhaps the hat he wore did, and the places he walked

did, and the ceremony around him did. But this was only given to facilitate what he could do.

But you see, like you, we knew Karol. He leaned into the wind of birth, too – just as you did. He was no different. And Spirit said to him, "You're going to have a chance to change the earth because the energy of this planet has the potential of being very different. There are potentials when you get to be a certain age where there'll be something called the Harmonic Convergence on the planet, and things will begin to change. You can fit into this as a world leader. Are you ready for that?" And he said yes.

No angel asked Karol if he wanted to be a Catholic, as he leaned into the wind of birth. That was simply the vehicle that got him into the position where he could change the planet the way he did. You couldn't have had the absence of the Armageddon that you've experienced without Karol. Did you know that [speaking of his direct involvement in the influence of the fall of communism]? So his belief system not only served him well, but it propelled him to a special place that was his alone to be in, and one that allowed him to touch billions all at once. And so it was that this great religious leader, who also knew intuitively what he was doing, had a love of humanity. His favorite thing was to be among common people – and he was, every time he could be. When he got to the position where he could make a difference, he did.

Now, there's something you don't know about Karol. The last decade of his life, he was very frustrated. Go look at the pictures. Go look at the pictures of the first 16 years. Then look at those from the last 10. The last 10, he was suffering – not just with his health – he was anguishing over a situation that none of you truly know about. For in his last 10 years, this man wanted to make some more changes while the time was ripe, but he knew he was too old.

Karol didn't have the energy to make the changes he really wanted to make, and those around him fought him to keep things the way they were. It was all very political, and someday this information may come out into the open, and you'll hear about those who influenced him in the last 10 years and helped to keep things on an even keel. He was too old to make a difference and he knew it.

Karol was not of a consciousness to make some of the changes that many cried out for – about poverty and the role of women in his organization (that will come later). But Karol cried out in his heart for the children that were abused by the priests, and he wanted to do something about this and make a difference. He believed that his Savior wanted him to make a difference, but he couldn't do it. So what might look to you like inaction was instead the pope suffering, for he was not allowed to do what he wanted – due to his lack of energy and those around him who made certain he didn't.

"Kryon, here we sit with a conclave of cardinals about to meet and select a new pope. What's the potential based upon the energy right now of the selection? What's going to happen?" I'll give you two potentials of what might take place in the next few days, because your future is always about free choice. There is no entity that can tell you about the future, since it's totally in the hands of the free choice of humanity. However, based on the energy of the moment, here's what we see: (1) You're either going to have an interim, temporary pope for only a short amount of time (relative to the last one), who will lead to a radical pope; or (2) You're going to go right to the radical pope. Either way, you're going to eventually end up with a man who's going to do things to shake up the establishment.

Let me give you some of the potentials of what the radical pope may be involved in: This religion he leads on Earth has doctrines that no longer "square up" with what humanity is seeing around itself. He absolutely has to address this issue, for the sophisticated Humans will leave the church otherwise. There will be those who may even call him "the evil pope" because he's going to go against tradition when he slowly starts a process that honors the Virgin Mary more than any pope ever has – therefore honoring women within the church, elevating them to higher positions… even to priests.

He will speak about family planning, and start processes that will slowly justify it in the eyes of God [this will take awhile], but it must come from the man who "sits in the chair" *[ex cathedra]* to change the doctrine of the whole organization. Because of this, he will also be in danger and will have to have constant protection.

Then he'll talk about what to do with priests who abuse children. Watch for this. Even if you receive the interim pope, he'll set the stage for the radical pope in this area. For this is in the energy aura of what we would call the *potential future* around this grand event. The earth is filled with free choice and it can go any direction, but I've just given you the potentials of what is here and now.

Death Isn't a Mystery Element to God

"Speaking of such things, Kryon, talk to us yet again about death. There are some who say that death is not what you said. They say you go to a place and sometimes you're stuck; some have called it purgatory. There are numbers of names in history given to the energy of a scenario where you go to a place and you either must work your way out of it or you're stuck there and you have to be 'prayed out of it' by others. Which is the truth?"

We will tell you what we have told you before, and there is no time we've ever changed this information. It has always been the same, for it honors the Human and the divinity within you.

Dear Human Being, when you pass to the other side of the veil, your grandness is seen, known, and accepted. There is nothing *out of control.* In fact, you are expected! We have told you about the Cave of Creation and the three-day journey. We've told you about the Hall of Honor and the grandness that's there when you're met by the family. You regain your entire knowledge of your entity and of the Universe, and you choose what to do next. There is no danger lurking in the transition, where you might be "stuck" somewhere and in trouble spiritually.

Now let me complicate it with new information: There are, and always have been, other journeys that you might take besides reincarnating, and many Humans choose this. They become part of the energy of the planet for a number of years in order to help certain situations. Some stop incarnating as Human for a while and become *guides*, but they're not guides with Humans. Instead, they're actually a part of the energy of Gaia.

Some go into the mountains – actual Human reincarnated energy on the planet, but not in Human form. And when that's done, they'll come back very much like they came back before, then reincarnate as a Human Being again.

We haven't discussed this before, because again, Humans, want a black-and-white scenario of what happens. They don't want to know about the energy part because many Humans will worry and say, *"Which one will I be?"* as if you have the mind of God and could decide now – and you can't. It's all part of a grand plan. It's beautiful and part of a system that honors the "now" of what is next at the moment.

Let me give you a hint about something: Are you one who loves the earth so much that you want to get down and roll on it? Do you hug trees? Are you one of those who the ground speaks to? Oh, there are many of you like this! I want to tell you that the *last time around* there is the potential that you were part of the dirt! Perhaps it didn't last long, but just long enough to put your energy in there so that when Humans walk on the dirt they will feel your consciousness, love, and feel Gaia's energy.

Oh, this is complicated, but it's true. No one is ever "stuck." And if you hear that, it doesn't honor the grandness of the angel called the Human Being, or the system you've set up to help the planet. You have full choice when you're not here. The Human-Earth scenario is the only place where you receive a hidden persona, where you don't know who you are and have to seemingly walk in the dark. When you're not here, you're a part of the whole of God. Death is a known transition, and not filled with uncertainty, error, mistakes or mystery. It's simply the closing of one door and the opening of another.

The War in Iraq

The next subject is filled with the potential for misunderstanding. Here we sit in the place you call Washington, D.C. And here we sit talking about Iraq. *"Kryon, did this war in Iraq have to happen the way it did?"*

Well, which reality are you talking about? Let me again give you the information that I gave not too long ago at your United Nations venue: Your event called 9/11 was not an accident. It set in motion something that only could be set in motion by the most powerful independent nation on the planet – one that doesn't have to answer to any other nation, or feels it's part of a consortium of support nations. That was the setup... no error in this. That's why it happened here [speaking of the U.S. and also speaking of the Pentagon].

The setup was to start a situation where the U.S., indeed, would change the Middle East. For part of the new arrangement of the planet, including the energy delivered both at the Harmonic

Concordance and the Venus Transit, demanded a new energy be started in stubborn places. Those places in the Middle East that had been the same for 1,000 years needed some kind of an energy stick inserted and stirred vigorously. There was no other way, and you were the ones to do it.

So the question instead might be, *"Kryon, did it have to happen the way it did... the way we have done it?"* And the answer is no, it didn't.

You're a very young country of free choice and you're all a race of free choice humanity. I'll tell you this: When you look backwards right now and see what the consciousness change did to the fall of the Soviet Union without firing a shot, you can see that there's always a better way. But you didn't do it that way and you'll be stuck, indeed, with the consequences of your actions for a while. There's no judgment here, but rather simple energy economics, because this is the way it works. Your method has delayed the outcome and the purpose, and has forced issues that were not quite ready and also created drama that will be with you for many decades.

You may not like what's taking place and the way it's taking place, but I'll tell you that historians will look back on it and say that the overview of the purpose was correct. The result of it will, indeed, stir a situation that needed stirring. For in the future they'll say that it started a ball rolling that you'll eventually call *The New Jerusalem*. You are part of that, United States.

"Well, what can we do, Kryon? Now that it's happened in a way that creates challenge... what can we do?" I'll tell you what you can do: You can shine a light to those who are making the decisions within your government and let them see the things that are unseen and hiding – beautiful things – by turning on the light in dark places. Not in anger or in judgment, but in love. For these are your leaders, and they represent the best you have at the moment. Anger and

frustration will only plant seeds of darkness for them and make things stop altogether.

If you can send light and balance to them, they can pick up the knowledge and the wisdom that's needed, and which hides in their own offices. It always did! Had you waited long enough, even the United Nations would have changed, you know? You were quick to call it names and render it useless. It was in transition, too, but you threw it away instead of being part of the transformation it needed. Watch it, for it's going to go through upheavals as well. When these shifts are in process, the U.N. will be stronger and you won't have as much trouble coordinating with it. Had you waited, you'd have seen this and you'd have created an energy of unity that would have served the same purpose as your war – without the suffering.

And so it is that we talk frankly about these things. And so it is we say that this is the route and the track that you've chosen in your own way to manifest The New Jerusalem. As you lay this track, the advice from Spirit is to be a little more patient. Your exuberance is part of your freedom and your American spirit, and this is understandable. But now you see that in dealing with the others, you'd be well advised to see how Gaia itself works... with patience and wisdom and time... just as with what happened to the Berlin Wall.

Good meals are cooked for a long time, then consumed all at once. When the Berlin Wall fell down in 1989, it happened seemingly overnight. But the energy of this profound change on Earth had been created slowly and deliberately by Human consciousness for a much longer time. Use this great event as a model for the kinds of miracles you need now in Iran, Korea, and the larger problems that lay in and around Israel. There are 10s of thousands of Humans represented in these places who desire exactly what you do – peace for themselves and their families within their own cultures, with freedom to worship as they please and to honor themselves and their divinity their own way... without hatred toward the West.

Believe it! There is support from the masses, which isn't reflected in the leadership you see. Let some of these things develop from within, and don't feel you have to force issues that are on the verge of taking care of themselves through the help of the new energy of the planet, with slight pushes and influences by your great American spirit of free choice.

Mass Human Death

The final one, dear Human, is the hardest one for my partner and the one we wish to leave you with in this channelling tonight. This is the one that my partner doesn't want to even have me talk about. It's the appropriateness of mass death. For you, built in to your very essence is the honor for life, and the sorrow when it passes. It's correct and appropriate that this is there, and never let it be tempered. But the wisdom of understanding is also needed to help you get past some challenges of the Human heart.

"Dear Kryon, was the tsunami really necessary?" Yes it was. Almost 200,000 Human Beings passed over. It's an event that for you is filled with horror, sorrow, emotion and challenge. Back in 1989, we told you of those that might have to leave the earth *en masse*, and here it is. Yet, even my partner [Lee] asks the questions, *"Why the children? Why the poorest parts of the earth? Why the seeming inappropriateness of all this death?"*

And I say to you the same thing I said with respect to Terri: Do you understand yet that death is often as precious as life on this planet of many energies and lessons? They are not gone! They're all here. [Speaking from Kryon's perspective] They're having a great time! They're joyful! It seems like a moment ago they leaned into the wind of birth with us beside them. We said, "*How would you like to participate in an event that will change the compassion factor of the planet so that energies can move forward and provide faster acceleration of vibratory shift? How would you like to help create peace on Earth through a consciousness shift within Gaia itself?*" And they said, "*Show us the way!*"

Do you understand why we are in love with humanity... that you would love the earth and the Universe so much that you would go through these things? So much of what you see is horrible tragedy, yet you're looking at the heroes of humanity as they deliver a gift that will change the very fabric of Gaia through the compassion created as a wave of humanity responds to their plight.

They knew the potentials and they went through with it. Even the children knew, for they're old souls within their divinity. There was so much compassion created at that time, in that one week, the earth has never seen anything like it in your lifetime. Billions of Humans were involved with a compassion that instantly went to the core of the planet. It went into the earth and it's still there. It changed the actual energy of where you walk and it planted seeds that will grow that will indeed emerge later in Israel, and those surrounding Israel.

And that's what it's about. Yet some of you didn't want to hear that, did you? But they're here, with me now... and with you as well. How could you fit them all in this room, you might ask? They can fit on the head of a pin! That's interdimensional talk. They can go home in your purse or your pocket! That's interdimensional talk, too. And they've got a message for you that we've given before, but you can't hear it enough: "*We did our part – now you do yours, Lighthouse! For the ones who remain are the only ones who can manipulate the tools we have helped create.*"

When you go home tonight, you're not going to be in a survival situation – in a tent in a tribe with no lights or clean water, with no food. You're not going to be in sorrow or despair. Instead, you go home to a warm place with plenty of food and friendship and the love of family. That's why you're the Lighthouses, because you have time for it. You've got the intellect for it. You're not in survival mode, as is so much of humanity on the earth. You have the education for it and the intuition for it. Now, do you understand why there are so many Lighthworkers in the western world? It's because your culture has created a situation where there's abundance of these things, and it allows you to lead the way in changing the energy of Earth, instead of having all your time spent just trying to survive. Does this help you understand the responsibility of what you have before you?

Strike the light and send it to the Sudanese. Strike light and send it to those dark places with governments where there's corruption. Strike the light and send it to the scientists and researchers who already have the cures for the more virulent diseases on the planet, but can't begin their work due to the barriers of certain leadership and their old ways. Strike the light and send it to Israel and Palestine and get on with this solution! This is why you're here, and this is the agreement you made when you arrived and selected the culture you live in.

Achievable in your lifetime, it is. Peace and compassion will prevail. You shall see. You shall see.

And so it is.

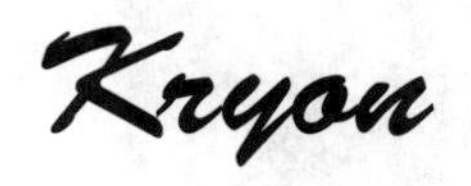

Kryon Cruises!
Held every year - Aug/Sept

Kryon Cruise #5 - 2004
Eastern Mediterranean

Kryon Cruise #5 - 2004
Venice, Italy

The End Times, Revisited

Channelled in Toronto, Ontario, Canada
August 2006

Chapter Six

The End Times, Revisited
Toronto, Ontario, Canada - August, 2006
Chapter Six

Greetings, dear ones, I am Kryon of Magnetic Service. I'm more than that, you know? For those of you who can see the colors, they're here now. They have come in quickly because those who sit in the chairs have expected them and want them. The entourage sits at your feet. They come into this place full of love, and I am more than Kryon of Magnetic Service. I'm an angel, just like you, speaking through a Human Being, and you call it channelling. We invite you to feel that in this place there is a sacred energy, which is beyond the sum of the whole. Some of you will not just feel it, you'll experience it; you will become it and you'll leave differently than you came. As you experience this energy, you'll slowly know that this message is real, and perhaps you'll wonder about who God must be. Beyond the doctrine of the religions that you celebrate and that you enjoy and that you love, there is a greater energy – one that encompasses you in a far grander way than you have ever felt could be so.

My partner remarked to you that in came the 11:11 energy in 1987 – the Harmonic Convergence. He spoke of that energy and how it drastically affected this planet and all who are on it. In free choice, most of you didn't feel it, and some of you didn't even know about it. And that's as it should be since it was an event that dealt with potentials, futures and energies that you cannot easily reach up and touch. But I'm going to ask you this: What happens now that you *do* know it? Does that change anything?

I'm looking at this group and I tell you this, I know your names. I know who's here. It's glorious to me to be here! I'm the one who said goodbye to you on the other side of the veil when you came in. I saw those colors, and how magnificent you were in transition. With the energy of a communication that is nonlinear, I spoke to you and I said, "Are you ready to go do it?" And you said, *"I've never been more ready. I'm going to go during a time of promise and make a difference."*

I'm going to tell you something, Human Beings: Those who are reading and hearing this are the ones who will change the planet and bring it to the vibration, which the 2012 is expecting. It is your lineage. It is your divine purpose in life within free choice. It is why you came. It is why you're reading the words on this page. I see those who are reading, even though you cannot. Stuck in a time frame, you are, which is appropriate for who you are. I see the potentials of those whose eyes are on the page and those whose ears are listening to this on their electronic devices. So I ask you, each one: Do you look at yourselves as a warrior of a light? Do you look at yourselves as a spiritual Lighthouse, or are you just making do, day by day? Do you think of yourselves as a spiritual person? Could it be that there's an angel inside of you? When you look in the mirror, what does it tell you? Do you see just a Human Being who's aging, or do you see divinity? Do you see something to love? We love to activate those energies within your DNA of awareness, of God in you. Layer 10 is the interdimensional DNA energy that allows belief... an actual layer of energy within you that cooperates with your spiritual curiosity to reveal God in you! Think about how complex and beautiful this it! It represents awareness of God in you. If you start looking at yourself differently, you will see the divinity inside. You will see the masters of the ages in your eyes. Then you'll know what I'm doing here is correct and true and timed perfectly.

All of the information I have ever given you was to allow you some choice of belief so you might steer this planet toward peace. I give this message in the middle of August 2006 [The flaring up of events in Israel on two fronts]. I rarely date these messages, but

I want you to know right now why I'm doing it. There are those who are afraid and they're stirring in duality. Their worries surface because there is trouble in Israel, they say, and the marker is that when there's trouble in Israel, beware of other things. The mythology of major religion will tell you that there's much more to it even than that. *"Get ready to go," some will say, "There's going to be a change on the planet when Israel is involved and the faithful will be removed soon."* So, to many it's about escape. To others it's about fear. To still others, it's about a signal to ramp up the light and get into the battle.

I will remind you what I told you in 1989. Remember these words, because we're going to talk about the Jews. "As go the Jews, go Earth." I said those words and they are still very meaningful. I wanted you to remember them and listen to what follows, for I will say them again and provide a review that may give you a hint that when there's trouble in Israel, indeed, there will be changes on Earth.

"As go the Jews, go Earth." What are you going to do with this information? Are you going to be afraid? I'll ask you some questions in a moment about that, but I want to do a review. This is for the Jews, too. Yes, there are Jews reading this. Yes, there are Jews hearing this. There are Jews here now in this meeting. Let me tell you yet again about this lineage and let me explain some things to the rest of you that may clear up some misunderstandings. I will present this in a way I have not before, with more clarity.

The Jews

The Jews are not a race. Anthropologists will look at the Jewish civilization and say it has every attribute of a race, but it can't be defined as such since it does not qualify scientifically. However, even the anthropologists and sociologists know that it has a different attribute than any civilization that's ever existed. Intuitively, they're picking up on the Akash. Here are the astral rules: There must be a core, karmic group that lies on the Crystalline Grid of the planet and never changes. It cannot change, for it is the hub. That means it is the staple of humanity. This is not in your science or your mythology, but it is very real and the proof is in the history.

In this particular case, the Jews are the hub. They have come into the earth for this purpose and they were called "God's Chosen People." And before you lift your head and say, *"Why them, and not others? Why do they get to be chosen instead of some of the other deserving kinds?,"* let me finish the sentence. They are "God's Chosen People" to suffer the hub energy… to be moved around the planet and be chased and hated. Wherever they go, others will be after them to wipe them out or enslave them. That's their purpose because they hold the hub of the Human Akash, a powerful position of astral importance.

All your history will show this. There is no other group who has consistently been pursued for annihilation through more than 4,000 years. Intuitively, the dictators, the masters, the Caesars all knew it. Intuitively, if they could eliminate the Jews, they themselves would take on the power of the Akash, or so they felt. They would become the core! That's how it continues even this day. Some will say, *"Well, that's an interesting story, Kryon. Do you have any proof of that?"* I say to you, just look at your history and tell me what other people have been pursued in this fashion all the way through their history? From enslavement by the Egyptians to elimination by the Romans, it goes on to the present day. From the recent events of the Nazis to current verbiage of Iran in the Middle East, they all wanted this "race" gone or enslaved. Oh, they all had their 3D reasons, but it's more than a coincidence that Jews are chased wherever they go. This is what they were chosen for. Are you beginning to understand? Now let me tell you the other side of that.

In return for this *Earth service* as a Jew, they have a pure karmic attribute that each time they return in a new life, they get to be Jewish again. How do you like this plan? It sounds unfair, does it not? But it must be this way. When Jews move into a non-Jewish lifetime, they never come back within the "race" of Judaism. It also has another attribute you can clearly see on the planet. Instead of passing around the torch of experience, as some of you have done through civilization, they've always been Jewish. Once a Jew, always a Jew, until they step out of that circle and then they cannot go back. The karmic attribute is a pure one. Now, perhaps in today's energy it's not politically correct to say it, but as you look around the earth, can you not see that Jews run things? They are in important places and seem to remain there. They're the masters of the shops and the corporate captains of industry. They understand how Human nature works because they've been there and they've done that for eons and eons. They have an edge on the rest of you, since their "experience jars" are filled with riding the same bicycle over and over and never having to learn on another one. But they pay for it. That's who the Jews are.

These End Times

This, then, plays in to these end times that we talked about in 1989. These end times are really the *beginning times*. How many of you have seen 11:11 on the clock? When you see it, does the energy of it say *"end times"* to you? Is it a fear number? Eleven in numerological terms is illumination. So 11:11 is illumination squared, if you want to say that. Illumination. Illumination. That's not the end of anything! It's a promise!

There are those who say that this is the energy of elimination. It's not. It's illumination. *"Then why are things so bad right now, Kryon? Why is there so much fighting? Why are there enemies all around us, raising their heads?*" And I'm telling you yet again, dear ones, that this is exactly what we told you about 18 years ago. In 1989, we told you about this battle. This is not new to those who have studies the writings of Kryon. You are approaching the "Bridge of Swords."

There are those right now who don't understand this and they're frightened. They're fearful of even calling themselves Lightworkers. So I say to these Lightworkers: Were you truly ever a Lightworker, or did you just give yourself that label? Maybe it's time to examine yourself. Are you claiming to be the chef and yet you're afraid to go into the kitchen because it's hot? Are you claiming to be the windmill that generates electricity, but you're afraid of the wind? And what about the lighthouse who is afraid of the storm? Such things don't exist. Dichotomous, it is. And if that's you, perhaps it's time for self-examination, since you can change it! That's why I'm giving you this message. Don't fear the energy of these times. Look upon these things with the wisdom of the ages and say, "*Here is what we expected. This is correct for the times. Now, let's temper it by sending light there. Let's make this a short battle because there is so much enlightenment present. Let me make a difference.*"

"*Kryon, how can we possibly do this when the greatest minds of this century are trying to figure it out and they're having trouble? Nothing is happening. It just seems like they never come to a solution. It doesn't seem to make any difference how hard they try.*" If that's your reality and your truth, then that's exactly what it will be. But I have another scenario for you to consider: You send the intelligence of the cosmos through a spiritual *beam of light.* You climb those stairs of your spiritual lighthouse, strike that light, and send this intelligence of the cosmos into those areas where those in frustration will have an illuminated area, exposing things they've never thought of before. What about that one? Be one who stands in your lighthouse and says, "*I have no idea how profound this light is, but I can feel the divinity in it. I'm sending messages that are so divine that the leaders at the United Nations and other countries will see their way through this. We may not be able to convince a terrorist of anything, but we can make the rest of the earth change in a way where terrorism is not possible any longer. This light is not logic, but the wisdom of the ages. It can surpass anything the men can do or can think of. It's divine light."*

I told you years ago about this battle, did I not? The old energy and the new would clash. I told you about spiritual rage [Kryon Book Eight]. In a day when you didn't use the word or the terminology, I used it. I told you spiritual rage was something you could watch for in these times, and here it is. It is the word these days as you sit here. It *is* the old energy. How many of you expected the battle of the ages to be about God? If you did, then you understand Human nature very well. These end battles will never be about land or oil. Those things don't change an age. But a spiritual shift will.

There will be those who will continue to say, *"In the name of God, the Jews must go."* But these who say this represent an old energy… the one you are in battle with. I want to remind you about those who chose the old energy by choice. You look at them in sorrow for what might happen to them, but it is their choice to have chosen it and to believe this way. It is their choice to turn to the energy they wish when there is plenty of choice around them. It's part of the battle. You may not like it, but go back and read the first transmission of Kryon in Book One. I told you that up to one percent of your population may have to transition on this planet. And if that is so, it's one percent that have come for that reason. Understand this, but do not fear this. Later, I told you that this potential had drastically changed, and it has. Through your free choice, it looks like far fewer will be involved, but there still is going to be challenge and death. Most see this and understand about those who choose it at a very high level.

The Potentials of the Future

And now I will give you another statement: 2007 looms as a pivotal year, and 2008 will be one that brings massive change. It's also an election year for the United States. 2008 is a 10 year and represents a one in numerology. It means *new beginnings*. 2007 is a nine year – completion of some old patterns will occur. This is all part of what we see coming through the energy of your own making. But it's not going to be achieved by those who are running the other way. It's not going to be achieved by those who are afraid to show their light, and it's not going to be achieved by chefs who never cook a meal. Instead, it's going to be achieved by those who fearlessly face it and say, *"Tell me what is happening. I want to know where to send the light."* These are the ones who make time in their day specifically for three minutes, five minutes, 10 minutes, to say, *"I don't know exactly how this helps, but I know intuitively that there's something to it. I'm going to gather my friends together to pray for our leadership."*

These Lighthouses are actually sending intelligent cosmic energy to places that need it greatly. That's energy that *knows* what to do. It's energy that cooperates with the Human mind and soul, and is uplifting in its perception. It's wise, balanced energy, and is the real ammunition in this spiritual battle. So many years ago, we told you about the battle and now it begins. Indeed! We gave you a phrase many times over the last three years: Lighthouses were never built in safe places! Are you OK with that?

You want to be a Lighthouse? You could be a Lighthouse here in this great city [Toronto]. Yet some say, *"Well, it doesn't seem to be a very dangerous place. How could I be a Lighthouse in the battle here?"* I'll tell you where the danger is: It's when you turn on your light and all of those who are dark on the planet see it. At some level, you become a target. You show yourself, do you not? You show yourself to your neighbors, do you not? You show what you stand for. When you turn on the light, suddenly you're no longer invisible, are you? Are you ready for that? What is your family going to say? What are those workers going to say around you? Are you ready for that? Let me give you some advice. You don't have to evangelize anything, ever. All you have to do is say to those who ask, *"I believe in prayer. Who wants to pray with me?"* Humans who believe in the love of God ALL have a light! Did you know that? You don't have to mention Kryon and you don't have to say anything about the New Age or any religious preferences. All you have to say is, *"Who wants to pray with me?"* Maybe you'll get some volunteers and the light will become stronger. They may be Hindu or Muslim. Do you care?

The Religious – Are You There?

I'm going to address this right now for the readership, for the earth, for anyone who wants to hear it. Dear Hindu, what is it your doctrine says you should do right now? What is it that you have been taught, that you are feeling, that is so true in you? Those who are the Hindu masters of the earth, what is it that your elders have taught you is appropriate right now? What should you do about this energy? Can you feel something happening? Are you working on it? Have you been told that you're a part of the earth energy in any way? Hindu, let me ask you this: Who are you this time around and why are you here? What is it that the accumulation of lifetimes has brought you that can help the earth right now?

Buddhist, what have you been taught that you might do? Are you truly part of everything? Is there really a oneness that involves all that is? If so, that puts you in the middle of the challenge, does it not? Through the energy that you generate, can you not see how you might affect the others? So sit and generate that energy, for you are powerful, my friend. You are a peaceful person in the middle of the storm, and your vibration is important on this planet.

Jew, what have you been told that you can do about this? You are in survival mode, as you always have been. You shudder in fear, but not all of you are in Israel. What can you do? Do you believe in prayer? Of all the stories of the ages, yours are known the best. You've seen the miracles of God. Remember how you escaped Egypt? Those things actually took place. You were fed from heaven. Those things took place. Isn't such a thing a miracle? Could it happen again, but this time in a way that delivers the entire planet? What does your faith say about it? Is there a limit?

Jew, did you know that your lineage was set up in this fashion so that someday these puzzles could be solved? You are part of the solution, not the problem. You are the core karmic race, the civilization that can make the difference and can help be the catalyst to peace on Earth. With that knowledge, do you shudder in fear? "*There is no solution. There never was. It's going to last forever. The problems are unsolvable.*" Is that you? Which one are you going to be, Jew? Look back on the words of your master profit, Elijah. Look at what a Human Being is capable of. Look at the wisdom of your lineage, and keep your eyes on Jerusalem. Temper your anger, for it is not commensurate with your magnificence, yet it is your major issue.

Christian, what are you going to do? What have you been taught? How about the light of the master, Christ? What did He say? Have you been taught that you could change things with prayer? Was there something about "moving a mountain?" The answer is, yes. Is it not so that part of everything you've learned is to start with prayer, end with prayer, go home and pray before you eat, pray before you sleep? What is that all about? I will tell you. That is communication with God. It is strong, and you are up to it. Join the Hindu and the Buddhist and the Jew and send that light to those places that need it. Now is the time. You're part of the issue – a profound part, a beautiful part. Your light is so great.

Muslim, you love the Prophet, don't you? All right, let me take you back to the cave. I'm going to give you something to think about. You pray as much as anyone on the earth and you do it on a schedule that is regular. You believe in prayer! So why not start these prayers differently. You will not violate anything that you've been taught, for you're going to be praying for peace on Earth. In the cave, the prophet Mohammed met with the angel, and I want you to remember what has been written and what the angel said to him, *"Go out and unite the tribes of Arabia and give them the God of Israel."* And that's the truth. Look at where the prayer rugs faced, for they faced Jerusalem before they were changed to Mecca for political reasons. Look at this. Look at the core information and the beauty of the unity that the prophet asked you to have... not just with Arabs. What can you do? You can pray! Powerful, you are. A billion strong, you are. Part of the solution, you are. Oh, there are others who I've not mentioned, and I invite you to place your name in this list. But I just included the majority of religious beliefs on the planet.

Time to Make the Difference

So, what do you think about God? Do you think you could make a difference or not? Do you think God is just pushing the parts around to make your life miserable? Some do! Well, if you're a reader of this message and you're a hearer or you're in the room, I invite you to feel the love that we have for you... all of you. We've known that you were coming to hear, to see, to experience. It's a beautiful time, for it's a precious time here.

I'm going to review for you, finally, who the Lightworker really is. Let me paint a picture yet again for who the Lightworker is on this planet. Imagine with me: There she stands, there he stands. Oh, look at them. They don't look like giant spiritual beings, do they? They look ordinary and average. But when you start going inside, you find things that the masters all had. These Lightworkers are balanced. That's the first way you can tell... they're balanced. They're so balanced that you want to be with them. Have you ever met someone who you just want to be with? You just want to walk with them? It's because they're not judging you; they're beautiful inside and they listen when you talk. They say things that are appropriate and wise. They're not judging anyone, or making fun of anyone. There's no drama around them. There's a radiance that you can feel. There's a joy. That's a Lightworker. And that didn't come easy; it's not natural in your busy civilization, and it takes an *activated DNA.* That's another phrase for "a Human Being working on themselves spiritually."

There's a vibration from the Lightworker that touches the Crystalline Grid. They know all about the Akash at an intuitive level, and pull from it regularly. This is a balanced Human Being! They've been able to solve the duality! Duality is a puzzle, is it not? You've got free choice, but you've got an angelic countenance. What are you going to do with that? You're placed upon the earth, where the darkest dark and the lightest light are working around you. How are you going to navigate your soul within it? It's a condition that you sit in for life. That's the duality. That's the *piece of darkness* that chases you around. It's the consciousness that you all joke about that makes you do things. For the Lightworker, it's a solved issue. They balanced it. They're centered. That's a Lightworker.

They stand tall, even though they may not be physically tall. Their countenance seems bigger than it is; that's the Lightworker.

They're sure of themselves, but they are not filled with themselves. That's the Lightworker. They look at you with compassionate eyes. They care about you, no matter who you are or what you look like or where you've been. That's the Lightworker. Perhaps this sounds like it's echoing some of the masters that you have followed? Does it sound like the Buddha or the Christ, does it sound like perhaps the prophet Muhammad? Well, it should, because those are the attributes of the masters of the planet.

Inside your DNA there is mastery, waiting for completion. The spiritual Lighthouse is intuitive; they know when to speak. They do not say inappropriate things. They're intuitive enough to know when to pray and what to pray for. They can look at somebody and know if they're telling the truth or not. They're not judgmental in all of this, but rather they use it to navigate through their own lives and they're no different than you are. Their lives are just like yours. One day they might be doing the laundry and one day they may be sending profound light energy to the Middle East. But they're a spiritual Lighthouse and they know how to do both with the same kind of divine approach. Did you ever think of that? Ordinary things in your life might not be so ordinary. Can you celebrate the ordinary? Can you send light to your country's leadership as you wash the dishes? A Lightworker can.

The Lightworker is one who strikes the light and walks up those lighthouse stairs when the storm approaches. They know how to put things in balance. They know what to do with a dark energy. Many say, *"Kryon, what can I do with that darkness in my life?"* The Lightworker knows what to do with it. Long ago, they put it in the back seat. They don't let it drive anymore. [Kryon smile] There's no more depression and there's no more worry. Anger? No. Against Human nature, the Lightworker is slow to anger, very slow to anger, and wise to respond. They look at life far differently, as the masters of old did... even while they do the dishes.

And you might say, *"That's a difficult thing, Kryon. Who are these people?"* They're right here. They're reading and listening. They're in the room. They may surprise you, what they look like and how old they are or how young they are, but they're here in various stages of training and action. They are like the warriors who train and train to be part of a perfect army, carrying swords that are not for killing, but for celebrating – the Bridge of Swords. We speak of this again. The Bridge of Swords is part of the final battle. Indeed, we speak in metaphoric tones, but it's the only picture we can give you, which is that this battle will indeed be solved and will have a solution to it. Lightworkers all carry swords. They will be held high as those who are the victors pass under them. And who are these victors? The civilization called Earth and the New Jerusalem, that's who they are.

Does it warm your heart to know that you all are part of this? Listen, reader. What are you going to do when you put the book down? Will you give God 30 seconds? Will you give God some time? Peace. No phones. No televisions or radios. Just 30 seconds. Now, would you perhaps even dare to say, *"I am that I am, and the divinity in me is going to make a difference on this planet. I feel the truth when I hear it and when I read it. Even my small efforts will create an energy that is larger than I can imagine, combined with others, to create peace on Earth."* How are you with that?

What about you right now in this meeting? Oh, there are so many involved today. You have no idea as you sit in this meeting. You think it's just Kryon, and you're in a channelling meeting, and that's all there is. You have no idea what is also happening. What about the readership in here? They're with you now – ask them! And so I invite you to join them, even though they're out of time with you, and I want you to celebrate their healing, for they're having some as they read this. They're having epiphanies, healings and revelations, just like you. They are important and there are far more of them than you. Perhaps you are one of them? [Kryon smiling at the thought of the paradox of time that a live listener could also be a future reader]

"Kryon, why do you talk about healing so much?" And I'll tell you this. It's because the Lightworker does a far better job of making a white light when the body is balanced health-wise. That's why. We want you to stick around a long time. But not everybody in this room thinks they will. I know who's here. I know what's wrong with you. How would you like to change it? These are the times for that, with the angelic entourage that comes upon you when you decide to attend something like this, or read it later.

We're going to leave. The message has been stated and it's a precious one. My partner reacts. [Lee becomes sad.] Every time we say we're going to leave, I give him the feeling that we have. Oh yes, there are indeed emotions on the other side of the veil – profound ones, mostly of love. And he reacts every time we say that we're leaving. He doesn't know how many times we're going to do this. Like you, he works a day at a time in his life, but he feels it profoundly when we say we're leaving. He feels the tug that we feel to the Humans who we have spoken to.

The readership, the listenership and all those who would spend a moment and look at these things are included in this blessing: Blessed are the Humans who have made it their goal for self-improvement… to know more about the vibrational level of where they are in the cosmos. Do not leave here with questions about how to do these things. Just do them. Sit in front of Spirit and ask the question, *"God, tell me what it is I need to know."* And then expect the answers and move forward with a cosmic intelligence that is there. Call it what you wish. You just have to be able to start, and the rest will be added by God as you climb the steps of your sacred journey.

That's the message of Kryon and always has been. Through all of these years, we continue to inform you that you're here for a reason. You have divinity inside, you have self-healing that is profound. You have the ability to solve the unsolvable in your life. Relationship issues, issues at work… you can get rid of the drama completely. You never have to experience worry again. You can become a very patient person. All of those things are yours, just like the masters said. Mastery is what we teach.

The magnetic grid has been in final alignment for years. Now you're in the thick of the battle. We are here as we always have been, to hold your hand, to wash your feet, to teach you profound things about how precious you are and how beautiful life is. Claim it every day. Look in the mirror and state your truth: *I am that I am*. Make each day of your life one filled with light. Cast out the things that do not belong in a life of light and claim your power, angel.

We pick up the bowls we've been using to wash your feet and we exit this place until next time. It is a profound time, a sweet place, filled with sacredness. Blessed are you who have heard and read these words.

And so it is.

Kryon Around the World

Tel Aviv, Israel
2005

Jerusalem, Israel
2005

Message to the Jews - Part One

Channelled in Tel Aviv, Israel

October 2005

Photos at: http://kryon.com/israel

Chapter Seven

Message to the Jews - Part One

Tel Aviv, Israel - October, 2005

Chapter Seven

From Lee: Kryon's full message to the Jews was spread over three days, given both in Tele Aviv and Jerusalem. In the re-channelling process for print, some of the concepts brought forth in the future day's messages were brought into the existing channelling for clarity. In addition, all these channellings were given live in a "back and forth" translation process from English to Hebrew. This kind of translation creates many short sentences in English, and to facilitate better reading, these have been put together and made to flow easier. If you wish to hear the original messages with the Hebrew translation, they exist on the Internet as free, downloadable MP3 files. [www.kryon.com/freeaudio]

Greetings, dear ones, I am Kryon of Magnetic Service. Since the last time you heard my voice, I have not left this room. [Speaking of the mini-channelling that morning] Humans often have an interesting perspective of what happens on the other side of the veil. You say that participating in spiritual things is like throwing some kind of switch. When you get spiritual enough and you throw that switch, on will come profound things. Then later, you feel the switch is turned off and you become a simple Human again. But you don't understand the real process. There is no such thing as a simple Human! We see all humanity as grand beyond anything in the Universe. Yet you still do not understand that you carry the seeds of God within you. Instead, you still feel you must "throw the switch."

When you're not here, you are indeed with me as a sister or brother. This is what you are blind to as you are sitting here. All you see is one life, your own, and sometimes it's a difficult one. You don't remember who you used to be and you don't remember the journeys that you've had before. But your DNA knows it, for indeed, it is responsible for some of the attributes of "who you really are."

Many years ago, we told you that there's something specific about the Jews. We told you that they have what we then called "pure karmic attributes of humanity." Difficult to explain, but they carry the core of the seed of humanity. If you are one that would believe that indeed you come around many times [reincarnation] and have many lifetimes that you cannot remember, the difference between the Jews and other Human Beings is that you have agreed to come many times in-a-row to be Jewish. Therefore, within your DNA is carried multiple lifetimes of this attribute of being Jewish, perhaps even thousands of years of it! When you decide not to come back into that family, then the "rules" are that you never return. Sometimes this shapes your attitudes and sometimes it shapes even more than that. This is different than those who come and go and have a much greater variety of selection within many karmic groups. You have mostly had only one.

Some of you are without hope because of this. It rings strong in your DNA. You have the same challenges every time, and often they are about struggle, life and death, and even the horror of those who would actively seek to destroy you. You say, *"We have never been able to do what we came for!"* And I want to tell you that you would be right, except things have changed. That is why Kryon is here.

My full arrival on the planet has to do with *you*. Let me give you the lineage of Kryon. But as I do so, I want you to understand it is the lineage of the history of a new consciousness on the planet. I am a messenger, and no more – a messenger that has arrived for one reason only, to give advice and help facilitate a changing Earth. But within this change is a great change for the Jews.

My message arrived in 1987. It did not manifest itself to my partner's channelling until 1989. My message responded to what you call the Harmonic Convergence. Some have even given it another name – the 11:11. For those of you who feel the energy of humanity, you know what happened then. Difficult to explain, it is, but at some level all humanity was given a choice at that time. Think of it this way: The higher selves of all Human Beings came together and were polled – voted, if you wish – on what to do next. And none of you remember that day, for it was done at a higher level than you were aware of. But it was *your* choice, and most of you hearing this were actually here.

The question was this, *"Does humanity stay with the original plan of being finished with its work, or does it proceed and do something else?"* I'll explain that in a moment. The vote from the spiritual parts of humanity was overwhelming. The planet had enough energy at a high vibration to accomplish a shift, a great change. And so it was that I arrived, the grid changed, and Gaia herself went into a different attribute to allow for what you had decided.

Now I want to remind you of some of the things that took place then. Almost immediately, politically, the world changed. One year later, one of the greatest political forces on the planet collapsed. The consciousness of what you called the Soviet Union was doomed. And it's important that you understand why, and I will get to that in a moment. Look at these things, for even within the doubter, there is so much proof of this shift within what you can see around you. A new consciousness was your choice, and it is already upon you.

In 1989, when the channelling began, we gave you information about the energy of Kryon. We told you that the energy of Kryon had arrived to give you messages about the new energy on the planet. Therefore, my arrival is all due to what *you* had decided to do with the planet! And if you will look at my first messages, you will see the messages about the Jews. I even made a statement, "As go the Jews, goes the earth." That's never been truer than now! It has to be this way, for you are the seed and the core of a great process. You are the bookends of the entire Human process. Your lineage brought the planet the core energy of mastery, and now I'm telling you that the new energy places the task of completion upon you. Peace on Earth will start right here!

We told you that the energy of Kryon was an 11. In the language of my partner [English], the numerological aspects of your alphabet spell an 11 in the name Kryon. We also told you of another energy of Kryon, the nine. If you would look at what these numbers mean, the nine means *completion*. And we like to say that the 11 means *appropriate illumination and action*. Now, that's not my energy. That's the energy of my message. What is completion and completion of what? It's the completion of an old energy that you are finished with. Hard for you to believe, but you hold this potential in your own land. It's all about the Jews, and always has been. Did you understand that the "end of days" would begin here? Well, the beginning of days will also begin here.

We told you interesting things back in 1989. We said that the magnetics of the earth would have to shift in order for this to work. Many asked, *"What does magnetics have to do with spirituality?"* And you still don't understand. Your DNA is the source of your Human mastery power. Your DNA is the source of your enlightenment and your spiritual awakening. That's why the layers are given the names of God in Hebrew! Don't you find it interesting that I chose an American channel to give you information about how grand the Hebrew is? For you wouldn't have believed it otherwise, and we know that. It had to come from another source in another culture that looks at you, and is honored to do so.

Magnetics changes your DNA. Even your science now acknowledges this. The magnetic grid of the earth had to move greatly in order to create an atmosphere for technological and inter-dimensional DNA change. Your magnetic grid had to shift so that you could have the ability to sense the spiritual changes in your DNA. Indeed, the magnetic grid moved, as we said it would, because it was you who made it so. And you can go to the scientific records, if you wish, and review for yourselves how it has moved in the last 12 years.

I know what you're thinking. *"Why so slow, Kryon?"* You are an impatient lot, aren't you? Oh, read your history. God moves very slowly, but there is a reason. Human consciousness does not change overnight. Sometimes it takes generations to forget what has happened. It is not the first time you've experienced this. Kryon has always been here, but only now do you receive these messages because of the shift that you have created. Sometimes generations must pass before you can forget whom you're supposed to hate. Sometimes generations have to pass before you forget that you used to be a slave. We speak of a new Promised Land called peace On Earth, but what a difficult journey it will be. And because of the past, you say, *"Impossible. It cannot be done."*

Many of you will be the ones who get to see the beginning, and might have to return to see the fruits. Sometimes it takes a generation or two. Those who walked in the desert for 40 years had accomplished the impossible, freedom from slavery. But in all their grandness, they then had to pass on the reward to those who came later, and only the offspring got to see the land of promise. Do you understand? If you wish to give your offspring and the earth your greatest gift, then you will have to first acknowledge that it is here to give. Can it be that you are in the same situation yet again? Indeed! Then begin the process of the creation of freedom for yourselves and those around you. It's in your lap.

We told you that the weather would shift on the planet. Have you seen that yet? Indeed, it is here! *"And why should that be?"* you might ask. I'll give you more information on that in a moment, but it has to do with your affect on Gaia, the energy of the planet. Indeed, the planet is vibrating faster because you are vibrating faster. We gave you all manner of information 16 years ago and some of it wasn't pleasant. But it was the truth. We told you to expect severe weather, even earthquakes. Many of you don't remember one of the statements we made, that perhaps up to one percent of the planet might perish before this is over. And, of course, so many of you said, *"Well, that is obviously going to be a war."* No, it isn't. You didn't understand about Earth shift.

We also told you that this planet has increased its vibration even faster than we had expected, as such is the way of humanity to surprise us all. This increase has actually tempered the message we gave you 16 years ago, and now much of what we told you might have to happen need not. More and more Humans want to create peace. This consciousness shift has revised the number of those who might have to perish. And that should tell you who's in charge, shouldn't it? It's you! As you shift the vibration of this planet, all the prophecies of the past will fall on the floor. You create a new future every day.

Still some would say, *"Then, what was the appropriateness of the hurricane Katrina? It was ferocious, so much damage and death. How could something like that be of God?"* So I will say to you yet again, that for spiritual answers, you must get out of 4D in order to understand. Put on the hat of the prophet. Place yourself in the shoes of Elijah (Eliahu), think with his wisdom and overview, and look at this from another perspective. If you do the numerology in English on the word Katrina, it is an 11. What does that tell you? *Appropriate illuminated action.*

"Kryon, it doesn't make sense that there would be destruction and death as part of a spiritual theme." Really? Put on the hat of the prophet and look at your own history. Sometimes it's a Human agreement to go through these things in order to change the planet for the betterment of the whole group. Surely your group can see this? Did you ever think that perhaps what your karmic group has gone through was a core issue of the planet? And that perhaps your sacrifices have actually changed the way humanity thinks and acts? Think about it!

The greatest earthquake to occur on the planet since you have been alive happened recently. It happened under the ocean. It was so great that it even affected the spin of the earth. Was that a spiritual event? Yes, it was. And it created a tsunami, which was responsible for the loss of almost one-quarter of a million lives, and all the sorrow that went with it. And regarding that, I'm going to ask you the impossible just for moment. Oh, just for a moment.

[Pause]

I want you to greet these Human Beings, all of the children, too, for you see, interdimensionally, they're still here. If you understand the cycle of life, you understand they're still here. They transitioned quickly and they knew in their DNA that they had a contract for this potential death when they came to this planet. I was with them in what I call the wind of birth, the place and time when they came back to Earth. On the other side of the veil, all of the potentials are seen in advance of what you might experience. God does not know the future of your planet. The future is predicated on your own actions, but the potentials are there for all to see. You know, therefore, before you arrive, what might be in store for you. This is one of the greatest reasons we love you the way we do, for all of you "see" these potentials as grand, and look forward to helping the planet. On my side of the veil, you don't see death the way you do on yours. It's a cycle, a transition and an appropriate way of creating energy. That's exactly what happened.

At the wind of birth we spoke to those who lost their lives in the tsunami. Before they were even born, we spoke to them and said, *"Are you really ready to go through this?"* And there was excitement as they said, *"Send us down there! Because what we're about to do, potentially, is going to change the planet Earth."* Dear ones in this audience, put on the hat of your prophet and listen, for when these precious souls came back after their transition, there were many smiling faces and much joy! The first question they asked was, *"Did we accomplish what we went to do?"* And the answer was yes.

But you might say, *"Well, what could that possibly do for the earth?"* Perhaps the teaching my partner gave you today will help you to understand this more? [Lee taught about perception.] On that day of the tsunami, and the following week, there was more compassion generated on this planet than for any other event since you've been alive. Hopefully you have learned about Human DNA, and how powerful it is over the elements. What happened that day changed the actual dirt of the earth. For that Human emotion called compassion went right into Gaia! And that, dear Human Beings, will affect the consciousness of the children that are going to be born from now on. It's all part of a grand plan called the New Jerusalem. Did you know that? Did you ever think that perhaps some of these things are actually linked to you and your task here?

Let us speak of prophecy. I want to ask you to look around you. None of the old prophecy has come to pass. All of you were supposed to be gone by now under the old prophecy. Many religions spoke of this prophecy and it went like this. The year 2000 would bring about a world war. You can find this in writings of the prophets all over the planet. What was going to happen was clear. There would be trouble in Israel, and there was, remember? But in the old energy plan, the old prophecy, there would be an immediate honoring of treaties between the Warsaw Pact and NATO. And this required the Soviet Union to be a lead player. But in 1987, the Harmonic Convergence changed that, and one year later in 1988, the Soviet Union was gone! Did you ever put this together?

Therefore, the war and the interchange that would have resulted because of the trouble here never took place. Did you understand and realize in prophecy that the year 2000 was going to be the end? This plan came from Humans and was foretold for centuries. But in 1987, humanity changed it all. Therefore, a completely new scenario developed.

In the year 2000, I came here (Tel Aviv) with my partner to channel, and some of you might have been here that time. You might have heard the words of my partner as he repeated a phrase I had given to him. I told him nothing significant would happen on the planet until the *draw to zero*. This was not given in channel, but rather given to him in on-stage dialogue. This was on purpose, since it was potentially frightening information, and it was only for you to hear and not for the whole planet to see. At that time, he had no idea what that meant. He was asked many times, *"What does draw to zero mean? It sounds like war."* And he did not know until 2001, in September, when the *draw to zero* became *Ground Zero* in Manhattan.

And that's when the world was brought to the realization of what the Jews have always known. They have to see the impact of *spiritual rage*, something we told you to look for within the scheme of the new energy [Kryon Book 8].

My partner took me to what you call the United Nations and I spoke there. And I asked them to see if they could find any prophecy at all about what you call the 9/11 event. There should be, don't you think? This event will affect two full generations of humanity. What the most powerful nation on the planet does with that event will affect two generations. And you think that was an accident, with numbers like nine and 11? *Appropriate illuminated action of completion.* It gets everyone involved, doesn't it? *"And why should everyone be involved?"* you might ask. It's not about war. It's about involving all humanity in the understanding and realization of what must be changed.

"Oh, Kryon, it looks so ugly. It looks so ugly. Everywhere we look on the earth it seems like things are getting worse and not better." And that's very relative for a Jew, is it not? For you have seen all of it. My dear brothers and sisters, you've seen all of it. When you turn a light on in a dark place, it reveals all of the dark things that are there. You're looking at a renovation of humanity. Now, everyone can take a hard look at what is really there when the light is turned on. We'll call it the "Years of Revelation." Things that were not known by all, are now revealed. We've told you before that conspiracies will be broken. There can be no secrets kept, and you will see many in high places fall. The way corporations and governments are run will change. And you've seen this even in the last few years. When did you ever think that you would see the energy of integrity prevail over conspiracy? It's happening everywhere. That, my dear Human, is a new consciousness. It's slow, but it's happening.

Let me tell you about Gaia. Gaia is an entity you call planet Earth. Think of the energy of the entire earth as having a personality, perhaps even an angelic form? How many of you, when you walk on the dirt of the earth, feel the energy of Gaia? Do you honor what you would call Mother Nature? Did you know that Gaia knows about the Jews? Did you know that Gaia is waiting for your action?

I'll tell you something else. You're not going to be able to do it alone. And this is where, as my partner says, this story gets good.

There are millions all over the planet who cast their eyes upon this land, and they are not necessarily pro-Israel. Instead, they're pro-peace. And that is meaningful for all of you. You won't have to do this alone, for your support group is willing and ready to send the light to illuminate those areas where you need to work in the light. But *here* is where it has to begin!

The greatest irony of the ages is that the spark of difficulty in the year 2000 was supposed to create what has been called the end of civilization. Instead, we are saying that the spark that will come from this area is going to cause peace on Earth. Oh, there are many that say that there is so little hope, and such frustration! *"Who are you that you can change the potential of the earth?"* You ask this as though you were simply the victims in some kind of odd game. Is that your attitude, is that your consciousness? Is that why you came here? Have you been so callused in what you've experienced that you go from day to day just saying, *"I hope it doesn't happen to me. I'll just move forward and keep my eyes down."* Oh, Israel, we need you to change that! And you'll know it's being changed because we can see some potentials of your future here, grand potentials that speak of heroes of Earth.

Let me give you a real potential, a potential picture that you can't imagine. We see a new leader here. This is a potential that sits here ready to be fulfilled. A new leader here, that will give you, for the first time, a majority party. Something you don't know anything about, since you've never had this! That leader has the potential of eventually being called *The Hero of Israel.* This new majority will be called many things, and experience much resistance to it. It will go against a great number of fundamental traditions, but many will call it the *Party of Peace.*

Let me tell you what will result. It will create the lines of demarcation on many borders through wisdom and understanding and cooperation. These borders will stay and remain borders, not an armistice or a temporary unstable "fix." It will be a final border of a land called Israel. And history will show that those on the other side will welcome it! For its their border, too, and they need it!

Go ahead, ask the mothers of those of you and those on the other side what they really want. Ask the mothers, the growing force on this planet, and they will tell you they want peace! They don't want your destruction. They want their children to play in safety, without the threat of those who argue with them within their own lands. It may take generations for them to look at you without hate, but they will agree about peace. That's what you have in common.

When the borders are established and there is consensus, it will disengage so much hate all over the earth. It's all about Israel! The spiritual rage that is rampant all over this planet has its seeds here, and when you disengage this situation, it will take the wind out of the sails of this hatred. Slowly, but it will happen this way.

Is it true that the world will revolve peace-wise around what happens here? Could it really be that you are the catalyst for it all? What do you think the third temple is all about? It's the New Jerusalem, and it's a concept, not a place. That is the theme of all of the days of my partner here in this place.

Number one, what happens here makes a difference for all. Number two, you are not alone in your endeavor. And number three, the pure lineage of this planet, which is called the Jews, is where it must begin. We'll say this again: metaphorically, the third temple is being built and we'll say it again, that the name of this process is the New Jerusalem. And we'll say it again that this name means *peace on Earth.*

As go the Jews, goes the rest of the planet. And that is a profound message when I sit in front of Jews. Blessed are you who have come to this place. Blessed are you who have come through the wind of birth deciding yet again to come back and make a difference. Blessed is this place called Israel. Against all odds, this is where the seeds of peace are. And yet you say, *"When? Could it be tomorrow, please?"*

God is slow and you, of all humanity, will know that. You hold the light for the planet. Let me ask you this: If it isn't in your lifetime, can you still hold the light of hope and promise? Well, we say this. If you can say that, then it will be in this lifetime.

Until tomorrow, and so it is.

Message to the Jews - Part Two

Channelled in Tel Aviv, Israel

October 2005

Photos at: http://kryon.com/israel

Chapter Eight

Message to the Jews - Part Two
Tel Aviv, Israel - October, 2005
Chapter Eight

From Lee: Kryon's full message to the Jews was spread over three days, given both in Tele Aviv and Jerusalem. In the re-channelling process for print, some of the concepts brought forth in the future day's messages were brought into the existing channelling for clarity. In addition, all these channellings were given live in a "back and forth" translation process from English to Hebrew. This kind of translation creates many short sentences in English, and to facilitate better reading, these have been put together and made to flow easier. If you wish to hear the original messages with the Hebrew translation, they exist on the Internet as free, downloadable MP3 files. [www.kryon.com/freeaudio]

Morning Surprise Channelling

Greetings, dear ones, I am Kryon of Magnetic Service. There are those of you who would believe that this cannot be happening, that Spirit or God talks to humanity like this. Again, we remind you that this has always been the way of it, no more profoundly shown than in your own history. The proof is how does it feel? Do you know what is going on right now? All of the scripture that has been written on Earth of all of the religions that exist has come from Human Beings. All of the messages that have been written to you, even from the angels, have been brought through Humans. Therefore, it is a partnership and always has been. Think about this – the process is taking the divinity that is inside the Human Being and marrying it with the energy of God. The result is a glorious message of release. So I invite you to feel it.

Did you ever wonder if your ancestors could look at you now, what would they say? What a vision that would be! Go as far back as you like with your lineage. What would they say? Well, I'm going to tell you something. They are here! Even the prophets are here. And the reason they are here is that you are the ones who will accomplish what all of history up to now has led to.

Are they proud of you? Not only are they proud, but they stand behind you. You are never alone, and your own ancestors sit next to you. Even those you recently loved and lost in your lifetime are here. We invite you to feel them. Let me ask you this – can you feel the love of them and of God beside you? Is it in your power to feel this? Let me also ask you this – with all that is going on right now outside, with the potential of the future unrest that is in your lap, can you say, *"It is well with your soul?"* Can you do that? If you can, then you've joined the lineage of your fathers and their fathers who said the same thing.

They understood the principle of divinity within, and they understood love and the incredible power of it. We are speaking of the love of God for humanity and the love of Humans for Gaia. Some have said even today, *"Kryon comes and speaks of peace on Earth. Now, look at the new developments! It's not getting better; it's getting worse."* [Speaking of the violence that has happened even as Kryon arrived in Israel]

When we were here the last time [2000], we made a statement. We told you that before the New Jerusalem could be created, the foundation of the temple must be scraped clean. This is a metaphor, yet I tell you what is going on outside [the violence] is indeed *the scraping*. It is not pleasant. It has created anxiety, and it's frustrating. So, in the process of being here next to it, can you say, *"It is well with my soul?"* If you can, then you'll understand that you hold energy in the midst of crisis that feeds Gaia's wisdom. And in this particular new energy, you are working with the planet to allow the future to go somewhere positive.

All of what you are seeing is the beginning, not the end. And you might say, *"But why us?"* The answer is because you are the chosen ones. You have been chosen to go through the frustration. What if you were the ones chosen to do the heavy lifting of this planet? What if this is what "the chosen ones" means? Well, we're going to give you a statement and then we're going to close.

God's chosen ones in this new energy will create peace on Earth. That's indeed what you have been chosen for. Again, we'll say, it starts here. Do not despair. Hold the love of God next to you so that in the worst moments of your life you can say, *"It is well with my soul."* And when we come back in a moment, we will speak more of love.

And so it is.

Evening Channelling

Greetings, dear ones, I am Kryon of Magnetic Service. One more time, I come into this sweet place, a place with a gentle countenance. These few moments are spent letting the entourage come in. Esoterically speaking, these are times when an energy greater than yours flows into this place. Although I do not speak of it often, let me tell you what this entourage is here for. Some say, *"Well, it's ceremonial."* Some say, *"It's the placement that matters, where they are, next to whom."* But you must understand that they are interdimensional. There is no such thing as *where* in interdimensionality. Distance does not exist, either. Time does not matter. Yet here they are, out of time and space.

So, let me tell you their function. All of them come in with the knowledge of who you are, and each knows your name. Metaphorically, they sit next to you right now. Some of them stand behind you.

Oh, I know, I'm speaking in an esoteric way, and there are those who would say, *"Can you prove any of this, Kryon?"* I will not, but you can. That's the way of Spirit, you know? The Human must be the one to prove it to him or herself. Let your own heart discern what is happening.

These who I speak of are arriving right now. You might say, *"But there's no space between the chairs."* To us, there's infinite space between the chairs. They are very large and very small, and they are almost in place around you. Dear Human Being, you have free choice, and *the rules* are strong with us. They are not allowed to touch you unless you allow it. And only with your heart connection can you allow such a thing. Only with a firm commitment of belief that says, *"Yes, I know there is more."* Slowly, then, they are allowed to touch you.

Once that connection is made, let the proof be seen! Some of you will be touched tonight. Some of you will feel it on your shoulders and on your arms. Sometimes, it's your legs and head, but this is a connection that is made that enhances the message of Kryon. It lets you *see* beyond your sight, like being plugged into an interdimensional place. That's why the entourage is here, for you, honoring you and your free choice.

Again, we say that there will be those here who doubt any of this is happening. They doubt such a thing is possible. You might say they are unbelievers, but the irony is that they have this entourage, too. They are loved just as much as any of you, and with free choice, the unbelievers will leave this place never understanding or believing that there were those who surrounded and loved them. The love of God is this way. It allows the Human to walk from place to place, undisturbed by Spirit. Wherever they go, they have the opportunity of spiritual discovery with their free choice. Only if they open the door themselves, can we show ourselves and begin a process of enhancement, a process that brings peace and health. It starts with intent, and these who come for you are all in place to do just that. That means we are ready; all of us. Let this message be one you will not forget.

This is the fourth time we have communicated within the energy of this auditorium. And now I'm going to speak about the grandest and greatest subject of them all, one that has many facets, many directions. It is a lesson on the power of love. You might say, "*Well, what does that have to do with the situation?*" [To the Israelis, *the situation* is used to mean the struggle with the Palestinians, as well as with those who openly hate and despise their land.] As I lead you through this teaching, you tell me the answer to that, for it should be obvious.

Every Human here who is an adult has felt at one time beloved feelings for another Human Being. It is Human nature no matter what race, no matter what culture. Humans fall in love with Humans. What a glorious feeling! Do you remember it? Do you remember when you first felt it? Humans do odd things when they're in love, you know? Do you remember? They jump up and down with joy. They make fools of themselves and tell their friends. Humans in love are fun to watch! What an energy between them! Your psychology doctors have said this about being in love: They say, "*It is so amazing, it is like a temporary insanity.*" What an energy to be in love! And I bring this to you first, because so many of you have felt it and remember the feelings. Remember the first time you laid eyes on the one that meant so much to you, and all the emotion that followed beyond that time. Now tell me, is that a falsity or is that true? It is real or imagined? And what is it that happens with your body? There's chemistry. Your very brain is affected. All of these things, together, create energy between the Human Beings that can be felt. And you know of what I speak. It's pure energy and it's thick with reality!

And is this also true with animals? How many of you are in love with an animal? I already know the answer, for I know who is here. Don't you love the unconditional love you get back from an animal? When you look in their eyes, you see the preciousness there. Are you surprised that the animal feels this? So often, the love is returned. How is it there can be love between a Human Being and a simple animal, some very small and some very large. Here's a creature that has no intellect and cannot even speak your language, yet they have love. What if this energy called love was a universal property? I'm going to ask you some questions in a moment about that.

It's a very energetic and powerful thing, this love. When even the animals of the planet can feel a Human Being giving it to them, do you think that there is actual energy being transmitted with the emotion of love? When my partner gave his presentation today, he showed it to you. When the researcher who deals with water did his experiments [Dr. Emoto], he asked the Human Beings to direct their thoughts of love into the water, and you saw the visual proof that the water changed. Indeed! What if nature responds to love? What I'm telling you is that there is a very strong field connected to this emotion. It can change the chemistry within a Human. It is a field that is felt by the animals of the world. Nature even responds to it. So is it a stretch of your imagination to think of what it might also be doing esoterically? What if love, and the emotion of love, were interdimensional? What kinds of effects might it also be generating around you? What if you could somehow direct the affects of this interdimensional love energy to a place? Would it make a difference?

Let me ask you this – do you think the angels know what you're thinking? Indeed, they do! There is no judgment, only beautiful understanding and wisdom. But the angels surrounding you now are waiting for something. I'll tell you what it is in a moment. The very emotion that is love and compassion has an interdimensional field.

To you, that might mean nothing, but I'll tell you what it means to us. It's like a bright light that illuminates the darkness. Can you allow the thought, for even a moment, that the emotion of love might be able to change your own DNA? *"Oh my!"* you might say. *"That's way too simple and trite. Here is Kryon saying we're going to love ourselves into health!"* Well, it's a good beginning, and it's filled with profound truth.

Examine the new energy work on the planet for a moment, and the teacher Peggy, and the work she has been given to guide her information to the planet. [Kryon is speaking of Peggy Phoenix Dubro, of the EMF Balancing Technique™, who is part of the Kryon team and has presented earlier in the day.] Look at where she begins her teaching. She must first teach how to be compassionate. She starts at the beginning of her lessons with love. Why should such a thing be? Is this really part of healing?

What I'm asking you to understand is that the energy of love is absolutely universal, that it is global and everywhere. Is this a basic rule that you have never even considered? What if, before you could do anything else, you had to learn to love? What if I told you that this love energy turns on a light that actually starts a process of higher vibrations. Did you know that? What if this love energy is the catalyst for almost every process of growth the Human wanted?

So many Humans want to touch God. They'll climb as many stairs as they're told to to accomplish this. They'll walk the miles, they will move into the odd positions, speak the words, sing the songs, say the prayers, and do the chants. Then, at the end of the day, nothing happens. Then they will do it again, thinking that they were not worthy of God's attention.

I am telling you that the core of God's attention is much simpler than that, even simpler than the processes that men assign to it. It's about the compassion of love! *"Well,"* you might say, *"what kind of love? There are so many kinds of love. Where do we begin?"* So I'm going to ask you some questions. Plug your own answers in when you hear them. These questions are given to you so that you might do self-examination and have realization and revelation as the result.

The Earth

Are you capable of loving the earth? Are you capable of loving Gaia? You're going to hear more from Kryon about Gaia. As the planet vibrates faster, it includes you. Some feel that the planet is out of control with the storms and the earthquakes. Now, this may sound odd and strange, but how would you like to bring the planet under control? If so, then turn your love upon Gaia! What an odd concept, you might say. Can you be *in love* with the Earth? Yes! Some of you can. Some of you know of what I speak. Can you love the Earth as you would another Human Being or God? Yes! Here's an invitation to try, for an interesting thing takes place. There's a circle of energy that, when you put your love into the Earth, stays there. The compassion and the love that you put into the planet are then shared with those who are born onto the planet. In other words, the children get it! Think of it as a depository of love that the new children of the planet will see and use.

This is complex, but we are endeavoring to simplify it. Think of what this means. How would you like the future generations here in Israel to feel what you deposit into the ground? We've not spoken of those kinds of things before, but project this. What feeling do you give your children now? What do you tell the earth that your future generations will *feel* and pick up and work with?

Your Own Cells

Here's another odd one, a challenge to you. Can you love your cellular structure? I'm talking about the individual cells of your body. "*That's too odd,*" you might say. I gave you information through my partner yesterday. He reported the results of others that there is, indeed, a code in your body, and that this code says that you have God in you. [Speaking of the work of Gregg Braden and the God Code] Every piece of genetic material has this code in it. And this code is actually a receptor system, ready to respond to the field of energy you give to it. Therefore, I say to you, if you can love the cellular structure of your body, it will *know* it and respond.

How many of you have ever taken a little time to celebrate your elbow, for instance, or your big toe? It sounds funny, but they are every bit as enlightened as you are! The whole body needs to be included when you're going to love Gaia. You are trillions of cells, all with *God within*. There is strength in numbers, and these trillions of cells together, if they receive the *code of love*, are going to cooperate with you. I challenge you. Can you love yourselves? If you can, the actual cellular structure of your body will respond and balance itself.

Family

Now consider this. Can you love family? You're not going to like this. I'm not talking about your relatives, but rather I'm talking about the Human family that is karmic. Did you ever wonder what that might include? The struggle you are in right now includes them. [The Palestinians] You're not going to like this. How much can you love them? You say it's impossible for an Israeli to do this. There has been too much history, too much hate and too much death. And I will tell you this, dear Human Being, if you have the wisdom and the courage to love them as Humans, even from a distance, and mean it, the very dirt of the Earth will change around them and you. This is how the new consciousness gets spread. This is the esoteric core foundation on which peace can be built.

It's interesting to consider that free choice is never interrupted. Think of it this way. Your love is a light. It's sent to the places that are dark. And with free choice, those who are in the dark can choose to see or not see. The light of your love is so much stronger than any dark place that they might be in, that they will sense what you're doing. Things around them will be revealed that they have never seen before, like wise choices and reasonable thinking. This is the truth. Did you know it was wrapped around love? Are you starting to see where we're going with this? If you're going to do the heavy lifting on this planet, it's not about suffering or enduring the hate of others. The hardest thing we ask of you is to take those on the other side and surround them with a bubble of love and light. That's the most difficult of all.

Humanity

Can you love humanity? How much do you think of those around you in other places? Perhaps you think your problems are so deep that you don't have time? Blessed is the Human Being who can look past his own situations and share his light with those who need it. How much do you love humanity? Oh, if you knew the truth, when you leave this place through what you call the process of death, which we call an energy adjustment, you take on your magnificence and return home. On the side of the veil from where I speak, I tell you that I can see *family* all around you. Every single person on this planet you call a Human Being is a collection, a part of your actual energy when you're not here. Family is like a giant pot of soup – called God, if you wish. You're aware of all of them, since you really *are* all of them. You know when even one of them does something, because the one represents the whole. One Human represents the complete wholeness, since the connection is esoterically a bonding of everything to everything. Difficult to explain, but we see humanity as one soul. Can you?

Do you have the wisdom to do that? From the smallest cell in the entire earth, can you love humanity? If you can, you're putting energy into the earth that you're not even aware of, energy that establishes the core foundation for peace.

God

What about this one – can you really love God? I'm not talking about ceremony anymore. There's a new energy on this planet for you. It's the one that you deemed necessary in 1987. [The Harmonic Convergence] You're the ones who put it together, and now I'm asking you, can you feel the difference? This is not a God of law we speak of. This goes beyond men's rules of what you eat or when you work. This is a God of love! This is a 100 percent connection to the essence of the core of the Universe, which is love. Can you love God?

Do you have the wisdom and the courage to do that? And I will tell you, if you do, this spiritual entourage around you knows it and they will enhance your experience, and those cells you love will start to vibrate higher. You'll begin to become another person, the one that has mastery within.

Yourself

And here's the last one. How much can you really love yourself? Not your cells, not your elbow or your big toe, but who you see in the mirror? Can you love that? Here's the challenge, yet again:

Stumble from your bed in the morning and go into the room with the mirror. Turn on the brightest light you can and look into your own eyes. Say these words, "*I am that I am. I am a piece of God. I love myself as I love God with the wisdom and the honor that goes into it. I deserve to be loved, and I will love as well.*"

And why do I tell you this? Because, chosen ones, this is the process that is personal for each of you. This is a process that you must begin to understand before you can do the heavy lifting in your area. We have called you Lighthouses; we have given you the metaphor many times of where lighthouses are built on the planet, and we remind you again that lighthouses are never built in safe places.

Let me talk about the Israeli lighthouse. It is in a constant storm, shining a light that is very bright. And if you could interview the lighthouse, it would say, "*I've got a light on top of me that is love. Although I may be in a dark place, I don't have to worry because I've got my own light. I am not afraid of the storm because I am a chosen lighthouse and I belong in the storm. I'm here because I can make a difference.*" And that's the truth. Can you let that light shine bright? I know it's a metaphor, but if a lighthouse has a very bright light, without saying a word to anyone else, it can steer ships into the harbor safely. Without saying a word. Do you understand the metaphor? This light you carry, Israeli, can be the light for the whole earth, but it's got to start with you first.

You can't just leave this place and go out and say, "*Well, I love the premise, now let's go create life and light and peace.*" Instead, you're going to have to have a meeting with yourself first. And in this meeting, you're going to have to ask the question, "*Who am I?*" And when you understand that you are a piece of God, a chosen piece, at the right time and in the right place, that's when the Lighthouse starts to flicker. That's when the light begins to shine with the wisdom of the love of God that begins to create energy. I would not tell you these things if they were not so. It begins with you. But you knew that, didn't you? And that's the heavy lifting. All the other things will be added onto it when you begin this self-realization, and life itself becomes easier once you can love those that don't love you.

Oh, the principles never change, do they? The greatest masters who ever walked the earth told you about this. It is not new information. And here's a sideline you want to know about. When your light becomes brighter, that's when the healing begins within you personally, and you're going to live even longer because of it. You're going to stay here longer, and some of you may even see peace in your own time, one you have created.

With time speeding up on the planet, the very words *Human generation* may actually be far shorter than you think. And I say that for those who already heard me say it may take a generation to create peace. Well, why don't you just shift some time and make it sooner? (Kryon smile) The light you carry also helps to temper impatience. That's what the love of God does. Do you understand what we are saying? We're asking you to receive and generate a light that is part of God itself. And if you look back in your history, that's what your prophets did.

"Kryon, are you telling me that we are a generation of new prophets?" That's what I'm saying – masters each one. Could such a thing be so? How can you doubt it? Look at what your lineage has produced? Did it stop somehow? No! You are still a grand part of the movement of this planet into other lands and other energies, many of them promised. Let me again tell you what the potentials are. Right where you sit now, we see you on a track that will eventually bring solution and peace to this planet. We have seen that track since 1987. So continue what you are doing, and I told my partner that

he should look around very carefully. For he's in a place most sacred for the entire planet, a place unlike any other. He is in Israel!

The seeds of peace are within all of you. It makes him look at you differently. He is not a Jew, but he is like a coach who stands cheering you on while you win the game. And then he cries tears of joy because he knew you could do it.

And so do we, so do we.

And so it is.

Kryon Around the World

Mexico City, Mexico
2006

Lee Carroll and translator Leslie Pascoe

Message to the Jews - Part Three

Channelled in Jerusalem, Israel

October 2005

Photos at: http://kryon.com/israel

Chapter Nine

Message to the Jews - Part Three

Jerusalem, Israel - October, 2005

Chapter Nine

From Lee: Kryon's full message to the Jews was spread over three days, given both in Tele Aviv and Jerusalem. In the re-channelling process for print, some of the concepts brought forth in the future day's messages were brought into the existing channelling for clarity. In addition, all these channellings were given live in a "back and forth" translation process from English to Hebrew. This kind of translation creates many short sentences in English, and to facilitate better reading, these have been put together and made to flow easier. If you wish to hear the original messages with the Hebrew translation, they exist on the Internet as free, downloadable MP3 files. [www.kryon.com/freeaudio]

The time in Jerusalem was very special. It was promoted as a world peace meditation with channelling, and was a shorter meeting without the entire Kryon team. For months, many were asked to join us from around the world at this Israel time, and meditate with us all around the world where they were. We definitely felt their presence. Mr. Robert Coxon, a world-class musician and composer for our Kryon tour, supplied the music and also a guided meditation. The following part of that meditation of the day was translated into Hebrew, Arabic and English.

Robert Coxon:

Please focus your energy from wherever you may be… for we are here together in the thousands, the millions, an infinite number of souls together creating this new future. Feel a new energy being delivered to this small but troubled part of the world. Give the intent to create balance, understanding and compassion.

Visualize the old conflicts being solved, new solutions emerging, and a long-awaited peace manifesting in this land. Visualize a new freedom being born… an equal honoring of the earth, God and the Human angel.

In that breath, hold the children in your hearts and allow them to lead you into a new, bright, peaceful future for our planet – the New Jerusalem. Don't try to figure it out or try to analyze how centuries of trouble can be solved, but instead see it already solved and visit that place that is the potential of the future where these things are now part of history, not the present.

Visualize it the way it will be… peace… peace… peace.

[Pause as the music continues]

Kryon:

Greetings, dear ones, I am Kryon of Magnetic Service. Let me tell you that I know what is happening here.

Again, we say that many will tell you that what you are hearing is simply the voice of my partner [Lee], who you've been hearing for hours. But there are among you those who can feel the energy and see the colors. There are even those among you who can see the faces change [the morphing of Lee while on stage].

Some of you actually have interdimensional sight, so we invite you to use it right now.

This is the way God speaks to humanity and it always has been. Messages given through angels to the ancients are the way of it, and it represents messages given to humanity so that they could pass it on to others. It is no different for these current times, except the messages have changed. And you are the ones who have manifested this change.

I know what is happening here. I am the only one among you who knows how many have joined this gathering [speaking of the world meditation invitation over the Internet]. And you would be delighted to know that they are in the tens of thousands. You have an alliance with minds right now in many places on this planet. They turn their light and their consciousness and their thoughts toward you right now as you sit here, and all that there is within that energy is "seen" by Gaia. It actually goes into the planet and it changes the energy there. It changes nature itself.

Are you aware you are never alone? There are those around you who some call "guides" and "angels." Some of you say it is simply energy, but have you ever asked yourself, *"Does every Human have this around them?"* And the answer is, "Yes." What does that tell you about what might be happening in those difficult areas not too far from here? You want to change things, dear Human Being? Then change the energy of Gaia! As you change the energy of Gaia, the energy of the guides also changes around all of the Human Beings involved. Some of them actually temper their ideas and their thoughts. They start to think differently. Oh, this is not an elimination of hate. That may take generations. No, instead it's energy transferred into a new focus – the desire to live on this planet together and make it work. Did you ever think of that – that perhaps the light that you shine puts a light in the darkness, allowing others to see more clearly?

So we say again, you don't know what these [on the other side of the fence] really think, do you? Ask the mothers what they want for their children, and none of the hatred words will be there. They will say, *"We want our children happy, educated, abundant and joyful."* What a concept! This is what we are telling you that you must look for. Not all things are what they seem, and we know who's here.

Let me give you some guidelines for personal peace. Let me give you some guidelines for a personal path. And let me give you some guidelines that will help you to achieve a higher vibration. Don't be surprised if these guidelines have a dual purpose, for they're going to sound like personal guidelines for your own path. But they're also guidelines for peace on Earth. Are you beginning to understand that there is no one else who could do this work but you? You wander among your land wondering when it will get better, looking at the others, hoping they behave. All the while you have no understanding of the power you have to change it all. It's time for Israel to begin a process that has wisdom within it. I'm going to give you some guidelines.

"Well, Kryon, first, why should we even do this?" you might ask. *"What is the reasoning behind a personal path of enlightenment?"* Some have said, *"I am fine just like I am."* And we say this is why the earth has free choice, is it not? And I'll also say you have no idea how you are until you realize how you *can be.*

Some Guidelines

The first suggestion is this: ***If you're going to go on a journey of enlightenment, then you must pack your bags.*** Now this, of course, is a metaphor. We're not literally asking you to pack your bags. But metaphorically this means to collect the things you're going to need around you as you begin the journey. So you will get ready and prepare yourself. What does that mean for a personal path? It means that you start to collect the things you think will be meaningful on a path of enlightenment. Learn what you can about the things that have been presented in front of you. Perhaps these will be books, perhaps various meetings. With your pure intent, you may wish to learn how to meditate better. Perhaps there are processes that you might be interested in or meetings you might attend to learn more about the energy of God. Look around and see what is presented to you that might give you sustenance and prepare your journey better. If you want to create peace on Earth, you've got to get up and pack your bags. Remember, it's a metaphor. It means that you are taking a major journey – personally, not with those around you, not with the government or family or anyone else. As you clean the actual DNA residue of your own selves, you activate energies for peace on Earth, one Human Being at a time. If you are, indeed, a piece of God, this means that you may make a difference. So you are now packing for this trip.

Now, the next three things I'm going to tell you, you won't understand. They will be confusing and not necessarily what you thought. Here are three steps for your packing preparation.

Number one. ***Do not make any interim goals.*** You know you want to walk a sacred path and the Human Being loves to make plans. *"I'm beginning a sacred path,"* you say. *"And here are the goals: I'm going to do this and I'm going to do that. Perhaps I will go here and I will go there."* It's a simple thing, and you are told that it's good to do.

It isn't going to work! Make no interim plans at all. Oh, there would be those who would say, *"That's useless information."* However, it may be the best information I've ever given you. Humans have a remarkable talent for canceling the good things that God has planned for them. By deciding in advance what's best for you or deciding that you know far better than God does, you void the plans of God! Oh, be the tool that has not yet been shaped. You are the tool for peace on Earth. You begin a sacred path, but you have no idea what the tool is yet. It's like purchasing a ticket for a train. The ticket says it's for a destination to an unknown place, leaving at an unknown time. But the ticket is still good for the ride.

Difficult to imagine? Yes. But then I say, celebrate this process. Celebrate the unknown! Some may come up to you and say, *"What are your plans?"* And you smile at them and say, *"I have no idea and I'm so excited about it!"* Can you do that? Is it silliness or is it the way of God? Why don't you talk to your ancestors about that? Some call it faith and say that there is a bigger plan.

So let me present number two, and it's going to sound a lot like number one. ***Make absolutely no assumptions about anything.*** You've got it all figured out, don't you? You say, *"I'm on an enlightened path. It's going to be much like that person over there. I'm going to do what they did."* Then you make the assumptions to do what they did, since you feel they did it right.

Oh, you are a unique piece of God! As you activate these things around you, the energy changes in your life in ways you cannot conceive. The moment that you have started your process, things out of your reach or abilities begin to change. We're not going to reveal number three just yet, but this does relate to it. Make no assumptions!

I'm going to give you an example. Some of you might even be shocked or very disappointed at the example until I show you what I mean. Remember, make no assumptions. *"We're going to have peace in this great land,"* you might say. *"It's about time."* So I'm going to ask you a question: What if somebody came along and made this suggestion to you about the situation?

They say, *"I have a good idea. Let's go and take a Palestinian from the refugee camp and put them in charge of everything. Let's ask them to solve it all and come up with the plan that will work."* Most of you would quickly distance yourself from that person, would you not? What a crazy idea! How could that ever be? Let's get real. That's the last person who we would trust or put in a place of power to change things. However, make no assumptions.

I want to briefly put you in the place of your Jewish ancestors. As you slaved in Egypt, you were praying for a Jewish hero, someone who would take you out of slavery to the Promised Land. What if someone suggested that you enlist the help of an Egyptian? *"I see the prophecy ahead,"* they might say. *"We're going to take a prince of Egypt to lead us out of the desert."* What a silly idea! Everyone knows they're the enemy. They are the occupiers and the conquerors. They are the enslavers! What a bad idea! You're going to take one of their princes to lead us out?

Well, dear one, that's exactly what happened, as you recall. And I want you to think about this for just a moment. That odd and unsuspecting plan was in place a full generation before it was manifested. For the prince that I speak of, who was actually Hebrew, had to be placed correctly and grow up as an Egyptian before it could happen. More than 25 years were invested to manifest the answer that was perfect.

That's almost like a generation, isn't it? [Kryon smiles.] Make no assumptions! Make no assumptions on how you think Israel will find its new leader or its peace, for out of the strangest places may come the answers and it will be nothing that you ever thought of, or considered could ever be. Never throw away an idea that seems to be impossible, especially if it comes from a young person.

Let me tell you something that you don't know. This odd solution is actually being manifested now. Just like in the past, the potential is there for those growing up who are going to make a difference here. They don't know it, and neither do you. Neither did the prince of Egypt until it was time, did he? This is the way God works with you, but you continue to deny it.

There has been a shift on this planet, one of consciousness. Those who pray for peace are helping to manifest this. And some day when the plan begins to work, you will look backwards and you will say, "*Look what went into this seeming coincidence! Maybe it took even 25 years.*" Right now you think you're going nowhere and you're frustrated. You don't know what's happening that's invisible. But can you celebrate it? Can all of you celebrate the unseen? I know, it's like asking the slaves to celebrate something years before it took place. Against all odds, the prince of Egypt will lead you to the Promised Land!

And here is the third one. ***Don't make up your mind what the timeline is going to be.*** "*Kryon, I've tried this energy you've spoken of, of a higher vibration. I've given pure intent. I've done all the things you told me to. I know something is happening because I'm feeling it in my heart. But now I'm stuck. Nothing is happening. And I know it's supposed to happen.*"

Human Beings are very impatient. You think you're stuck. You think your politics are stuck. Nothing is going on that is good. Oh, dear one, I'd like to tell you something personally: The moment you gave pure intent for the change in your life, things went into action. Invisible to you, these things are. Action is taking place and movements in other areas that will affect you later. And while the energies you've set in place are moving around you, all you can say is, "*Woe is me, I'm stuck.*"

If you could interview the fetus in the womb, it would say the same thing! It can't see the upcoming miracle of birth. It only knows is that it is trapped and uncomfortable… more so each day! Our perception is that your miracles are taking place right now. We know what's for supper, but to you the meal hasn't been cooked yet!

How many of you can sit and enjoy "being stuck?" Perhaps it's time for you to start thinking of this differently?

The one who is hungry waits for the meal to be cooked. Getting hungrier by the minute, he blames God, the cook, that the meal isn't ready yet. He says, *"God, if you don't do something soon, I'm going to just leave. I'll try something else... go to another kitchen."* This person is like you. You never understand that those in this area are manifesting the answers, even as you sit there hungry for the meal you call peace! You are frustrated, waiting for the cook to finish the meal – something especially nice and complex, you hope. You can smell it being cooked, but you don't know what it is, and you have no idea where the kitchen is either.

There are so many who are frustrated. Your perception? The earth is stuck. Israel is stuck. *"We never have any good leaders,"* you say. *"There are no heroes here,"* you say. *"Too many political parties to choose from... too many zones, too many rules."* Maybe it's time you took the mantle of Eliahu, my Jewish brother! That's what this is about! Place the mantle of the master upon you so firmly that there's no question what you're supposed to do next! Make this time "well with your soul." Be peaceful with the unknown.

Say to your friends, *"I know that there's an answer and I'm working on it, by the prayers and the lights that I send to others."* And that's what this day is about. There are others praying right now. They're not like you. They believe that one prayer is worth 1,000. [Kryon is speaking of those who were praying with us at the end of Ramadan. Muslims and non-Muslims were meeting together that night and had contacted us to join them. They believe that on this day, one prayer is worth 1,000! Many, all over Jerusalem, were praying for peace at this very moment.]

In this energy, I'd like to tell you that these others are correct. You see, what you do here in this room makes a difference. You make a difference. They make a difference. Together, you are all united. So, in our final words, we would say this: Israeli and non-Israeli, leave this place differently than you came. Take the mantle of God with you and stand tall and acknowledge that you personally are a part of the solution.

And now we'll just take a moment to ponder this thing that you call promise.

[Meditation music continues for several minutes.]

And so it is.

Speaking to the Jews...

"Go ahead, ask the mothers of those of you and those on the other side what they really want. Ask the mothers, the growing force on this planet, and they will tell you they want peace! They don't want your destruction. They want their children to play in safety, without the threat of those who argue with them within their own lands. It may take generations for them to look at you without hate, but they will agree about peace. That's what you have in common.

When the borders are established and there is consensus, it will disengage so much hate all over the earth. It's all about Israel! The spiritual rage that is rampant all over this planet has its seeds here, and when you disengage this situation, it will take the wind out of the sails of this hatred. Slowly, but it will happen this way."

Kryon

Tel Aviv, Israel

How it Works

Manhattan, New York City
February 2005

Chapter Ten

How it Works
Manhattan, New York City
Chapter Eleven

Greetings, dear ones, I am Kryon of Magnetic Service. And so it is that you thought this room was warm to begin with? Just wait! [Referring to the lack of space and the way everyone is forced to sit close together.] There's an entourage in here that begins to push upon you. It starts from the back of the room and then moves to the front. It has been here on this 11th floor for some time. On Thursday [three days ago], something happened in here, very late at night. The room started warming up and entities started arriving, some of whom you know. A three-day preparation of the room began so that all of you would fit, and so all of you could be here to listen to the family.

I know who you are! This is not a fear-based statement. I *know* who you are, family members. In this room there is only one who is a first-timer on the planet. And oddly enough, that first-timer is one of the first to accept the energy, being fresh from somewhere else. It's not unusual and it's not uncommon that this first-timer is already on the path. The rest of you have come and gone and come and gone on this planet so many times! We call you "old souls," and some of you are even Lemurians – and you know who you are. All of you gathered in one small place.

All of you know of the transcription being taken at this moment. This transcription will reach the eyes and ears of many readers and listeners. So, dear ones in this room, let us greet the readers and listeners, for they're here right now, too. Let them join you in this room... there's going to be tens of thousands of them. This particular message will be available for those on Earth long after the vessel of the channel is gone and is home with me. The readers on the page, you see, are ones we know who will participate in this energy through your future, which we call history. [Kryon sees the future of Earth as "history" since the future becomes the past only due to time passing, and Kryon is in the "now."]

So, reader, we greet you and we say the words of today are for all of you. Listener and reader, I'll address you now and I'll ask the question we've been asking so often: Why are you here? Why are your eyes on the page, and why are your ears hearing this? Perhaps you came for healing? Oh, this would be a good place for that. Have you accomplished it all, or are those the things you're working on? Are you interested in progressing through something that we've described as enlightenment? You want to be a Lighthouse?

Completely, with free will, we give you this message today. It's about free will and the choice to move forward spiritually. It's a basic message, a simple message, but it answers some of the questions, yet again, all in one place for you to ponder. Many have been asking about enlightenment. So let me speak to you – all of you, reader, listener – and say to you: Did you come for a healing? It's a common theme right here today, isn't it?

Reader, what are you doing looking at this? Is there something here for you? What's surging through your body that you'd like to alter today? Divinity now presses upon this room. There are guides that you don't know you have who are here. Perhaps you'd like to greet them? Maybe you'd like to begin feeling them, for they have permission to touch you. Some of you might even smell them... the ones you don't expect to be here.

I've repeatedly told you of a system, but you still don't understand it, and you still don't believe it. Maybe today you'll be touched in a way that you finally will. We've told you that those you've loved and lost become part of your guide-set for all of your life. Did you know that? Do you believe it? Oh, this is the mysterious concept, is it not? *You*, when you passed over the last time on the planet, became someone's guide who is still alive today. That means that you planned a dual role on this planet. You think you're walking around singularly and you look in the mirror and you see one face. But let me tell you something yet again: You're in many places doing wonderful things on this planet. You're still with other people in your own karmic group as their guides. Did you know that?

You might say, "*How can that be? I don't feel that.*" Yes, you do. It's responsible sometimes for what you've called twin flames, or soul mates… all manner of connections you feel with some people that you're not aligned to, that you'll never be with, but who you meet along the way. And when you meet them you say, "*There's some connection, but I don't know what it is.*" And you have no idea that what you share is a quantum bond – perhaps you're even each other's guides. So complex is this that we don't intend to even begin to try to explain it. There'll come a day when you understand all of it yet again. We mention it only so you might begin to understand the real relationship you have with one another and even with myself. Later this year, I'll tell you all about it.

You come in to this earth prepared to help humanity and you think you're alone, and you think you're singular. Do you want to know why you're here? I'll tell you. Let me revisit it yet again. There was a time when you leaned into the wind of birth, when we were holding your hand, and we were next to you, holding you back for a moment. You hadn't moved *in* yet, and it wasn't yet time to go, and we were questioning you, "Are you sure you want to go? Do you really want to be received into the earth?" And you said, "*Yes. Look at what's going on down there, there is the potential – the potential that we can change all of it.*"

Did you understand, did you ever realize, did you ever think that maybe all your past lives, cumulatively, were like classes you attended for graduation? Would you have ever missed this graduation? That's why you're here. Everything you did in all your past lives has ramped up to this. There you were, leaning into the wind of birth, with all your magnificent selves. The interdimensionality of you glistens and sparkles in what you would call the holographic part – spinning, a diamond within a diamond. Gorgeous! Surrounded by entities who were going to come in with you for your support, you're like a little troop, you are. The big one and all the ones surrounding. You at last let go and started the trip, and as you were dropping into that place that you call birth, you were talking to us all the time. "*This is it,*" you said. "*This is the time I planned for. It doesn't matter what age I'll be when I awaken to my higher purpose. I'll be the perfect age and I'll have free choice and I hope I see it. This time around I hope I see it. I don't know how old I'll be when I see it, but I'll be the perfect age to find the mastery within, to become a Lighthouse for the planet, and to make a difference.*"

There isn't one here who is reading and hearing that didn't have that scenario, yet you wonder why we love you the way we do! I paint a vivid picture, do I not, of the way it began? It's even more glorious than that. You can't imagine it. So blessed are you among beings in the Universe! All of them are connected to you and know your name – not the one you have now, the real one – the one we sing to you in light when we see you every time.

The purpose of life is to discover life within life… the divinity hiding within a 3D existence. Could it be that this is what you were born for? Do you feel a calling to find out? Some do. Some don't. This is the free choice at work.

Why Begin?

And so let us speak of that free choice and what you have before you. The intellectual Human mind asks logical questions about the nonintellectual, interdimensional self. The questions are always the same: *"Well, Kryon, we'd like to do this, but you know, there isn't a whole lot of proof. Give us some proof and we may begin this journey of enlightenment."* This is an interesting subject for Humans. There's no real feedback, you know, in an interdimensional way, because you're not yet interdimensional.

Think of this: When you come into the planet in 3D, one of the first things you do is know how to eat. It's instinctual and you do it. You know how to begin and you know when to stop. It doesn't seem to bother you that you have to eat every single day, even though you ate yesterday. Isn't that odd? And you always have 3D feedback, chemically, informing you when you're full. You all *know* about eating.

What if there was a hunger, as well, that was interdimensional? Many of you are beginning to awaken to that because the veil is lifting. What if it's like a spiritual hunger and you're asking, *"How do I start? Where's the food? What do I do? When am I full? When am I too full?"* And so we say to you this is a quandary. It's like the chicken and the egg – there's no interdimensional feedback until you become interdimensional. So the first question is, therefore: *"How do I begin? Where do I start? Is there proof that it's real?"*

The only proof we offer before you is this: Why would you be here asking the question? Why are your eyes on the page? Is there, indeed, some kind of interdimensional spiritual hunger that visits you now and says, *"Is there more than I was told? Is there something else?"* Let that be the proof for now – the fact that it's here before you, and you're looking at it. Or do you all think this is a coincidence? Dear one, if you sit here or you read these words and there's no spiritual hunger, then stop this endeavor. It's not for you; it's not time; it may never be time. It doesn't matter, since we're dealing with free choice. You're created with a duality. When you ask the questions you're asking, in all appropriateness, and the answers don't ring true, then put all this away. And in a moment, we'll tell you what will happen to you if you do that.

"Kryon, how do I start?" The most difficult thing we've ever talked about is starting, and if you recall, we've discussed it before. If you're ready to begin, then find the food of spirituality that soothes you the most. Is it in the channelling? Is it in history? Would it be in the study of ancient religions and what they had to say about God? What would feed your spiritual hunger the most? Where do you begin? It's sometimes possible to sit all alone and say, *"Dear Spirit, with pure intent I ask you to open the door and begin the process with me."* Without reading anything, studying any history, without opening a book or talking to anyone, it can begin. There are as many different ways as there are eyes on this page and ears hearing this. The processes are individual ones, just as you are unique, and they will suit the consciousness you came in with – no right or wrong, just divine, interdimensional food.

Starting the Path

"Dear Kryon, how do I start? What is it like?" There's a linearity, the way things work in your three dimensions, that often causes an interesting, practical problem. You open that door, you pray to God to begin the process, then you sit there waiting for something to happen. Some of you complain it's not happening fast enough. *"I opened the door; I've been sitting here a long time, yet nothing's happened at all."* And you don't understand and you don't realize that *you* are God. What if I told you that you are on the other side of that door as well as on the side you're on now? Would you understand that?

Now, if that's true, and you're really in two places at the same time – a dual creature – that means that you actually help yourself open the door! Are you starting to get the picture? Perhaps it's you who are the master of the door.

Don't sit around and wait for God to do something! Pick up the tools that are handed to you through the door by the angelic realm (intuition), paste them upon yourself, and start the work! *That's* how you start. You don't just sit around. *"Well, Kryon, how do I know if I have this? You know, when I eat food, I know when I'm full. But here I don't know what I've received and I have no idea how much to ask for. What do I do?"* You don't understand yet. There's a coat of many colors that has your name on it. It has been handed to you through the door. It's *your* coat. It's the mantle of Spirit, and when you take it, you may be troubled knowing which arm to put in first, but it fits you perfectly. You know you have it, because you *feel* it on you, and you're warm! It couldn't be a more perfect fit. See, it was tailored for you for years! The colors all represent your life, the solutions to your challenges, and why you came here. So, the answer is that you experience the proof. You *feel* it at a heart level. You may not feel the coat on you, but you're spiritually "warm," so you know it's there.

Then you might ask, *"So when do I get the tools, and how do I know I have them?"* The answer is this: If you can give pure intent for these things, then you have them. They may not be given by your clock, either. And they may not feel the way you think they ought to feel. Some say, *"I've been meditating for a long time. I know what it feels like when I'm 'in tune.' I get in this position, and while there I hold my mind a certain way in consciousness. Is that it?"* No. Unfortunately, you can't use this method to validate an awakening experience. We've told you the metaphor before. This radio station you've been tuning in to is moving off frequency. The frequency is becoming higher. You're going to have to spin that dial and find the new frequency almost every time you sit down to meditate! Now, that's kind of difficult, isn't it? That's a lot of work, isn't it? I agree. So why don't you do it automatically? Why don't you get into a mindset that says, *"I am a divine creature of Spirit. I'm in a position to tune in to the station no matter where it is. I will sit here and it will come to me, because I attract the light. The coat I wear is a divine one, and the color I have is one that will create the marriage of the very frequency I seek."* And indeed, it will!

All of this to say, dear Human Being, that you don't have to ask the esoteric questions about how much, how many, or when or where. It's going to be like the coat that fits perfectly. I hope I'm making myself clear. You'll *know* because it fits, and intuitively you'll feel the warmth of it. There's a great deal of trust going on within the starting process. Many look for 3D and are disappointed. They don't understand that the result of starting the ascension process is a "knowingness of Spirit" that fills you and lets you know that you're beginning the process. This simply can't be explained, and even after you've experienced it, it still can't be explained to someone else. Explain to a space creature who doesn't need to eat what it's like to be full. He'll have no reference, even to food! Quite difficult.

Too Much!

Sometimes there are some who say, *"I've got too much of this! I did all of these things and suddenly I've got too much. I can't sleep at night and it's interrupting my work. It's got to slow down. How do we slow it down?"* Let me tell you something. When you open that door and that beautiful coat is given to you, you're surrounded by an angelic realm of brothers and sisters who you know and have known, all willing to go to work for and with you. Oh, I know this sounds simple, and it's a metaphor, but it's the best we can do in 3D.

When you open the door with your pure intent, there's going to be a whole lot of us pouring in and we'll push just as hard as you allow us to, because we've been waiting a long time for you to open that door! Ever since you were born, pieces of you that wish to reconnect have been there, as well as all of us! So the answer to that question, if you're receiving too much, is to simply tell us so. Guess who's in charge? You are. Did you think it would be some God in the sky? No. It's you. So all you have to do is say, "*Go slower. Dear Spirit, I appreciate all of the attention, but I'd also appreciate it if you didn't have the disco ball in my bedroom with all the angels dancing around while I'm trying to sleep! Go slower.*" And we will. We'll tune to you, for you are the boss of you. We'll give all this energy to you at the speed that's appropriate for your learning, for your attitude, for your sleep. You are in total and complete charge.

But let's review this idea, yet again, that perhaps there's you down on Earth, then there's God in the sky. In this approach, when you start doing things, God in the sky is going to come down and do things with you, to you, and for you. So this approach says you can't really control that, since God is bigger than you are. The truth, as we've told you for 16 years, it that there's no God in the sky. Instead, there's divinity inside the cellular structure that wants to visit the piece of God that resides in *you*.

There are energies in Gaia who are God, too. The very air you breathe is interdimensional and has life, and it's also called God. And the indigenous knew it and they tried to pass it on to your new cultures, who simply didn't believe it. There'll come a day when even science will prove it. The earth is alive! Most of nature is, too, even the things you think are not – like the air you breathe… all coordinated for life on Earth and a divine revelation created through pure intent.

The Ascension Factor

There are those who still would say, *"I'm really interested in opening this spiritual door in my life. I haven't read a whole lot about it, but it sounds like I can have ascension... true ascension. If I do all these things correctly, that means I can get out of here – I can float away. I don't have to be a Human anymore, and I'll disappear just like Elijah did. Sign me up! I'd like to do it."*

Let me tell you, yet again, about this. You forget the plan because of the duality, and, in all appropriateness, you forget everything you planned for when you were leaning into the wind of birth. I remember. We were talking to you, holding you back, making sure you really meant it and were ready. Now you look around and begin to remember that indeed we're telling you the truth, but you also read in past history that *ascension* means disappearing into thin air and "being with God." This isn't the way of it in this new energy, but many seek this anyway. They feel that if they embrace this spirituality, they can get away from everything around them... and many do!

Have you ever heard the expression that another person is too spiritual to be of any earthly good – they have their "head in the clouds" and there's not a practical bone in their body? This is the kind of person who wishes to use all this spiritual information to *escape*. Does this make any sense to you? It won't if you recall why you're really here – and that is to build a bridge called peace on Earth. You're here to hold the light, one that will shine in dark places that need to be illuminated so that free choice can be clearer for all. You're here to be an example and to stand alone, quite often, on the most dangerous shores of the planet. That's what ascension is. You don't float away, you don't "poof" in the night and become an ascended being that leaves the planet. It's far grander than that! You actually "die to self" and have a rebirth of sorts with your name and your existing body, but with a brand new interdimensional countenance. That's *ascension*. And you walk from place to place with new spiritual tools. People see your light, and you don't have to romanticize it, evangelize it, and you don't have to give them any Kryon books. All you have to do is have a light that's so bright, they'll fall in love with who you are. And, dear ones, it's not that hard when you carry the love of God with you to that degree.

That's what you carry from place to place, you know? It's the love of God. And what it does is *not* invade anyone's space. It does the opposite. It creates a space of balance that many want to be within. It's a special place, so powerful with peace, that you attract those who don't have the balance. They desire to be with you because you're balanced! Oh, we've given you so many parables about the way this works! Take care of yourself, and all the other things fall into place.

Just the Good Parts, Please!

"Kryon, I just want the good parts. I've been told that there might be some rocky things along the way." Oh, yes – let us be clear on this. Think about it. What will happen around you if you do this, if you begin a spiritual change? If you start shining a light in a dark place and you're with others who are used to the dark? They may not like you. They're of an energy that's not going to be what you're heading toward, and so there may be some adjusting to do. That's their free choice, but it also might be a rocky road for you. Are you ready for that?

What about your friends? Are they ready to accept you? *"Not if I get strange, Kryon!"* How about you don't get strange, but instead you become balanced by turning on your light? Blessed are the Humans who are not afraid of striking a light and taking on the mantel that's thrust through the door, represented by the coat of many colors. When they put that coat on, even the little ones [children] will see them differently. Blessed are the children who understand an enlightened mother, father, grandmother or grandfather. There will never be better quality enjoyment with your children and their children than when you decide to spiritually balance. They won't run from you. They won't shy away from you. Of all the humanity on the earth, it's the little ones who'll see your light first. Don't fear losing your family, since this isn't part of any requirement for enlightenment.

But it's still a difficult road. *"Kryon, I just want the good parts. I don't want those other parts. Isn't there a process where we could just go to the good stuff?"* Dear one, it's all good stuff! You have predetermined that challenge is going to occur, and you have predetermined that "challenge" is negative! What if challenge is simply scrubbing the foundation so that you can build a new house? What if challenge is simply going through the steps of learning? Your request is like a woman saying, *"I don't like the pregnancy part and the delivery part of having children. I like the stork story a lot better."* Well, that's mythology! So, indeed, you must experience all growth, since it's something that is yours alone to do. That's what the duality gives you.

What If I Ignore All This Spiritual Information?

"Kryon, what will happen if I don't do this? What if I just ignore everything you've been telling us for the past 16 years?" I'll give you an example, dear one, of the way it is. This is a beautiful story and it's the next to the last thing we're going to give you in this channel. There would be those who would read these words or hear this message who then say, *"This isn't for me. I don't really want it. But I believe in God, so what will happen if I don't move forward on a spiritual path? I want to leave here and forget this meeting. I want to put down this book and forget I ever read this. What's going to happen to me? Am I*

going to be punished? Will there be darkness in my life? Will things go poorly if I simply ignore it all now that I've been exposed to it?"

Let me make something clear, and it's something we've covered before. We give it yet again since there are still those who need to examine it in the context of this message. There was a parable we gave you many, many years ago. It has been published, and it's called, "The Parable of the Prodigal Son." It goes like this: The father, who you see metaphorically as God, sends two sons into the world. This is the metaphor for being born on Earth – two Human Beings come to the planet. The story/metaphor continues and one son becomes a minister and the other son becomes a hedonist. They both sow their own kinds of energies and their own kinds of seeds on the planet.

In this story, they both are in the same culture, and they both grow up to be adults. One seems to do everything right and has a wonderful life in integrity and spiritual growth. The other one seems to do everything that feels good and has a life of self-indulgent pleasure – often at the expense of almost everyone he's with. They both die when appropriate. Then they come back *home* across the veil and present themselves before the father (God).

So here's the information you should examine: What happens to them? We ask to revisit your scriptures. Go read this again. You see, both get the same party! When they return to the father, they're both honored with the same energy! It's not about what they did, or their works while on Earth. It's about being in the test of free choice. It's about being on the planet and going through the test of duality. God isn't here to punish you. You're not running around the earth in a rat maze for God. Your duality test has been described as when angels come to the planet and don't know who they are. With free choice, what will they decide? And the energy of this test is what is then applied to the very vibration of the planet. It changes the planet itself! In other words, the very scriptures of your own culture shout that there is no judgment!

All your energy now is about what happened in 1987, called The Harmonic Convergence, what is often called the 11:11, celebrated in 1992. It's the acknowledgment that the earth has changed its vibration and that humanity will never be the same. So the answer to the question, *"What if I don't do it? What will happen?"* is *nothing*. There's no negative thing that you will create by not being interested in this spiritual aspect of yourself. Your free choice is accompanied by honor of your choice.

Dear one, perhaps you're one that leaves the room and makes no decision, or puts down this book without any choices being activated. Perhaps you really don't want anything to do with this spiritual energy. Let me describe something: You're going to be welcomed back to the other side just as firmly and strongly as any other family member. *"Well, then, Kryon, why should I do it? It sounds like a lot of trouble."* Why would you eat, dear Human Being? The answer is because is sustains you in life. Your spiritual food is the same, but many are simply not hungry! Indeed, it is the sustenance of God within you.

Those who choose this path will end up lasting longer with a sweeter life, without frustration, and with little or no drama in their lives. They will solve the challenges slowly, little by little, clearing the way until they're satisfied within themselves that, indeed, they carry the energy of Spirit in their bodies. Their personalities will begin to change ever so slightly. You see, something happens when you put on that coat. All the ego that was you is forced into the pockets of that coat, and then you sew up the pockets! Oh, those Human things are still there, and will be all your life, and they want to get out. But as you wrap your own hands around yourself and wear that coat, your ego stays put right where you trapped it. And because of this, people don't see that ego anymore. Instead, they see the coat and the mantel of Spirit and the love of God.

Why not be balanced and live a life of meaning? Why not help the planet at the same time you're helping yourself and those around you? These are the real questions. Why not do what you came for? It's not about judgment and things that may or may not go on in an afterlife. It's about living to the fullest while you're here, being supported by an entire entourage standing behind that door who will assist you in this.

Did you come here for a healing today? Did you pick up this book hoping for answers? Well, let me tell you something right now, reader, listener: If you're one who says yes to this, now would be a good time for that healing. They're all here, you know? All the colors of your coat.

And with this we close. Blessed is the Human Being who has come here and whose eyes are on this page, who understands what is taking place in his body and the potentials thereof. For right now, we say this to you: You can leave this place differently than you came. You can stand up from that book and actually feel the rush of intent to change. Let the seeds of the healing you came for be implanted upon you now, so that when you rise from the chair, whether you're listening or you're reading, you'll be different.

What's troubling you? Are there challenges with your body that you can't control, that you can't seem to get a grip on? Why not leave here with a complete new countenance for that? Why not have this the gift today? What about the habit that's killing you? I know who's here! We want you to last a long time, Lightworker, warrior of the Light. We want you to stay here in good health and last a long time. We've given you the tools right here for it; we've given you suggestions on how it works, what to look for, and how to know you've got it.

You can have control over all habits, no matter what the chemistry of your body yells at you! When you start this path of enlightenment, a whole troop comes in and helps you with it. It re-adjusts the chemistry so the addictions fade away. Again, I know who's here! Do you doubt this? I know who's reading! I also know who came for a healing.

Blessed is this Human Being who has given pure intent for the healing they came for. Let them never be the same when they leave this place. Let these meetings, which appear to be channelling meetings, become healing meetings! With Human permission, let there be changes in the cellular structure of all those in this room who may give intent for this, for it is why they came. Not one came in fear. All came in expectation, so let them be solidified, amplified, balanced and healed!

The problems that you came in with will stay on the floor when you leave. That is the message, co-creators. It has always been the message. *"Kryon, when are you going to give us some new stuff? Every time we hear you, it's all about the same things. Different words, different parables, different metaphors, different stories. It's always the same."* I'll make a deal with you, Human Being: When you fully implement what I've been giving you for 16 years, I'll move on to something new. My message is about mastery. And when the masters stand and create the New Jerusalem, I will move on to the next phase. And when that happens, I'll celebrate all of you even more than I do now.

And so it is.

Kryon in Manhattan...

"Here we sit in a very historic place, and I'm not talking about this church [100-year-old structure]. I'm talking about the fact that we are so close to the event you call 9/11. Think of the loss of life there... in your own city, in your own town, in your own neighborhood. It's such a profundity of energy shift on the planet and it happened right here. I want to revisit with you for a moment these thousands of lives, lost right here. You know, out of time, they're still here. Some of them turned around and reincarnated immediately into a new "expression" on the planet. If you could interview them, I'll tell you again, what they have to say: They will tell you at some level, 'We agreed to this.' They will tell you that they knew about the potential, for it was in their interdimensional 'possibilities jar' when they were born. They will say, 'We participated in it, and it is part of what we came in for. We did our part. Now you do yours.'

Do you have the courage to take a look at the smiles they have on their faces right now? They are eternal, dear Human Beings, just like you, but you may not wish to look and it may be sorrowful for you, but the fact is that there is joy in their energy because they are known by God... every single one. Just like you."

Message For the United Nations

Channelled at the UN, New York City

February 2005

Photos at: http://kryon.com/UN05

Chapter Eleven

Message for the United Nations

United Nations - New York City

February, 2005

Chapter Eleven

This channelling has been "re-channelled" (a channel on top of a channel) by Kryon to enhance the meaning of the words that were given live on February 18, 2005, at the United Nations. The information that has been added is subtle and is intended to make it easier for readers to understand the message, which was clearer to the listeners of the live channelling.

"We seek to inspire, inform, enlighten, and uplift your spirits." This is a quote from The Society for Enlightenment and Transformation (SEAT), part of the United Nations Staff Recreational Council (UNSRC), a group of clubs sanctioned by the UN for members, guests, employees and delegates of the organization. Having previously presented to the group in 1995, 1996 and 1998, Lee Carroll was invited again this year to the Dag Hammarskjold Library Auditorium in the UN building in Manhattan, New York, to share Kryon's message. This message is especially significant, as it marks the 10-year anniversary of Kryon's first visit to SEAT. We thank Lina Arellano, president of SEAT, and Susan Bastarrica, vice president, for this wonderful opportunity.

Greetings, dear ones, I am Kryon of Magnetic Service. Indeed, we sit in this grand room yet again! It's no accident that you hear this voice here, for the core of this place is the core that will eventually help bring peace on planet Earth. Yet you don't know that at this point. Oh, you might hope so, since it's the reason for this building, but you really don't know it.

This is what we wish to describe in these few moments, and this visit, to put a cap on all the things we've said before [referring to previous times Kryon spoke in this building]. This angel [Kryon] will give you the lineage of some energies being delivered to you, and also of some central issues of this very organization – for they are aligned with Spirit.

The year 1987 – it's remarkable for what humanity did, what you called the Harmonic Convergence. Did you know that the attributes of the Harmonic Convergence align with the core issues of this United Nations organization? Let me itemize from this list that humanity has created at a cellular level, what goes on here in the halls [referring to the UN].

Most of those who would attend this building and call it "work" are into everyday humanitarian issues. Humanitarian issues cause a change of consciousness on the planet, and they're what the UN is about. Yet many people forget what you do here, and many feel that this organization may be outdated or ineffectual. I wish to remind you of some things.

Hunger: The elimination of hunger for all humanity has been the UN's goal since the beginning. Through your efforts, thousands of lives have been saved and improved in health. Working around warring neighbors, you continue to feed those in need.

Education: Educating others in their own tongue, so they can speak and read their history and see the wisdom of those who went before is indeed a humanitarian issue. And you create this here!

Disease control: Because of your efforts and the core issues that are here in these hallways, diseases that used to kill tens of thousands no longer occur on this planet. Think about it! Before you walk around wondering whether you've done anything good here, know this: If you belong to these hallways, Earth resounds with what you've accomplished!

Poverty: The elimination of poverty is ongoing. Some have said it's like a cat chasing its tail – it can never happen. Yet it's a goal pursued with vigor. Indeed, it's difficult. Strides are made in one place, but the population increases all the time and keeps you on your toes, doesn't it? But your intent is honored, and the results are seen. And the way you do it is often through education.

Empowering women: You've helped created equality for humanity in cultures that never had it before. Look at the strides you've made! Look at how this is happening on your watch. Even in the last decade, have you not seen the results grow exponentially? Oh, dear ones, before you believe those who would discount what you're doing, look at this.

Economic security: It's a phrase that literally means "a stability of government so that people may have clean drinking water and electricity of their own making in places where they never did before." And you do this.

I just gave you six attributes that are the core of what you do here in these hallways. Then there is the seventh one – the big one. That goal? The elimination of war on the planet... the creation of peace on Earth. And some here might say, *"Well, we haven't done very well with that. In fact, the world is in chaos at the moment and it's getting worse."* Yes, it is, and we told you that it would be. So before you discount these United Nations and declare, *"Well, it hasn't been able to accomplish its real goal,"* I will say that this elusive goal is the most difficult, and will remain so for at least four more years.

The event that happened not far from here, which has been called 9/11, should have validated what we told you in 1989 about the shift at hand. September 11 was not in your prophecy, and you won't find predictions of that event anywhere. It wasn't in the quatrains of Nostradamus. [Some said it was, and later this was shown to be a hoax.] It wasn't in your scriptures in this culture [The Holy

Bible], and yet this one event will shape humanity's future for two full generations... and it's right on schedule. This may not be what you felt you wanted, but sometimes a stick must strike the nest for the awakening of those who are asleep.

How could something that will affect the earth so dramatically be absent from prophesy? The answer is that you're not in the future you designed when you were born! The shift we spoke of – the change of energy on the planet – is here for you to see. Look at the logic in this, and begin to see the truth of it.

The Light Lineage of Earth: A Delivery Schedule

Let me give you the lineage, yet again, of what we call "the delivery of light" on the planet, starting in 1987 with the Harmonic Convergence, as we mentioned when we began. This 1987 event set the stage for a shift. The Harmonic Convergence was the beginning of a powerful and profound reality change for all of humanity. It was filled with the honor of choice for all Humans on the planet.

In 1989, the Kryon "grid group" arrived and began teaching what you might look forward to, and what you might do with a beginning new consciousness. That's when many of you believe Kryon came, but I have been here since the beginning, and you can find those who channelled me even before that time. I told you at that time that the magnetic grid of the planet would be moved, and it has been. [This was validated in 2002 – see www.kryon.com/grid.] This was to allow your DNA to shift with the new path of Earth. We told you that the grid would be settled in 2002, and that's when the real Kryon work would begin. Those are the attributes of 2002.

In 2003, we gave you the Harmonic Concordance – a bookend to the Convergence in 1987, and a time that represented closure, so that a posturing of energy could remain on the planet. Call it a graduation, if you will.

In 2004, you got the Venus Transit, another implanting of energy into the planet that was a balance of masculine and feminine. And not everyone liked that! In fact, the many who actually create their reality from an old paradigm didn't like it at all. The Venus Transit brought the beginning consciousness of a balanced planet, where humanity would start to shift the imbalance between masculine and feminine attributes of the planet. What this means is that Humans will begin to "think differently" about the way things are in regard to this attribute, and begin to change them. But unlike the past, the energy will support these ideas.

Next month, on the fifth of March, there's another delivery. We won't name it at this point, because it has many names within many cultures. It's not necessarily solar system based, as many of the others were. If you search, you'll find spiritual history that said it could happen. The March 5 delivery will again be subtle like the others, yet not so subtle for Gaia [the energy of the earth]. Call it an "implantation of a feeling of originality to the planet – the original idea of paradise." This, then, is a remembrance energy of the goal of the creation of planet Earth. This will begin to visit you on March 5, 2005. If you're participating in these messages via transcription, you're not too late, for this is a beginning energy and it will be increasing from now on.

Think of these events as a series of lights being given to the planet very slowly, when it needs it the most. Yet some of you might say, would you not, "*With all this light, why is there chaos? With all of this light, why isn't there peace on Earth?*" And now I'm going to give you still another metaphor so that you'll understand better what's happening, and why it's so difficult for any kind of peace at this time.

Metaphor of the Bowl

We give you the metaphor of the bowl. Think of a bowl in the sun, but with a veil upon it. The veil is creating darkness or dimness inside the bowl. In the bowl, there are billions of entities dwelling in this darkness. Many of them survive within a "dark paradigm," for they've been in the dark for eons. Some actually "eat" darkness [a standard Kryon metaphor that means that darkness sustains them and their biology]. Therefore, their lives are accustomed to the dark, and depend on it.

These entities, which survive in the dark, stay away from light because they can't survive in the light – not with the "dark biology" they have developed. Now, in this bowl, there are still some who seek the light and hold the light, but they're fewer, since darkness is the way of the bowl and has been for a very long time. Therefore, those who choose the paradigm of light struggle more. It's a harder life.

Now, in this metaphor, we'll say that suddenly the veil is taken away, and the bowl is flooded with light. The very first thing that happens is chaos for those who can no longer find dark sustenance! They'll be very angry that their "norm" has been upset. Next, many more light entities develop in the bowl because they've seen this light and they're absorbing it. Like seeds planted at night, they were waiting for the sun to come up, and they're responding. These are the ones who were never quite pleased with the dim light of the past.

Let me ask you, what would you do if you were one of the dark entities that depended on eating darkness, and suddenly it was tough to find? I know this is a metaphor, but this is simple and understandable. I'll tell you this, dear ones, that when you turn on the light in a place that's been dark for a very long time, all of the ugliness shows! It's like taking an ancient forest and suddenly defoliating it and lifting the rocks up to see what's underneath.

Things that have always been there are now showing clearly, but you never knew about them before.

And why is it that this bowl has to be exposed? And why is it that this must take place? It's due to mass decisions from humanity called the Harmonic Convergence, as we discussed, and it started a ball rolling that will flood this planet with light. In the process, many will fall by the wayside, many in chaos, many in anger and many won't make it. Others will adjust, but the ones who will "feel" the change the greatest will be those who are hearing and reading – the ones who have been waiting for this light. We call them Lighthouses and Lightworkers.

We spoke early about a war between old and new energy. It's *before* you, and it'll be *behind* you if you follow the instructions we've been providing you, for peace on Earth is attainable in your time! The bowl is the earth, and it's in chaos because it's in great transition. Dear Human Being, it's falling upon you individually to create divinity from within. Individuals who stand in the light will create a large light source. The ones who have been feeding on darkness have a choice, just like you do. They can understand and accept it – a new paradigm on the planet – or they can fight to the death, and many of them will... and many of them will.

Years ago, we told you that up to one percent of the planet might have to leave before the energy is shifted completely. Later, we altered that. The energy had shifted yet again, with you in control, and we told you that although one percent was not needed, many would be lost. We told you that the very earth changes themselves would be involved with some of that, and they were, just recently. Perhaps it didn't seem fair in your eyes, but you got to see it.

In your lifetime, in these last few months, Gaia has shifted more than in the past 100 years, just as we said it would. You think this is an accident? These things are all there for you to see, and many were predicted.

And so we say to you a number of things before we close. The first is this: The greater you hold your light individually, the more the earth will respond wherever you walk. As you increase the light, darkness must recede. And I know we are speaking metaphorically, but it is to say this. Take care of your own integrity one by one in this grand place, and the place will change! Hold your lights individually, and watch what happens.

And now the prophecy: This is given based upon what's happening right now on the planet. In these next four years, this organization may play a major part in disarming a major war. Get ready. Sharpen the tools of negotiation. Hold that light strong, for the thing that the building was built for 60 years ago may very well happen next. It will take place in the grand assembly, where the decisions are made that literally will shape the earth. Do not despair, some of you. You may wonder what's happening, whether your organization is as viable as when it was designed. It is, and it will continue to be. Peace is not "out of date." You're currently going through the winter before the spring. Believe it.

Blessed are the Human Beings who are brought to this place and call it their home, who work in these halls for humanity, for they are greatly blessed and that is why they came. And that is why they came!

And so it is.

"Strike the light and send it to the Sudanese. Strike light and send it to those dark places with governments where there's corruption. Strike the light and send it to the scientists and researchers who already have the cures for the more virulent diseases on the planet, but can't begin their work due to the barriers of certain leadership and their old ways.

Strike the light and send it to Israel and Palestine and get on with this solution! This is why you're here, and this is the agreement you made when you arrived and selected the culture you live in."

Message For the United Nations

Channelled at the UN, New York City

February 2006

Photos at: http://kryon.com/UN06

Chapter Twelve

Message for the United Nations
United Nations - New York City
February, 2006
Chapter Twelve

More than 10 years ago when very few, if any, were familiar with the *Society for Enlightenment and Transformation* (S.E.A.T.) within the United Nations organizational structure in New York City, Lee Carroll received his first invitation to come and channel. It was a profound visit for him, with attendance limited to guests of the organization plus employees and delegates to the U.N. The general public could not attend.

Subsequently over the last decade, many have been invited to speak and channel. Lee also has been invited back repeatedly. The below channelling represents his 2006 visit, the fifth time he has made this trip to that famous building on First Avenue in downtown Manhattan within the last 11 years. Held in the Dag Hammarskjöld auditorium in the secure areas, Lee again found himself in a meeting where only delegates and guests of S.E.A.T. could attend.

Greetings, dear ones, I am Kryon of Magnetic Service. Oh, as always, there would be those who say this is not possible; that Spirit, which you call God, cannot give messages like this. *"It's not part of God's protocol to speak so simply through a Human Being,"* they say. *"You've got to do things to create sacred energies. You must bow and call upon God in special ways, in order to get this kind of straight-forward message to arrive from the other side of the veil."* Perhaps this was true in the past, but not anymore.

The short time we have in front of these who have come to this auditorium to see and to feel Spirit is unique. I invite those here to see and feel the energy in this room. The entourage pours in here in a way that some of you are going to recognize – you're going to vibrate with this, for it's real. This is the same energy that so many of the prophets felt in front of angelic beings, but you are the selected prophets of the modern day... potential masters, each one.

When we come into a place like this, we say to you, *"Known to God you are, every single one."* Your angelic names are shouting to me in light within this place. When you come and go from the veil into this planet you call Earth, in the form you call Human, this light name is known to us. Indeed, you are family. We know who's here. You can never hide that fact from God. It's an eternal truth that you are known to God, wherever you think you are, and whatever dimension you think you're in. Family is like that. Even the one who is here for the first time in disbelief, saying this cannot be so, is blessed beyond measure, for he is family with a free choice "not to see." So it is no accident that you are here in the room with me – some in belief and some not.

Perception of the Way Things Are Today

We're going to walk you through a lineage of what we would call perception of what's going on today on the planet. Then we're going to give you what some will say is prophecy about tomorrow. It isn't. It is just the potential of energy manifestation. It "could be so" if the potentials are manifested into reality, which is a very strong possibility at this moment. We have told you before that this is the way of it – tthat Spirit, God, knows all the potentials of your future, but does not know which one you will select. Therefore, in one way, the future is actually known by God. In another way, your particular one is not! It's part of the "Human free choice" axiom that we refer to so often.

Many are telling you that you have failed, Lightworker! They tell you that you have missed some junctions along the road, and that Spirit has moved the timetable as though we were in charge. We are not in charge, you are. They will tell you that things have moved backwards, and that a centuries-old energetic time window for enlightenment has also been moved. It hasn't. It's spectacular information to get you stirred up, and it simply isn't so. It would be like saying that the clocks on Earth have stopped because you were late for an appointment. Some things just keep going.

The Aztecs and the Mayans saw it, and so did many others who studied the movement of energy on Earth: The energy of 2012 will arrive on time no matter if you are here or not! Remember, in an older scenario called the "Armageddon," you would not have been here at all! It doesn't matter what you do, Gaia will deliver this renaissance energy to an empty planet if that is the case, and would have been! The entire Human test is about the vibratory consciousness of humanity, and how ready it will be for what will occur anyway. For the energy clock ticks the plan of the solar system, and that won't change. All of our work is about how much you will change in anticipation of taking advantage of it.

I know where I am. It is no mystery to me. Eleven years ago, you led me and my partner into a committee room nearby [the first United Nations visit] where literally hours before, there was joy in a solution – a treaty, as you would call it, that represented a solution for peace in Bosnia. Smiling faces were there because that's what you do here, you try to work on solutions to almost impossible Human problems and interactions. It's one of the main reasons this organization exists.

Oh, we are familiar with your work on disease – the work for children – things like fresh water and Human rights. We know what you do here. But when you put the treaties together, when you can create something that was not there before, because two cultures come together – two consciousnesses – agreeing not to fight, that's the gold, isn't it? That's what everyone wants here. That's what they look for here. It's what they want today here.

In 1989, I began telling you that your Armageddon would not happen and it did not, if you noticed. All scripture was poised to give you the end of the earth scenario. Trouble in Israel about 1999 to 2001 would activate both NATO and Warsaw Pact treaty obligations to go at one another, creating World War III. You can read that in Nostradamus, and also in your religious Christian scriptures. It was prophesy, and you were born with it already published.

However, shortly after 1987 and the Harmonic Convergence, the Soviet Union fell over all by itself. No one had set any times for that [there were no prophesies for that]. Against all prophesy information, it fell over by itself – a consciousness issue that did not support it anymore. And you shifted gears. The entire earth had great potential at that moment. The U.S.A. did, too, since its major competitor had disappeared almost over night after 50 years. Some say that a potential was missed, and that the U.S.A. should have done things differently at that time. However, if it had, you would not now be where you are... in a struggle to define civilization and raise the energy of the planet accordingly.

Human nature is well understood, and governments have no surprises for God. I tell you that just in case you felt that one day Spirit woke up and wondered what had happened! It doesn't work like that.

I told you the last time I was here about the meaning of the 9/11 event that happened some blocks from here [speaking of downtown Manhattan]. Many of you are afraid of what 9/11 has created, and what the U.S.A. is doing with it. Many are afraid of what you call "a new world order." Fear seems to be the product of change, even when the changes were foretold. Many of you think God is asleep somewhere and that all this is happening "in the dark," so to speak. Many cry out for help.

Let me speak of the fears of today and let me remind you that in 1989 we told you to expect these things. We told you that darkness would be with you for a long time before it would get better. That's what happens when you take and expose the darkest things on the planet to a very bright light of integrity. Reality for you had to shift. We called you Lighthouses, and we told you that it was time to go to work. We reminded you years ago that you were here NOW for that very task. Still, many are shocked and hide in fear. Many who actually came to be warriors are shaking in their closets, with their shields at the ready and their battle armor on, but with no idea who they are or why they came.

Let me take you right now to the words of the fear mongers, for they create the conspiracies that are everywhere. They're here in the hallway outside, you know? They abound. Anything that happens on the earth right now creates conspiratorial views around everything. Let me tell you this is because when there is no guidance and there appears to be no core-good and no center, conspiracies abound everywhere. When there is no central guidance, information flies in all directions. And the thing that often wins in the darkness is fear. It's strong and with you now. All you have to do is tune in to hear it, for those who like to expound on what you are afraid of will win if you stay in the dark with the others.

Do you now see why we call you Lighthouses? You are Lightworkers who create light so that fear cannot and will not take charge. But some of the Lighthouses that are reading this are consumed with the dark, not realizing that they are their own salvation. They are starving to death, while their pockets are filled with food.

The United Nations is like that. There are many who say it has been relegated as irrelevant. *"It doesn't work anymore and it shouldn't even be here."* That's what they say. They don't know the work it has done in the halls of the building we are in. They don't know the lineage of the workers who have spent their lives here and what they visualized and what they did. Instead, those who would dismiss this organization see instead a perception of what has happened in these last years. Darkness seems to have pervaded the hallways, even into this very group [S.E.A.T.] and then out again [meaning that it was eliminated]. It's everywhere, you see? And there would be those who would say, *"This is proof that the world is going into the dumper [Lee's word]. War and struggle is everywhere."*

They tell you that these things are not in any prophesy; therefore, it's proof that we have failed. For if we had done well, then scripture would have prevailed and things would have happened as they "should have." Many say it's hopeless. Take a look at Israel and Palestine. *"The worst of the worst,"* they say. The fear mongers say, *"Take a look. We now have lost Prime Minister Ariel Sharon." They say, "He was the hope of Israelis."* And then against all odds, Hamas won the Palestinian elections! *"That is the worst news,"* they say. *"It couldn't possibly be any worse."*

Indeed, Lighthouse, what are you going to do with that news? *"Look,"* they continue to say, *"it's not getting any better; it's getting much, much worse."* And then they say, *"Here is the organization you sit in [The United Nations] and you can't do anything about it here either! It's proof," they say, "that everything is going badly and is going to result in the end of everything."*

Then they say, *"Look at Iran. It won't be long before they have a nuclear capability and the first thing they're going to do is bomb Israel! They have said as much. You'll have a nuclear war in the Middle East!"* It's the very thing that would have created Armageddon, so therefore, it has just been postponed. Many say that, you know? Many have said it's going to happen next year [2007]. Even though clearly in scripture it was told how it would happen many years earlier – and now the players aren't even there anymore to create it – the fear mongers want to stick to the old negative news, you see? It somehow feeds the drama of the darkness.

And then they say, *"You know, the Mayans and the Aztecs said that in 2012 we'll have the end of time. That means we'll all be gone in a few years!"* And that, dear Human Being, is the picture that is painted by so many who watch you and this organization. They look around and all they can see is the darkness.

It's an odd thing about darkness. There are three kinds of Humans who lay in the dark. The first group is the ones who tremble in fear, since they can't see anything. The second group takes advantage of the first one, since they understand that a fearful Human can be controlled. The third group is the one that has a light in their pocket, but are not certain that it will work... afraid to turn it on, since it will show where they are, and they won't be anonymous anymore.

When you tune into your news broadcasts, those are all enhanced with the same information, are they not? It's all bad news. Drama is riveting to the Human Being, and solution is not. That's simple Human nature. That is what you receive in your media, no matter what happens on the planet. Get used to that and listen "in the cracks," so to speak, of what else might also be happening.

Now, I want to tell you about the Lighthouses. I'm going to give you some potentials that some will say is prophecy, but, as we said earlier, it's only a report of what we see as potentials of what you are doing on the planet... something that is not reported by any news media.

We see what you might call *under the hood processes*... things working within a system that you could not have foreseen and that you will know about only later. There are things that are going on that have vast potential to change everything.

For those conspiratorial ones, let me give you something that you didn't expect. We have spoken of this before, but this is the time to speak of it more clearly. The Illuminati. Are you afraid of them? Do they exist? The answer is, of course, that they do. Conspiratorial ones will say that the Illuminati has been responsible for controlling stock markets, elections, commerce… perhaps even the U.N., for decades. Indeed, there is some truth to all of this because in an old energy, especially one of darkness and fear, this was not difficult by those who controlled shipping and oil.

In a new energy, where light is being turned on and everyone can talk to everyone, it is very difficult. So let me tell you what the Illuminati are doing these days. They are about to change everything and become the earth's "benevolent uncle." Oh, they're still interested in getting money and power, of course, for this is what they do. But they are beginning to realize that the old ways are becoming harder and harder to control. They were based in Greece, but they have moved to Africa.

In a not too secret move, they are moving billions of dollars from Europe to fund the curing of a continent. It is the Illuminati who will supply the funding for curing Africa of AIDS. The funds are there. Oh, Humans! Did you know that? You won't have to worry about that… one of the biggest puzzles of the past decades is on the verge of being funded and solved – the curing of an entire continent.

And why would they do such a thing? Because if they could become part of large, emerging governments, they will be on the ground floor of everything that happens from then on. Part of every tax collected will be theirs, do you understand? When you cure a third-world continent, it begins to fill with healthy Human Beings who can buy homes, have commerce, and trade with other countries by land. Do you understand? They'll have a piece of all of it. Tens of millions of Human Beings will be cured over the next decades. It's unexpected, is it not? Like it or not, it is in the works, and the result will be the saving of millions of lives.

You think that you have something going on with China regarding trade that is unique, don't you? Wait until you see Africa! Imagine, if you will, a continent full of workers that have never had anything to work for in their recent history. What do you think they're going to do? They're going to compete with the champion – China. Watch for this in the future.

This is the potential for those involved in conspiracies. *"It's too good."* they might say. *"It doesn't fit the old norms,"* they say. The villains of the past are taking on different modes of accomplishing what they need, and often it may actually benefit humanity. We'll leave it to you to decide the "new integrity" of it all, as is your task of free choice. As you have seen in your history, your judgments of "right and wrong" seem to move about with your advancing cultures and awareness. Indeed, welcome to a new energy!

Let me tell you more unexpected good news. This U.N. building and these workers are old. The United Nations is poised for a resurgence, a renaissance with new blood and new people and new ideas and new leadership. It will have gone through the darkness and if history will do what the potentials show it could, there will shortly be no one who could doubt the viability of what they do here in these halls. The delegates come and they go, you know? But the ones who've dedicated their lives who work in the buildings here are going to make the difference. The potentials are here for things that the U.N. has only dreamed about, including those that would bring together groups of different consciousnesses and cultures to ponder and provide solutions.

It's time to do what the U.N. was designed for – not a peace-keeping team with colored helmets, but a group of those who have the wisdom and the light to put things together, shine light on untenable situations to bring them to solution. That is the potential here. It's in the works, as they say, working right now. Still, there are many who say, *"I cannot see it, therefore, it does not exist."* Is that your reality? Or will you be a Lighthouse that's actually creating the light so these things can happen?

There will always be wars and rumors of wars – it is Human nature. But in the future, there will be fewer of them, and a general stability that has not been present before. The influences that the U.N. might have in bringing many various sides together is very important, and we'll say it again: The more that you trade together, the less tendency to go to war. In fact, a group of countries that is dependent on each other for goods and services can't afford war with one another.

Years ago, we told you two things to watch for in Israel and they're now happening. But the fear mongers don't want you to put this together. We said to you that before Israel and Palestine can put anything together, you have to have two leaders gone from the picture – Arafat and Sharon. They represented old energy enemies chasing each other around the globe for more than 25 years. At some point, both were in their battle uniforms as soldiers, even trying to kill one another. This was before they became leaders of their countries. It's an old energy concept that dies very hard within the Human and we told you that their departure would begin to facilitate a rapid change.

Literally months after my partner brought my message to Israel last year, two things have happened. In the meetings we told you that Israel was going to shift and change greatly, and it now is. Ariel Sharon is gone and Hamas has won the election for the

Palestinians. There are those who would say that is awful news. The terrorists who have declared the destruction of Israel have won! But you don't know about Human nature like we do.

The potential exists for Hamas to morph into something entirely different. We have said this before: Terrorists don't do a good job running a country, you see? When they are faced with turning the electricity on and building schools and hospitals, their former consciousness tools cannot do it. Opportunities are there for them to change or lose power. Oh, it's not going to make them love Israelis. But rather, a new goal may occur to them that asks, *"What do we have to do for our people to stay in power? What is our responsibility?"* And this will lead them eventually to lose power or change into those who understand that a fast track to getting everything their population really needs is to promote the road to peace. Ironic as it seems, this group may actually be a catalyst that provides the ability for Palestine to have its own state, and even be represented here at the U.N. before long.

Fear monger, reader, are you understanding this? For us, the reader is as present as the listener, you know? Are you fearing what's going to happen in the world? Are you fearing what's going to happen in Iran, in China? Your perception is only what you see on the news. It's a reflection only in what the leaders say, and their bravado attitudes. It does not represent the "soul" of the population. We'll say it again. Potentials also exist for what we call a *soft revolution* in Iran and also in China... but not within the same timeline.

The consciousness now is far different than it was 20 years ago, even 10 years ago, and some of the things that you would expect are simple Human nature, but they may shock and surprise you since it is not the old way of things in government. The young people are becoming more active all of the time and there's a lot more of them than there are of you. Don't be surprised if you hear from them in some of these issues you think are being controlled by conspiracy theories. It will boil down to these young ones, you know? Many of them do not agree at all with those who run their respective countries.

2012

Lastly, we will tell you again about 2012. If you will look at the real Mayan and Aztec calendars, you will see what they really had to say. What they foretell are patterns of energy potential that are all part of the time clock of Gaia. They're not calendars at all, as you think of them, but rather energy markers.

2012 represents a renaissance in thought, where light will come onto the planet. This new energy will not support war or the potentials of war. The *time* that will shift and change is "the old time." Some of you have seen this and you have been in your metaphysical belief long enough to see the changes and the shifts beginning to occur. You know what I'm speaking of.

How many of you consider yourselves Lighthouses? Let me remind you of something we told a group last week: 3D lighthouses on the planet [the actual cement ones] don't know anything about storms. Nothing. They don't know how big a storm is going to be, or how dark it's going to get. They don't know how strong the wind is going to blow, or how long it's going to last. But they and their keepers can see the storm coming, and they know when they're in it. They're built for it, you know? They don't care how dark or how long, since they are built for any duration! They don't care because they've got a light that's strong enough to help anyone troubled by the situation. You see?

That's why you're here! You don't have to analyze this current storm to deal with it. All you have to do is stand where you are and keep the light going. That's why you came to this planet this time, and that's why you're here. Spirit promises you that you have enough light and that your lighthouse will not be destroyed, for it was built for the storm. In fact, it was built for exactly this storm. Do you understand what we're saying? You don't have to understand it and you don't have to figure it all out. The last thing we'd expect a lighthouse to do is to turn off its light, close its doors, and run the other way because the storm is coming. It doesn't make sense, you see? And that's the good news of the age.

These are the potentials we see. And yes, it may get darker before it gets lighter. Remember, 2008 is a pivotal year. We told you that in the year 2000. There are potentials in that year that, if they should manifest, will change much, including what happens in this building.

Are you willing to smile? Are you willing to stand up and strike the light and say, *"I don't care what it looks like. I'm not afraid of the storm. I care what it's going to be when I'm done."* And that, dear Human Being, is why we love you the way we do.

This has been a message from the angelic realm. It's practical and real. We celebrate you, and the entourage in here celebrates you. And so it is.

Becoming Masters

St. Augustine, Florida
March 2006

Chapter Thirteen

Becoming Masters
St. Augustine, Florida
Chapter Thirteen

Greetings, dear ones, I am Kryon of Magnetic Service. Yet again this meld takes place, does it not, between the Human Being and the Higher-Self. The process you would call "melding with family" may sound a great deal like what you've heard for the last few hours [speaking of listening to Lee] – the Human Being in lecture mode. But it's not that way.

In these next moments, I invite you to feel the energy of a legion of what you would call angelic beings fill this place. They will "sit" upon you in a way that makes you know this experience is real. For by intent, each one of you have invited this situation into your reality at this time. The multitude can sit upon your lap and surround you, can hug you, can hold you around the neck and the head, yet the person next to you who gives no intent whatsoever will feel nothing. Here is an interdimensional attribute: you can sit in the stadium with us or you can sit alone, and that is your free choice. Therefore, you might say that your intent is your reality creator, for many will "go somewhere" tonight with it, while others remain static.

There are so many at this moment who have come prepared – have come ready. Wouldn't you like to move to the next level? Wouldn't you like to know more about the divine master inside you? Wouldn't you like to know who you used to be, who you are, and who you'll be when you're finished with this expression of humanism? All of that information is available. Did you know that? This is a precious place that is sweet beyond measure.

My partner makes fun and he makes a joke. He talks to the rug. He talks to the ceiling. [This is a reference to Lee, telling the audience earlier about his dialogue with a new hotel room almost every other day. He talks to the elements in the rooms.] Well, I'll tell you, the elements in here are talking to you right now. All of the things that you think are static and without life-force are part of the bigger picture. It may shock and surprise you to know that they are all in support of you. The trees that went into making the pieces and the parts of the wood here still have their interdimensional life-force. The fibers – even those pieces of what you would call inanimate metal – have a life-force. The air you breathe has interdimensional life within it, and all of these know the master who is inside you.

Many of you want proof of this, don't you? It's just too strange in your 3D reality to think that "things" can have awareness. How about proof that comes from an internal engine of discernment? Is your own validation of awareness and intuition proof enough, or do you need an outside authority? [Lee laughs, knowing there is no such thing as an authority on "thing awareness."] Why not ask your Higher-Self? It knows all, and each of you have this. It's actually a spiritual part of you, but Humans love to think of it as a separate part. This helps to separate the 3D from the multiple D… something you almost have to do to maintain sanity in a 3D perception.

Right now, this room is a safe place – an ultimate safe place. You can silently talk to your guides and ask them the questions you've always wanted to ask them. Many of you will receive interdimensional answers. Oh, not necessarily the 3D ones you expected. Instead, sometimes you may only get hugged and touched. But I'll tell that if you get either, you've allowed a two-way conversation through the veil and that's just the beginning.

Reader, are you getting this? This is a safe place for you, too… while your eyes are on this page. Get used to it, for as you read this, we know what is happening and see you as you do it. You think you are just reading something that happened in the past? Think again. These words and the energy of them will last an eternity if those in charge of the legacy of my partner's words wish it to be so.

Tonight some of you may ask for one thing, yet will walk out with another. Do you believe in divine intuition? It's a guidance system that will help you to know how fast to go and which way to turn. It won't happen in advance and you won't have the answer when you leave. It's going to happen when you least think it should, at the point in which you need it the most. Humans don't like that, but that's the now of it. They would rather have advance information to "tuck it into their pockets" and then use it when they need it. So think of it this way: We are giving you a package that is interdimensional. You will walk out of here with more than you came with. The reader will, too. But it won't manifest as a specific answer until you need it the most. Indeed, it's a bag of valuable treasure… but you don't get to see it until you need it. There is a legion of angelic beings here, and yes, they're all invisible. [Kryon smiles. Lee teaches the difficulty of proving invisible things to those with a 3D perception.]

Before we even begin the teaching, the invitation goes out: How many reading and hearing this message would like to leave differently than they came in? Isn't that why you're here? I am Kryon. I am your sister, and I present myself when you leave this planet and arrive on the other side of the veil. I am there when you lean against the wind of birth and are placed into the birth canal. That's where I say "goodbye" to you. That's what I do. I'm well known to you, since I am related. If you read my words and you feel something within them that you recognize, it's because I am your brother. I know all about you. We all do, and we sit in awe, not in judgment. We sit in awe that you would do this at all.

Perception of Past Masters

The masters of this planet all had something in common. Have you put this together yet? They walked this planet in divinity. They healed people when they touched them. They went from place to place and gatherings arose. They had miracles of matter manifestation. Some created things out of nothing. That's what masters do. Some continue to do that on this planet, right now. They are alive now and not parts of history, performing the same kinds of miracles. All that was, in the way of the energy of master-hood, is still here.

What do you do with the knowledge of these past and present masters, and how do you look at them? Ponder these things for a moment. All these masters seem to have a divine complement. The Human perception is that it is manifested divinity – from God, whatever that word means to you… "from God." God has touched them and that allowed them to have control over matter, over disease – ahh, control over seemingly life itself. What do you think of that? They are worshipped and most of them in the past were killed. That's what Humans do when they have things they don't understand. They worship it or get rid of it… or both simultaneously. Even in the new energy, this fact is so.

So I ask you to ponder for a moment what it is that they had – for this pondering has created every religion on the planet! Humans often ponder their prophets. And if they didn't have prophets, they ponder their Gods – and the pondering creates the doctrines, and the doctrines create the religions. Every one of the many religions on this planet was created through the pondering of the masters… what they said and what they did… what they taught.

There is an assumption that all divine things are separate from Human Beings. This assumption actually makes good sense, for it follows three-dimensional thinking. It's logical. You know how to separate the tangible from the intangible, and the things that are marvelous, unseen, invisible and miraculous belong to God. Things that are mundane and ordinary belong to you, the Human. And that's an old energy concept, if you know that or not, and it's a paradigm that's about to be shattered. What if those masters who walked this planet, who did grand things, were just like you?

"Oh no," you might say, *"No, they weren't like me."* Yes, they were! Have you heard the term, "Made in His image?" They were just like you, and you're just like them. The only difference is that they had activated certain parts of their Human interdimensional DNA, the divine parts that made them seem supernatural to you. And as you viewed that, you called it "God."

Here is the truth. In the old energy of your past, when you had masters appear, their lives shined like a lighthouse in the dark. Everyone saw it, and everyone considered it unusual and God-like. There is now a new energy, which I'll go on to explain a little more about in a moment, that actually promotes mastery. It invites you to take the light and enhance your own process to the degree where you begin an ascension process that has your DNA vibration ascending to a level of master or near-master. It's an energy that was actually present in the body of those who you worship.

It's not here so that you might walk the earth as prophets, as the old masters did. No, it's so you will walk the earth as your own prophet, answerable only to your own mastery as you walk in the light and the love of God – able to heal yourself first and foremost – and able to move from one place to another without being affected by other Humans or the drama of the moment. In a new-energy perspective, it's an attribute of divine power that I have been teaching you, and in an old energy perspective, it's what the masters told you that you could do.

So the truth is that you are just like them, but you haven't got the internal knowledge of what to do next to activate the toolbox that will begin to change the interdimensional layers of your DNA. This is appropriate and falls into the category of free choice. But the age of illumination approaches, and fulfills the circle of energy that the ancients saw in their calendars.

Perception of Good and Evil

You have this odd perception of good and evil, for it's biased in 3D and imprisons you into a concept of mythology that you feel is real. You think things that are good belong to God and things that are evil belong to another entity called Satan. Somehow, according to your beliefs, they are both supernatural, and they are after something you have, in a struggle of the ages.

In the middle of this dark and light struggle there is the bulk of humanity, and God and Satan are locked into some kind of a struggle to get your soul. Odd as it might sound in the overview of this dark and light, the Human is seen as worthless, born in sin, and will be discarded unless they somehow find a form of God known only by those who are in charge of the mythology. What's odd is that the battle for the Human's soul is so intense in this story. Does it make sense that the forces of good and evil should battle over the souls of worthless Humans? No. So even in this dichotomy, there is a hint that for whatever reason, the Human is precious to God and Satan both.

Oh, how convenient this all is! It explains so much. It excuses you from taking the responsibility, does it not, to create light or dark yourself? Supposedly, you just sit there and wonder, "*Who is going to get you.*" What if the darkest of the dark on this planet, the most evil you can imagine, the supernatural occult... was Human generated and sustained? No devil, no Satan, just you. Would that bother you?

What if the most divine thing on the planet, the brightest white, the lightest light was also you, evolved and sustained? What if the most awesome healing power on the planet came from within instead of without? I will tell you: This is the way of it, and I have just explained the power of the Human Being to be whatever he wishes… free choice with supernatural abilities.

In a darker energy of the past, things that were of a lower vibration were easily sustained, easily developed. And now the light starts to turn on and burn them with truth. There are less opportunities for those things to be sustained and developed and far more opportunities for the masters to emerge and the light to be turned on. I'm telling you the truth, and it puts the responsibility of good and evil into your lap. Which direction do you want the vibrations in *you* to go? Which kind of energy do you wish to have around your family and your work place? You totally control how dark or light your soul energy will be. It's part of the test, you know? It's part of the free will.

Many have doubted that this could be so. They say, *"If we are angels disguised as Humans, what possible system would allow us to create evil and go to the darkness? It simply doesn't make sense, Kryon. Angels can't do that."* However, you totally ignore your mythology in the process, where an angel somehow magically falls from grace and becomes Lucifer… Satan, and the lord of darkness. You see? The system is there even in your story telling. The metaphors of your spiritual history gave you that, but you took it as reality instead of seeing it as your own potential. Does that give you a hint that you have the choice to choose to develop either side? You do! But the mastery in your DNA is suddenly awakening you to what is coming on the planet… a time of awakening and renaissance.

How are you going to do this? How are you going to create a change in your own DNA? We have told you over and over there are no steps. It's an interdimensional puzzle. It has no answer. You want an empirical answer and you desire the exact steps in a linear system. You want a clear generic answer, but it's different for every Human Being. Where are you in this chain of events? Some of you are ready and some of you are just awakening. Some need time to think about it. Some are ready to jump in right now. You want to know more? *"Kryon, at least tell us what to do first!"* you say. We have... many times. You can read it and you can hear it. For 18 years, as my partner says, the same message has been given over and over by this entity you call Kryon. We'll never run out of ways of telling you about this. It's precious information: You start with intent, and the door opens. Then it starts to become difficult.

The History of Planetary Change

We're going to tell you a little bit about some of the things that you're facing. But let me remind you of the esoteric history involved. You have the various stages that we have put you through since 1987. You have the 11:11 experience, which you really acknowledged in 1992. The 11:11 experience had to do with the decision to change history... to wipe away the prophecy, which you did. It was a decision that was made, by the way, not only by all of you, but by all of you who had ever lived on the planet or who would ever lived on this planet. We're talking about a decision made at a level that is beyond Human understanding, by those who hadn't even been "born" yet. This decision affects everything on the planet, including the Gaia energy. Don't you think you would have to include those who would be born into it? Indeed!

The 12:12 experience was the passing of the torch. We've told you this before. It is the significant expression that described those of you who passed the torch from the old to the new. It's significant because it was needed and necessary as a symbol of moving into a new dispensation. Now, you see these numbers repeatedly: the nines, the 11s, the 12s. It is not a repeated coincidence that you see the 11:11 on your clocks. It is a "wink" from Spirit to remind you why you are here.

The Harmonic Convergence, the Harmonic Concordance, the Venus Transit – all of these things were deliveries of energy. One year ago, the most magnificent one happened and few even noticed. It's too esoteric and unexpected by all but a few. On March 5, 2005, it happened. We told you about it, too, and we'll tell you again because you ought to know. It was called the Paradise Matrix. We described it as a time of revival when the masters who said they were going to return to Earth all did. Not in body, not even in spirit, but as an energy delivered to the magnetic grid of your planet! And now, perhaps you understand why I am the magnetic master? It took 12 years to prepare the magnetic grid. Now you know what we were preparing it for.

We gave you the dates 18 years ago... when the magnetic changes would start, when they would stop, and now even your science showed that it did. Your compasses showed that the magnetics of the planet had changed oddly, mysteriously, in a way that it never had before in your lifetime, or your parent's lifetime or even your grandparent's lifetime. The movement of the grid was complete in 2002. And now, you know why it was moved.

In an esoteric way, but one that involves the interdimensional attributes of magnetics, we've prepared your planetary grid for the masters to come back, to begin the tool kit you will need to proceed. They are here – all are back – and they sit here with you who are hearing and reading.

Why you? Why are they looking at you? That's because they're talking to old souls, who have come for a reason and a purpose. These are old souls know they are here to become metaphoric Lighthouses to a changing planet. They are the catalysts for you to use to start your DNA shift and develop this mastery to whatever degree you can, to move forward, to create the energy called, "The New Jerusalem" on this planet before 2012. That's only six years away, you might say. But things are not always as they seem.

When the lighthouse strikes its light, it does not measure the storm. It does not judge the storm. It does not say to itself, *"I must understand where this is all going"* before it shines the light. All it knows it that it was built to endure darkness, mighty wind and the waves that will crash endlessly over its structure. It's not afraid, either. It doesn't know when the storm will end, how powerful it will become, or the reasoning behind its creation. All the lighthouse knows is that it's safe, and that it must shine a light in the darkness to help others find the safety of the harbor. It never questions how it became light, either, but it knows who it is, and what it's for. It also knows that the light it carries is expected and those in the dark are looking for it. Do you see what I'm saying? You knew all this when you came in. Profound, it is! Emotional for my partner, it is!

[Lee stops for a moment.]

This [Human emotion] is because, when I talk about this, I show him the potentials of the planet! I show him smiling faces in Iran. I show him smiling faces in Palestine. I show him laughter and joy in Israel. I show him things that you would think are impossible, created by individuals who sit here right now. The news has a profundity to it that makes humanity weep with the joy of the potential.

Three "Impossible" Tasks

How are you going to do it? I'll give you three impossible tasks. They're not really impossible, but they're going to be impossible within an old way of thinking. And you're not going to like them either, because they fly in the face of old Human nature. When I start to tell you about them, you're going to say, "*This is tough,*" and it is. You're going to realize that it requires you to drop the "old Human" and also drop almost everything you have been taught from the beginning of your life and rebalance it.

I'll give you three examples of things that you're going to have to deal with in order to begin this journey. In each example, I ask you to compare it to the master of your choice and you'll see I'm right. They had to throw away Human nature to become the masters they became. They had to rebalance all they were given into a new paradigm of humanism.

Number One

I invite you to ***get rid of survival instinct***. Are you ready for that one? You come in with that built into every cell, don't you? It's imprinted upon you, isn't it? Indeed, it is, but it's an old energy imprint. Survival instinct has a powerful message to each Human Being. It silently fills the Human mind with these thoughts: "*I am alone. Everything that I do, I must do myself. I've got to clear the path before me because no one's going to clear it for me. Therefore, I will survive by knocking over the ones in front, or on the sides, or in back. I will compete for the space on the planet. I have to to survive. Otherwise I'll be overrun by the others who know what I know. I'll compete for relationships, for food, for money. I'll compete for love. I've got to do it. I've got to take care of myself because I must survive.*" Sounds like a song, doesn't it? [Kryon smiles.]

What about this thought from the mind of the master? "I now understand and realize that I am not alone. I have divinity in my pocket for the asking. I have the power of the Universe at my disposal. I have interdimensional tools that will clear the space in love, and everywhere my bubble is spread in light. Those around me will see better and in free choice will steer a safe path into the harbor. They will survive with me and will be part of a family that I help create with my balanced light. I am the master Lighthouse. Everywhere I go, I'll be blessed. I don't need survival instinct, because I represent ultimate survival. I am the definition of survival... a master of humanity. I am light."

How about that? This is the master's voice, but it's also yours. You begin to realize that you can trust in interdimensional forces that are mastery forces that you don't understand, but know are always there. You begin to realize that in the mastery department, you've got deep pockets when it comes to love. Ahh yes, deep pockets when it comes to survival. How about that? That's number one. Drop that survival instinct. It's an old energy that says you have to compete for everything. You don't. There's plenty. But it's against your old Human nature, isn't it?

You've got deep pockets when it comes to energy and miracles. You could walk out of here differently than you came in. You can change before you put this book down! Is it part of your belief system or does that matter... or does it matter? How would you like to go out differently than you came in? How would you like to go out healed? And that, my friends, is the potential of this evening's experience, is it not? And that, my reading friend, is the potential of why you picked up this book, is it not? That is called free choice. How much can you put away of the old baggage you think is imbedded within you?

Number Two

This one will be even harder than number one for some of you. You're going to have to ***dispense with, then balance, your ego***. Did you hear that? How can you balance something you get rid of first? I just gave you the answer. You've got to toss it away. By tossing away your ego, you gain balance. Because you think your ego is one thing and it is not. I'll give you some exercises or examples of what it's like to have a balanced ego: Can you sit in a situation where somebody is calling you names and not feel it? Hmm? Even if they're right? [Kryon smiles.] Can you? Can you sit and take that kind of verbal abuse and not feel it? Can you smile in the joy of the moment while it's taking place? Can you be detached, watching the movie, as they say... can you?

I'll give you something to do, an exercise. The next time this situation occurs, I want you to try to disengage. And when you are looking at the person abusing you, in their anger, in their unbalance, in their turmoil, I want you to love them. At this moment, *they* are the ones who are out of balance, not you. Their abuse of you is an invitation for you to join them in an "out-of-balance experience." [Laughter] So sit there and endure their unbalance, don't join it. Then when they're finished, if they're within touching distance, you might touch their arm gently and say, *"I'm sorry you're having a bad day."* [Laughter] Can you do that?

Do you know what happens when they don't get the reaction from you that the drama they're putting forward is supposed to create? They are completely and totally disarmed. And that, my friend, is when communication can happen. That's when the love of God is best seen. This can only take place with a person who has a *balanced* ego.

A balanced ego is an ego that is present only in respect to a Human who truly knows who they are. It's a piece of divinity and survival that nothing can touch. No other Human can touch you in death or in life and change your mind about anything if you have a divine countenance. No matter what words are presented to you, no matter what situations are given to you, no matter how loud they yell... they can't change a thing because of your mastery. Remember the four attributes of love that we taught you? [Kryon Book Five] Your reaction will not be anger. It will be solution. As they are yelling, all you can think of is how to solve the issue, not how to yell back or get even. A balanced ego says to you, *"I know who I am. I'm a loving individual who can solve problems. I don't have to defend anything. I'm not in survival mode, and I am concerned about the one who is in trouble in front of me."*

Number Three

Let me give you the third one. ***Get rid of your gender bias***. You think just because you have the parts of a certain gender that you've got to be a certain way, don't you? Well, it's pretty laughable, since there are those in this room who have female parts who came from a male warrior background. They are used to wearing the armor and they have slayed large men in battle. And you know who you are reading this, don't you?

It's a joke. All of you have been both genders. What you do with your current gender is your free choice. But you have a bias within it to release. Most of you say, *"I am male or female,"* and this defines you. It's a giant bias, since you then act certain ways to conform to what is expected of you. Some of you even campaign for your gender, against the other, again, for survival and what you think is a fair and just placement in your culture.

On this planet, for thousands of years, there has been an unequal balance between masculine and feminine conscious energy.

It's been masculine heavy and you know this. The Venus Transit energy of last year was a tool that placed a potential balance into Gaia itself, to allow for those who wished to become more balanced in the masculine/feminine area. This would mean that men would be comfortable with a feminine side. They would see with a "sweeter countenance." Women would be more comfortable with the masculine side, looking at some things in a very different way. It's a balancing of the two, and when it sweeps your culture and the other cultures around you, it will start to create a better communication between the leaders of this planet.

We've said it before: There is a potential present for masculine, macho leaders of various countries to do dumb things just because they can. You will see their masculine bias, for it will drive their actions, rather than the idea of balanced solutions being considered. It's part of a macho club that exists, and has exited for centuries. Suddenly, however, these macho leaders are uncomfortable – more so than usual – and they don't know why. They are irritated, yet they don't know why – unhappy and illogical. And I'll tell you why – because Gaia just shifted and there's more feminine energy than there ever was before, and that will drive them crazy, for it doesn't work in the energy they are use to and wish to create! It affects their populations, their subordinates, and also their plans.

Watch for it. There will be last-ditch, dying efforts to hold on to an energy of control, but they'll fail. This is part of something new on this planet, but something we have told you to expect. It's coming very slowly, but now you will see what the reactions are.

Can you personal balance this within yourselves? It's against Human nature, you know? Women want to be feminine and men want to be masculine. What if you were both of these all the time, yet balanced in your thinking about the two? Think of the differences in relationships that would solve themselves far easier if they could see both sides and weigh them in their thoughts. Imagine what the leaders of the earth would be able to do together if there was a more balanced process of thought. But it's not intuitive, not easy, and against the way you have been taught to think.

That's three, only three. We have presented three "impossible things." Get rid of your survival mode, throw away the ego, and pretend your gender doesn't matter. That's a good beginning to what masters do. Look at your favorite master, dead or alive, and you will see all three of these things within them. Did you notice? Now, perhaps, you will see it in yourselves?

How do you begin? How do you create energies and emotions that are counter-intuitive to your Humanism? The answer? You give intent for it, and begin a slow process of working the puzzle. But your DNA is there, ready to be activated. The tools are in place, the masters from the matrix are on the planet, and they're ready to go. Therefore, there is far more energy available to work in your behalf than ever before. This is the real renaissance. The difference is that you now have so much internal help.

[Pause]

And so it is, there's only one thing else we want to say before we close. It's about one of the most misunderstood concepts you have today.

The Place of Emotion in the Divine Plan

There has been a question for some years about the actual purpose of Human emotion on the planet. I wish to set the record straight. There are those who would say, *"Human emotion is a horrible weakness. It's too bad we have it and it gets in the way of logical thought. Kryon is too emotional, and might sway your intellect."* Think for a moment. Pure love exists in a grand form on the other side of the veil. You know this, since you can't experience the joy of enlightenment and the love of God without the emotion of it. You weep with joy when you think about birth, the joy of healing, and even peace on Earth. Therefore, if you are one of these who wishes to eliminate this, you are going to alter a divine attribute that has been passed to you through the veil when you were born! It's not something that is a weakness, but instead one of the greatest powers you have.

When I come to you and I say, "I honor and love humanity," I have in me a presence, a female presence of motherly love that says, "I am so proud of you!" Where did this come from? You think that's Human? It is not! It's divine and from *Source*. That is universal divine love. Love has a place in your divine schedule and so does compassion.

Here's the truth. There are certain kinds of Human emotions that are designed to change Gaia itself. Oh, if you want to spin with anger, drama and hate, you'll get one kind of reaction. If you want to create compassion and love, you'll get another. It's all part of the free choice of dark and light, you know? But it is all given to you to use as a tool.

Human compassion, used through prayer and the sending of light, is perhaps the most powerful thing on the planet. It's why the tsunami happened... to generate compassion. It's part of the 9/11 scenario, too. These things and others have developed a compassion wave that has actually changed Gaia in ways you could never have done unless those things had occurred.

You might say, *"Well, Kryon, why does it have to involve so much loss of life and so much sorrow?"* That is your 3D reaction to these kinds of things. Again, we ask you to look at those that you've lost in these years. 2005 – an amazing year for catastrophe, yet all those who were lost, including those that perhaps you had loved, are still here. They're working the earth, perhaps in another way, but they are still here. Some of them have returned in Human form already, and some of them are staying as helpers. Who are you, in your limited dimension, to tell the Universe that's this is not the way it's done? Who are you to tell Spirit that you want them kept here? This is your Human bias at its best. If you were to interview them right now, they would say, *"We're fine. We are in joy. We did what we did and we're glad we did it."* It's a different perception than you have, and a far larger picture. It's beautiful! Life goes on forever… never terminated. It simply changes form in front of you, but you can't see it, since you are in 3D.

Those you lose in death, who you are mourning for, needed to leave because they needed to work in other ways, in another area, in order to push this earth toward peace. And you don't know anything about it! All you feel is your sorrow, yet I'm telling you that there is appropriateness in all things and they're working with you, next to you, side by side, if you allow them.

I know who's here. Listen to me. Why don't you form a partnership with those you loved and lost and keep going? It won't be long before it's your turn to do the same thing [speaking of again moving into death and rebirth]. Encourage this understanding within your children. Tell them in advance. *"When I'm gone from the earth, celebrate my life. Hold my interdimensional hand and keep going."* Because that is the truth. And that's the way of it, masters.

Healing energy is here. Are you receiving what I'm feeling you're receiving? Are you being touched yet? Do you feel the tingle yet? Reader, do you actually think this communication is just "words in a book?" There's far more here than you think right now, and it's precious. Some of you have been touched tonight. Some of you will put down the book and be different than when you picked it up. And if that's you, then you know we had an appointment, didn't we? Is it emotional? I hope so, for this is the compassion that will heal you, create a peaceful countenance, and help to heal the planet.

And so it is.

Co-Creation Revisited

Manhattan, New York City
April 2006

Chapter Fourteen

Co-Creation Revisited
Manhattan, New York City
Chapter Fourteen

This channelled message in New York was originally called, "The Many Yous." But after re-reading it a few times, we now realize that it's all about co-creation. In almost every Kryon book, there is at least one chapter that deals with this. So why change things?

Greetings, dear ones, I am Kryon of Magnetic Service. There are so many here whose names I know. Every single one of you is known unto God. This is just a phrase, *known unto God*, but you ask the ones who have been healed in these past months and years and they know what it means – *known unto God.*

They're here, you know? I know it seems trite, but I wish they could stand and give their testimonies – testimonies of the interdimensional soul who says, *"I know I am known unto God for what has happened to me."* I know each of you in this way, in this profound way, and I have known you forever, backwards. Imagine eternity, if you will. Imagine it in your 3D… a time line that goes forever. Now turn it around and push it backwards. It represents time that never began… a backwards eternity. That's how long I've known you.

Think for a moment. Use your intellect and your divine intuition. This is not biology I'm asking you to use in your thinking process, but rather it is your divinity – that spark of what you call intelligence and life, which is forever. It is divine and you all know it. You've even invented rules for your religions that echo it. Almost 90 percent of the earth has various religions that believe you "go somewhere else" when you die. What does that tell you about intuitive expectation of life? It's Human intuition, is it not, that shouts that you're not finished when life is done?

Eternal life is not a concept I'm giving you, but rather it's a concept you've given yourselves through your own divine intuition that life is forever. However, because you're linear, you don't understand that you always were and you always will be. Long before the earth was formed, you were with me and I was with you. We are connected and always will be. A system is in place that you cannot remember that is shielded from you because you're in duality and within the test. It's a system where I say goodbye to you before you come into this planet and hello to you when you return, but you can't remember it. But I do, dear one. I do.

I know your names because you're *known unto God*. You know who is here? The ones who awakened first on this planet for this renaissance that is coming. The ones who awakened first are the old souls of the planet. The Lemurians and many others like them. That's who is here. It represents expression after expression on Earth [past lives], but you can't remember any of them. Hidden, it is, from you, but I remember. Dear ones, I remember.

This puts you at a disadvantage since I know about it but it is hidden from you. But it puts me at a disadvantage also because I am in love with you, and yet I cannot show you physically who you really are. I must instead simply love you and give you the messages that you deserve to hear. That's what angels do with one another, you know? They are connected by love. In my case, I must love you enough not to show you more than you can know while you are here.

Love is thick. It is pure. It is real. It is an energy that you can see and you can feel and it pours into this place because it's precious and sacred. Blessed is the Human Being who seeks the truth, for that's why we come here, and that's a promise. Blessed are those right now, who can see the colors on the stage. For these colors are already here, yet we've not even begun!

It's a powerful thing when you recognize divinity in yourself. It's a powerful thing when you can trust your own intuition and your own emotions and put away what you've been taught is real. Some are asking, *"Is this really so? Could God speak to you like this? Could Spirit speak to you like this?"* I'll say it again: This is the way of it. Of all of the scriptures that have been written on the planet, none were written directly by God. All of them were written by Humans under the influence of the love of God. That's the truth, and that's channelling.

It's profound, you know? Think of it. You've always had this, yet it is still something many consider too odd. All of you can channel and all of you can connect to Spirit in this way. Every single one. *Known unto God.* Life is just waiting for you to take the hand of your Higher-Self. That has always been the invitation.

The Mayans and the Aztecs, they knew something you don't. Their calendars did more than represent the sun's predicted movements. Instead, they represented the energies of the past ages, and those to come. They had names for them, and the cycles they went through, and they all agreed that a new age would begin in 2012. Some even called it "the end of time." It was that profound. The Mayans called it The Age of a New Sun, meaning a new energy was upon you. We call it a renaissance.

This is a great shift. This is what many of us have been telling you for all these years, since 1989. They said, *"It's coming, you know?"*

And it's not the end of all things. Hardly. It is the beginning of all things and it will have taken you almost a generation to create it. 2012 is the beginning, a marker of a potential on the planet that we have called The New Jerusalem. And when that time arrives, I want you to look around and see the changes that you have wrought. Free choice is within you to do this, and create this. So far you have worked the potentials to match the predictions.

Now, let me speak about how this works. I'm going to speak about interdimensional things again – difficult things for you to understand, and we're going to work in a circle. I'm going to title this message, "The Many Yous."

Although you cannot see proof of this, and although it is invisible and will stay that way, you already have the concept of what we have called "multiple lives." However, you see them linear, in a stack of time, and we don't. To you, a past life is a life on this planet that you have lived, in what you call your linear past. You are currently in a life that you call your present life and if you are astute, you understand this is not the last one you will have, even though some of you think it is.

Oh Human, you're so quick to pat yourself on the back and say, "*Well, I've done it… I've helped the planet, so I'm not coming back.*" Yes, you are! Yes, you are. Oh, it's free choice, but I'll tell you what your choice will be: You're coming back! Why would you miss it? Why would you miss what you have spent so long creating? You *will* be back, dear one. But as a Human, you have a different perspective. You're in the trenches… doing the work, and some of you are so tired! But when you get to the other side of the veil, you'll turn and look at me and say, "*How soon are we allowed to return?*" And I'll tell you, "*How about now?*"

Two Places at the Same Time?

As my partner teaches, interdimensionality is very difficult to understand for a creature brought up in 3D. Let me define for you your interdimensional attributes. You're an angel. You always were and always will be. You are temporarily on this planet as a physical 3D form and that piece of you is Human. Now, you believe the whole intellect is with you, don't you? But it is not. Only a portion of it is here. The rest is kept hidden, but it's still connected and available. You're in a quantum state with yourself and the rest of you is somewhere else. The question was asked, *"Can you do a seemingly circus feat? Can you be in two places at the same time?"* I will tell you that, indeed, you can be in multiple places at the same time, and all of you are.

But first, let me tell you who's in charge: It's the consciousness of the one who is here in Human form. You don't have multiple brains, but you do have multiple interdimensional pieces... hundreds of them for some of you. I'll explain one of them, the one you know about. It's called the Higher-Self. That's the one that is closest to the Human-Self, which some of you have audaciously called *the lower self*, (but it isn't). That's how you think of yourselves, don't you? I'm going to call this physical part, *the Human divine self.* That's the one that longs to connect to the Higher-Self. And that, my friends, is the purpose of your life.

You spend your life trying to connect to the Higher-Self, and when you do, you become a Lighthouse. You fulfill what you came for. That is your purpose here if you want to ask what you're supposed to be doing on Earth. You connect! Get connected, if you want to say that. You are an interdimensional being, able to be in many places at the same time in a different time frame, but always connected to one source in this circle of life. Now, let me tell you what this means to the concept of past lives.

No Such Thing as a Past Life

There is no such thing as a "*past* life." That's what it really means. For when you leave this planet, you will be out of time [removed from the limitations of linear time]. There is no *time* on the other side of the veil. It's something that has been manufactured for your comfort and lifestyle in 4D [3D].

Let me tell you what this means. Listen carefully, for this is important. You think you've got past lives? You don't. You have multiple current lives all at the same time. When you get out of time, as you have known it, what are you going to call it? Think of it this way – it's a whole layer of lifetimes, but you're living them all once right now, so therefore they're all now lives... all of them.

But there's one on top of this layered stack who is in control, and that's the one that you are living now – the one you see in the mirror – the one that is currently occupying your body, who you think is the only one. This is the one who talks to all of the others in what you call the Akashic Record. This is an interdimensional concept and is also represented by one of the layers of your DNA... also invisible. This interdimensional layer of DNA reminds you that all of the other lives are still there being lived at the same time, but out of a linearity way. Why do I tell you this? Because there, my friends, is the storehouse of your power.

Isn't it odd how we must force interdimensional concepts into single-dimensional explanations for Humans? I wish to tell you about the infinite circle of lifetimes that are active within you, yet I must resort to an example of "stacking them up" in a simple linear fashion for you to understand it! Any way you can grasp this will be helpful for the next step.

How would you like to have the benefit of everything you've ever done as an angel, since you arrived on the planet? Lemurian, how about combing through 52,000 years' worth of experience for the best of it all? How would you like to have that, Lemurian? Well, I'll tell you, you connect to the Higher-Self and suddenly the quantum effect takes place and you're connected to all of these lives at the same time! Some of you know what I'm talking about and some of you don't. It hides from you... this wisdom of the ages. You can dig down into those lives that you are currently living all at once, and using the one who's in charge [who you are now], you can choose to pick the best parts of each, and bring many former attributes forward to use them.

Here's what I mean: We've broached this before in a different way, but I'm going to use my partner once again, even though he doesn't like it when I talk about him this way. [Pause while Lee considers what's coming]

About Lee

While in his early days, when considering being the channel that he is now, his exchange with Spirit went like this: "*I cannot write anything and I never have. I cannot speak in front of an audience and I never have. I'm basically an engineering hermit. I'm not social, either. I like to be quiet and unspoken, and I'm nervous in front of people. Therefore, how is it I'm supposed to proceed, since I don't have any of the obvious talents needed to do what I've been called to do?*"

Now, what we showed him, in a way he still doesn't understand, was that these talents were always there, but hidden as part of his personal Akashic Record. These are attributes that he carries hidden deep down into the past lives he thought were behind him in a linear spiritual history he thinks is over with. However, they are not gone at all, and are actually part of him, still active. In a process that is still mystical to him, he pulled out the one lifetime who was the writer. He pulled out the one who was the orator. He pulled out the attributes he needed, out of his storehouse, and you see the result. These were talents that always belonged to him, but that were not present when he was born, so he thought.

He reached down and pulled them out of the essence of the Akashic Record, which is alive and well and living within his DNA. The promise, therefore, from Spirit is that you can do it, too! But we use him as an example, since he sits in front of you, and you can see what we mean. So, which one of these things do you want, Shaman? Is this concept really that strange to you?

Rejuvenation

I'll give you something else to think about. If you don't believe in past lives, let me ask you something that only involves this current life. Do you remember when you were 10? The answer from most of you is "yes." Well, so does your DNA! How about that one? Think of it. Imprinted in your body is a memory that has a cellular stamp on it that remembers "10 years old." You see, it's still there. It's a cellular memory. How would you like to revisit it? And you might say, *"Well, why would I do that?"* When most of you were 10, your DNA was clean and pure and it was whole and young. Although that was long ago, your body has retained a memory of what it was like then.

So how would you like to instruct your body, in your next meditation, to *"Go to the 10-year-old DNA imprint, and replicate it?"* Why not? The body reproduces itself all the time, cell by cell. It rejuvenates. Let's go to the 10-year-old DNA – young, pure, fresh with the energy of the youngster – hard to even keep still. [Kryon smile] It's alive, you know? It's still there within the body's rejuvenation memory.

Concepts of the Future

Oh, and here's another one: This concept you have of the future. It's so limiting. Let me give you a snapshot idea about the reality of the future. *"Kryon,"* some have exclaimed, *"There's a dichotomy here. You say God can do anything, yet you also say that God doesn't know our futures. How can that be?"* It's easy. God knows all your futures, but does not know which one you will select!

Spirit knows the potentials of all of the things that you might do. It's extremely complex to you, but to us it is not. It's interdimensional and it loops around in a circle. We can see the potentials of every decision you might make throughout your life. Therefore, we know everything except one thing: In this free-choice situation on this planet, we don't know which future you're going to choose. That's up to you.

So I bring this to you so that you will think this through, and complete this circle of the "now." I've already discussed the past, so let's discuss the future in your mind. Do you agree that each lifetime is a graduate one from the one you had before? In other words, since you learn from each, and you reincarnate with all of the knowledge from what you call the past one, the next life is going to wiser. Do you agree? You learn, learn, learn. If this is truth, and if what I'm saying is the way it works [it is], and if there really is no time on the other side of the veil, then why not go five lifetimes *up* the Akashic potential ladder and grab the wisdom that you are going to learn in your future? Pull it down and use it right now! How about that? That's called Ascension Status, dear Human Being! Learning to become interdimensional, therefore, is an invitation to "mine your akash" and participate in the best of past and future. This process isn't for the faint of intellect... it challenges the very concept of what you have been taught are your 3D limitations.

This has been the promise since I arrived in 1989. You've got a new energy on this planet. Whether you call it the Harmonic Convergence, the Harmonic Concordance, or whether you call it the Venus Transit – call it whatever you want – you now have new energy to pull from. We even gave you the big one [speaking of past channelled information given]. We told you about The Paradise Matrix. Go back and find what that is, for it's profound. All of these are deliveries of specific energies to the planet to set you up for 2012, the Renaissance of a New Sun [as the Aztecs called it]. No wonder it seems so dark here to you. You're only beginning to turn on the lights! I know I speak in metaphors, but it's all we have to try and convert interdimensional information to 3D concepts.

Co-creation Using the Many Selves

Let me move on to another subject, and one you all wish to know about. Humans are possessed with a desire to know, *"How do I co-create my reality?"* Well, the first way is to get rid of your 3D sense of time. Understand and agree that you are a bigger energy than you can see in 3D. There are more of you than it seems, and although you're in charge of your life and your brain, think for a moment of these other lifetimes that are still happening, that you also have control over. *"Kryon, does that mean that I also have control over my Higher-Self?"* Yes, it does – because your Higher-Self is no more than a divine complement of your angelic being. It sits there in no judgment at all, and does not control you. It sits there ready to be connected to you and when you connect your thoughts, they are the enhanced thoughts of *you*, but enhanced by the wisdom of the Higher-Self.

Back to co-creation. In order for me to do this explanation correctly, I have to give you *the rule*. It's an axiom that you've always known intuitively is there, but now I'm going to verbalize it. It's about enlightenment, and here it is: No amount of enlightenment energy can be put upon another person to change them without their permission. Let me put it in another way. You cannot, with your enlightenment, spiritually steamroll over another person who doesn't have it. It's against the rules; it cannot be done.

Co-creation in the 3D sense might appear to be something you do with your own energy, which affects you and gets you something. That's not the way it works, though. You cannot, in all integrity, affect someone else's life with your own co-creation. Now, when you think about this, you might say, *"Well, how else can it work? Doesn't there have to be a winner and a loser? At least there has to be someone else affected by what I create. I don't live on a desert island. Everything I do will affect someone else."* The answer is no, there is not a winner and loser. Instead, there is a winner and a winner.

There is a huge concept you don't understand. As you co-create for yourself, you push energy around that never would have been pushed around before. When you do this, it helps someone else to move into a place that will eventually give them a light that they didn't have before, allowing them better free choice. At the same time, it creates the situation in your life that you have been working on. It's complex, but think of it this way – your energy is perfect for all around you when you are co-creating with pure intent. It never violates the rule.

Let me review so that you understand two things we have mentioned before. When you send light, it is the same concept. We told you this before: You are not asked to send light with a bias. If you know something is happening, and you wish to send light there to help it, don't send the solution! Don't send what you want to happen. Just send light. Get used to understanding that light is all you have. It has "cosmic intelligence" that knows what to do. That's what the Lighthouse has. It doesn't have an agenda. It only has light. It doesn't broadcast something on the light. It only has light. It depends upon someone else "seeing" what it does. You send light to a place in the darkness, and whoever is there gets to see better. Do you understand? And when they see better with their free choice, they can choose things that you have helped illuminate with your light. That is the integrity of sending light, and it also applies to co-creation.

The second review is we told you about prayer. When you pray for someone, don't put an agenda on it. This it tough! *"Kryon, if we can't put an agenda on it, how do we pray for somebody?"* It's easy. Imagine the end result of the prayer. If you're praying for someone's health and they are sick, see them in your mind as happy without the disease. Don't imagine how it's going to be done and don't tell God what to do. See the result. You are actually pulling upon the "now" of your potential futures when you do this. If you pray for peace, see an Earth where families are not in fear or worried, where they don't have war. Visualize the smiles of the children in a safe place.

It is your visualization that is your prayer, and that, my friends, is just like sending light. Send the compassion of your Divine-Self in places that need it. That's what real lighthouses do, except that they have physical light and you have spiritual light. That's not hard to understand, but the hardest one is about co-creation.

The only way I can do this is to give you this example, and one that you will all understand, especially in this town [New York City]. See, I know where I am. [Kryon smile] How many of you have heard of the Parking Angel? [Laughter] You've got Parking Angels here, you know? You probably have more than most. [big Kryon smile]

The Way it Works

Let's say for a moment that you're in your vehicle and you're circling the block. You're praying: *"Dear Parking Angel, I don't know how you're going to do it, but I need a space here."* You've all been there, haven't you? [Laughter] Suddenly, indeed, another vehicle pulls out right in front of you, and that driver leaves, and you pull in. You say, *"Thank you, Parking Angel!"* Now let me review to you what just happened so that you're not confused.

There are some who feel the scenario goes like this: Your arrival in the circling mode changes the energy of the block and, somehow, some poor soul who is in a store shopping gets ripped away from the store by the Parking Angel, and plopped into their car, where they're forced to put it in reverse and leave! Bewildered, they suddenly realize that they had no intention of leaving, but they did anyway! What happened? [Laughter] Then you pull into the space!

Oh, how 3D of you! Of course, what I just described simply doesn't happen. No, instead it's a synchronized *dance* done out of time and space. Do you know how complex this is? Think of this the next time you get "your space." Here is the correct scenario: Your arrival is about to correspond with someone else's departure, so all the Parking Angel has to do is to align the synchronicity of the dance. You're there at the right time, the shopper leaves, and you pull in. They're happy. You're happy. Everybody wins. However, this involves the many portions of you who are in many places at the same time, as well as the one who is shopping. The Parking Angel is actually a traffic director of the immense planning session that many parts of you are involved in all the time.

Now, think for a moment of the complexity and of the planning of all this. You've got a Higher-Self and you've got other selves above that... all knowing what time you're coming, what time you're going, when you're going to pray, and also the same thing about the others who are shopping. Did you ever consider that the other angels in this dance have to agree? They do! Did you ever wonder if your good fortune was someone else's co-creation? It often is... made much easier to synchronize.

There the shopper sits in her car. She is praying, *"God, parking places are really hard to get. Let this one go to another who really deserves it, and who loves you the way I do."* Suddenly, you show up! Now... who was co-creating for whom?

Do you understand how complex this is? Now, amplify this complexity tens of millions of times, because the process is about a dance of synchronicity. You're asking for relationship issues; you're asking for job issues; you're asking for travel issues... so many things you're trying to co-create in your life.

You're asking for the synchronicity of the dance and at the same time, so many of you don't understand how this works. You put rules on it. *"Oh, Spirit, deliver to me exactly what I need, and I've got this need and I've got that need and I'm going to co-create it. Uh... but I'm not willing to leave town, by the way, and I'm not willing to do this and I'm not willing to do that."*

"How am I supposed to do anything," your angel says, *"if you put restrictions on it?"* If you put restrictions on it, you're not going to have any co-creative ability. Restrictions stop the music.

If you want to co-create, let the dance begin! No restrictions. Don't be afraid of the love of God. You think you've got it figured out where you're supposed to be and what you're supposed to be doing? But you've all got something, don't you, that you don't want God to *disturb*. *"God, don't touch my family,"* some say. Let me tell you about your imprisoned thoughts. You're always afraid that God's going to do something to disturb your family or friends or something good in your life. What if, instead, we touched your family and made them fall in love with you all over again? What if they got an enhanced love wash? What if this family of yours that you don't want us to touch suddenly becomes interested in what you have found? Do you have the courage to let them all know? That's what I want to tell you. Things are not what they seem.

The Intelligence of the Universe

We've got one last thing. It's called quantum intelligence. We don't speak of it very often, but you've got to know what it is. Humans often put God in a box. You want to compartmentalize everything so that you can understand it. *"Dear God, teach me how to pray. I need to know how to pray."* We've heard this so often. And we've told you before. Soon, we'll tell you yet again a different place. But the real answer is: Don't worry about it! *You* develop the light, and *we* know where it goes! How about that arrangement? Free choice is the key. You develop the light and we'll place it correctly.

You want to pray for somebody in Somalia, but you don't know who because there are so many who need it. Go ahead and develop the light, then sit and with pure intent and send it. We know who needs it, dear one. You don't have to. Quantum intelligence means you're connected to God. All of you. You can develop the light without knowing who it goes to or any of the details. We know the address!

You can turn the light switch and expect light in a room without knowledge of how the electricity was generated, or the properties of a light bulb, or the physics of photons. This is because you are familiar with the process in 3D and you trust it. Now, extend this trust to the invisible, and become part of the interdimensional process of quantum intelligence.

This comes right down to the affect of what Yawee is doing with his interdimensional laser. [Speaking of Dr. Todd Ovokaitys, who is in the audience, and who gave a presentation on AIDS research earlier] When the information is transmitted to the cellular structure by his laser, Yawee is done! There is intelligence within that interdimensional process that addresses the exact cells that need to be addressed. This is very different than classic medicine. Instead of targeting a specific chemical or protein in a physical way, this seemingly mystical process does it by itself. However, there is nothing mystical about it. It is an extension of cosmic intelligence, and is part of the lattice that "knows" all about cellular structure and the balance of everything. The study of things in a quantum state in your physics will show that infinite connection [the opposite of infinite separation] creates a oneness that therefore has only one universal conscience... a way of saying that things in a quantum state *know* all about each other and tend to balance themselves.

Back to the Message

Are you here tonight, uncertain of how to pray? Do you know what to do for your own bodies? *"I don't know what to do next,"* many say. You don't need to. Don't you understand? Just sit in front of God and say, *"I am connecting with my Higher-Self. Tell me what I need to know. I'm sitting here and I'm ready."* Then stand back! All we need is your permission, dear one, and your pure intent.

Quantum intelligence will go to the places in your body that need it. Get used to meditating every day, even a short amount of time is better than none. Say, *"Dear Spirit, place in me what I need,"* and you'll save a lot of time, dear Human Being. Stop telling Spirit what you think we should know. Don't you think we're around? Oh, you sit in front of Spirit and you say, *"You won't believe what happened today."* Oh yes, we will. We were there, remember? *"Well, Spirit, I'm going to have a hard time paying the rent."* Don't you think we know that? Don't waste time. We're in love with you. Don't waste time. Just get to the point, and the point is this: *"Dear Spirit, give me wisdom to create what I need. Give me the peace that it has been accomplished and I'll just sit here and I'll be loved."* That's what brothers and sisters in Spirit do with one another. That's who I am.

Here we sit in a very historic place, and I'm not talking about this church [100-year-old structure]. I'm talking about the fact that we are so close to the event you call 9/11. Think of the loss of life there... in your own city, in your own town, in your own neighborhood. It's such a profundity of energy shift on the planet and it happened right here. I want to revisit with you for a moment these thousands of lives, lost right here. You know, out of time, they're still here. Some of them turned around and reincarnated immediately into a new "expression" on the planet. If you could interview them, I'll tell you again, what they have to say: They will tell you at some level, *"We agreed to this."* They will tell you that they knew about the potential, for it was in their interdimensional "possibilities jar" when they were born. They will say, *"We participated in it, and it is part of what we came in for. We did our part. Now you do yours."*

Do you have the courage to take a look at the smiles they have on their faces right now? They are eternal, dear Human Beings, just like you, but you may not wish to look and it may be sorrowful for you, but the fact is that there is joy in their energy because they are *known by God*... every single one. Just like you.

It's time for a shift. Let you be the ones to begin this. It's a sweet place here and the colors have been grand. Five of you have got the seeds of healing that you didn't have when you came in the door. I don't just mean physically, either. How about peace over something that you want peace over? I know who's here! Celebrate the peace that passes understanding... a peace you can't explain... waking up peaceful, no matter what is in your life... no matter what the threats are, what the conditions are... *known unto God.*

Let us in, dear Lemurian Lighthouses. You won't be sorry. Don't fear the love of God.

I'll see you again. You can count on it.

You can count on it.

And so it is.

"Does it warm your heart to know that you all are part of this? Listen, reader. What are you going to do when you put the book down? Will you give God 30 seconds? Will you give God some time? Peace. No phones. No televisions or radios. Just 30 seconds.

Now, would you perhaps even dare to say, 'I am that I am, and the divinity in me is going to make a difference on this planet? I feel the truth when I hear it and when I read it. Even my small efforts will create an energy that is larger than I can imagine, combined with others, to create peace on Earth.' How are you with that?"

The Winter of Spirituality

Edmonton, Alberta, Canada
September 2004

Chapter Fifteen

The Winter of Spirituality
Edmonton, Alberta, Canada
Chapter Fifteen

Although the title of this channelling says that it was channelled in Edmonton, Alberta, the truth is that it's a combination of two channellings. The first was done on the 2004 Kryon Cruise on August 4, 2004. Later, it was revisited and added to in September in Edmonton. So the most complete one was given in Alberta and transcribed. But the core of the information was given while cruising the Mediterranean Sea.

Greetings, dear ones, I am Kryon of Magnetic Service. We wish to pause for just a moment to enjoy the energy that pours into this place, one that's different than it has been in the past.

You may be unaware of it, but even in these few moments that you've gathered together, there have been entities arriving every single moment. Even though there are some who feel that this can't be happening, there are also those who will send their energy into the chair where my partner sits, in an attitude of communication with Spirit. These are the ones who will be communicated with today.

It's not an accident that you, or those who surround you, are here. There are far more of you than you think. For each one of you – senior, young person and all the others – represents at least five or more entities around you who've arrived for this moment... just for this moment. And that doesn't include the ones who come with you in your DNA! What? Oh, that sounds odd, doesn't it? Wait until you hear more about it in a moment.

We're going to present something. It's something we've presented before, but never in this succinct way. Now it's being transcribed, and before it wasn't ready. It was my request to my partner [Lee] that he transcribe it now. He had a warm-up for this message, a practice time in two other channellings, so this message was given in partial form before so that he would know more about the energy and accuracy of what to present. That's the way we do it. For in these last years, this information has become not just more esoteric, but far more difficult to explain.

Each of you has a different kind of life, and each is on a different path within your own time line of learning. Some of you would say, *"I'm very content with everything around me. There's nothing I have to decide, and there's no large challenge."* And if this is you, we say to you that you're thinking in 4D. The next level is for you as well. How bright will your light shine? How far can you send it? How strong can your light be sent and still not be evangelistic or inappropriate with respect to others' free choice? Do any of you understand that the energy of *right now* is why you were born? Satisfied and content, are you? Then why do you wake up at 3 a.m. so often with questions or anxiety? What is really next? Do you hear the Lemurian chorus within you yet? Indeed! Why do you sit here listening to this? Some of this is metaphoric, but all of it is happening.

Then there are the ones who have come with specific questions, and we know what they are. We always do. Oh, do not despair, Human Being, thinking that you're alone. Do not despair, thinking that there's no one around you who knows how afraid you are. God is always surrounding you, and when you can see that invisible shell and paste it upon yourself, you can stand tall and walk from this place knowing that you're protected. And when we say *protected*, we mean energetically and spiritually.

There are those who've come here who want specific answers to specific private challenges. We're going to say that you're going to get some of those answers today. Each of you is different – different choices to be made within vastly different life situations. Yet there's also a private answer for each. We've spoken so many times of this! There's a passion that you develop on your own, which only you know about, and which will guide you like a life's compass wherever you go. The *prophet* that so many ask for and look for is actually within you! The angel that's inside each of you is the one to follow. It's the most intuitive, the one who's written the only book for you. Those of you who want to follow a prophet and have a book to consult don't have to look any further than what's surging interdimensionally within your own life code. It's in there, it's yours, and we've told you this for 15 years.

Mastery is internal, and the masters you currently worship who walked the earth in past times had nothing more than you did, except a message that you continue to deny and misunderstand. They all told you the same thing in different words! Each told you that you were God! Each told you that you were sons and daughters of the Universe, and each told you that you could have what they had if you looked for it and followed the divinity that was there.

When you approach these things and search with pure intent, you're going to get the answers that are appropriate – not only for your life, but for those around you and for the Universe itself. Some of you have to make difficult decisions. There will come a day when you look backwards at this time and you say, *"It was correct, it was appropriate, even though it was difficult to do."* So be guided – not by the words of men, but the thoughts, intuitions and the spiritual compass you have inside.

Some have said, *"I have trouble listening for these answers. Where are they? What do I have to do to get them?"* It couldn't be simpler.

Sit alone on the ground and know that you're not alone. Then say, *"Dear God, tell me what it is I need to know."* Do you believe that if you approach God with pure intent that the family will walk away? Why should it be difficult? Let us tell you this: The difficulty in finding your own spirituality is based on your disbelief that it exists! Your perception is your barrier to God. You ask for lists and procedures, yet you don't yet understand that love has no list! The power of God has no manual. It is that it is. Where's your breathing manual? Where's the manual that instructs your heart to beat? Think of your spiritual abilities as intuitive and automatic, just like these body functions that you never have to think about, but which you depend on for life itself. Master-hood is alive and active within you. Now claim it.

And when you sit before Spirit in meditation and prayer, don't provide lists with the lineage of what's going on around you, because we already know all about it! We're there with you every moment. Don't give us the reasons why you need certain things, because we know all about them. You see, we're with you all the time! Do you have a prayer list? Forget it. We helped you write it! We've seen everything that's taken place. We know of your fear; we know of the challenges; we know of the decisions to be made. If you're praying for another, we helped bring that to your attention! Like a spiritual brother or sister who never leaves your side, we are there. We wanted to remind you of this fact before we go into this next discussion, which may be difficult, to say the least.

We sit before warriors of the light. We sit before those who've been called metaphoric spiritual Lighthouses. Oh, not all of you, but most who are here and are reading. So right now we address an entourage of humanity that numbers in the tens of thousands. You don't know they're there, but we do. For as we give this message, it's also being read by thousands of eyes. Now, you may not see that, but we do. So let us talk to the reader in real time. Reader, we see you now, and we know who you are. And what we've just said to this audience of listeners is good for you, too. The information today may be difficult to understand and absorb, but it's needed for you, too. There are challenges before you that you may want to weigh based upon what is said today, and some of this information is, therefore, just for you.

So the group is far larger than you think, is it not, as we prepare to give you the information of today? Sit in this safe place and know that all is appropriate. See the colors if you wish, for they are there now [speaking of those who always see colors around Lee on the stage]. The energies are in place. We're ready to go.

The Winter of Spirituality

We want you to pretend for a moment. Fantasize what it would be like to come from a planet that had an orbit around the sun that took hundreds of years to complete instead of the 365 days that you enjoy now. What if you were on a planet where you could live out your entire lives within just one or two seasons? That would mean that there would be only a few of you who would be in a culture or in a lifetime who would see a change of seasons at all. And when you did, wouldn't it be scary? It would be frightening, especially one or two of the seasons that had never been seen. Can you imagine going into autumn and winter when, for hundreds of years, humanity had only seen spring and summer?

Just consider how it might be: You lived all of your life, your parents before you and their parents before them, where the earth had always been mild. Warmth prevailed, with birds every day and sun and nature celebrating life. Then it happens: The trees drop their leaves! What's wrong? Are they sick? Are they dying? Where did the birds go? Look at the stark trees! Oh, what is taking place? Darkness, grayness… death. You never saw the fall before. To you, the trees are dead – just look at them! They're dead and dying all around. All the life has been sucked out of them, and they're becoming just skeletons of what they were before.

Then the sun doesn't come out anymore. You can't walk around either, because it's too cold. The water you drink from the lake is freezing. Your well is freezing! How will you drink? How can you grow food? The earth is dying, and so is humanity. You might even consider dying yourself! Wouldn't this be a possible attitude? Indeed! There would be mass suicide and much angst. Governments would fail and priorities would shift. It would be the end of the earth if you didn't know better.

Now, project your perceptions to that possibility. Then, can you even imagine what might happen after four or five generations went by and humanity saw the spring? Wow! Heaven had arrived! Miracle upon miracle – the trees weren't dead at all. They were just hibernating! Who knew? New growth, new life – the sun, the warmth and even the birds came back! Humans could sing again. The perception of a tremendous healing had taken place, and all humanity celebrated.

Silly? We present this to you because all of you know about the seasons. So perhaps this is a metaphor that you'll understand through familiarity of change. What we're going to tell you is this: You're sitting in the energy of something that you've never seen before, nor have your parents or their parents or even the ones before them. Dear Human Being, you're seeing a spiritual winter.

Never before on the planet has this kind of shift occurred in this way. Master after master came here with an altered DNA, with all of it enhanced and activated so they could give you messages about your own mastery. And they all said the same kinds of things, if you noticed. Even within diverse cultures, they had this message: They told you that there was more than you saw in 4D. They told you that there was interdimensionality, and that you were not to make decisions based upon what you see, but upon what your intuition told you was the truth.

They told you that you were not to trust men for your spirituality, but to trust yourselves. They told you that all of you were equal in your ability to create miracles, and that there was no real death. They showed you what an activated DNA was like, and they healed themselves and others around them. They spoke, and the elements changed. They gave intent, and the animals heard them. Then they looked at you and told you that you could do the same thing. Then many of them were killed because it was enabling information in a time that wasn't ready for it. Now it is.

Here comes spiritual winter. All of the lineage that you've been through, ever since Lemuria, has never given you this kind of change. The masters of the earth said that you could change your reality, and you did. There's been a shift of dimensionality occurring on this planet and this solar system, in this section of space, because of what you've done here. We've given you the primers of magnetism and gravity, and we've even talked about astrology being part of it. We've spoken about how interdimensional information rides on the solar wind from the sun, which then *talks* to the magnetic grid, and then to Human DNA.

This shift and change has brought you to a place where some of you say that it's very dark. When you look at the planet and you turn on the news, it's dark! It's there, is it not… the darkness? It would appear that this isn't an enlightened planet at all. It would appear that you've been born, and have lived your life up to this time, in a mild climate, but now the planet has changed tracks. You're sitting there holding your light in a very dark place.

What's going on? Isn't this supposed to be the new energy? Well, let us tell you that those appearances are real. It's getting dark. The trees are dying... the trees of civilized logic... the trees of peace... the trees of old energy thought. The birds' singing has also stopped, and it's uncomfortably quiet, isn't it? Anxious, are you? You're in a spiritual winter, and it's the first one on Earth!

What's happening? We'll tell you: That's what happens when the earth decides to shift dimensionality. We said to you in the year 2000, in a place much like this, in Israel, in Jerusalem, that the potential of this was real. We told you that the temple would be rebuilt, and that's a metaphor for the planet's consciousness. We told you that for the third time it would be rebuilt, but that you'd have to *scrape the foundation clean* first. That's what you're doing, and it's called a spiritual winter.

Everywhere you look, things don't make sense, do they? Do you feel a disconnection? Think about this: A disconnection with spiritual things hasn't been that uncommon in spiritual writings. It normally happens right before a shift. Humans who make profound transitions feel this kind of disconnection, also. Go read about it. Even in current situations, there are some of you who've moved from one level to another only to feel complete disconnection until you're taken into another consciousness. But a disconnect had to be there for a new dimensional perception to occur. Sometimes it's frightening, if you didn't expect it.

This is what's happening on Earth. Let us give you some examples of things that don't make any sense. It might help you see the bigger picture and provide some evidence of what we're speaking of. Let's start with the big one. Let us take you to a place right now that's precious. It's called the Temple Mount. Four grand religions of the planet all share it. It's sacred to them all. Christ himself walked there, and so did Abraham when he almost sacrificed his only son. [There are two versions of this – the Christian one and the Islam one.] This makes it precious to all Christians and Jews on Earth.

Mohammed was also said to have put his countenance there when he ascended [where the gold dome of the mosque is today], making it very precious and sacred to another billion people on the planet. Yet it's in the middle of the most unstable area of Earth... Israel.

Can you imagine such a challenge? Intermingled with all those of differing faiths who are "walking on the religious eggs," so to speak, the Palestinians are still looking for their state. Many, in a generation far removed from the actuality of it all, believe that they should reclaim land that was taken from them. Others disagree. Many feel that there's "men's law," and others are following what they feel is "God's law." And the argument rages, as it has for 50 years.

Now, we want you to sit in that place for a moment and feel the anxiety and the energy of its sensitivity and potential for explosion. For this was the spark that was to create Armageddon at about your 1998 to 2001 time frame. Don't believe us? It's written in prophecy in many places over hundreds of years by many priests. This isn't something Kryon brought you. It's a strong potential that you had for a very long time, and many of your religions spoke of it and warned you about the end times coming from this.

But it didn't happen, did it? For after the Harmonic Convergence in 1987, which was then celebrated by the 11:11 in 1992, things started changing on the planet. Very, very quickly after 1987, the geopolitical structure crumbled around some of the governments that were scheduled to be principal players in the prophesied Armageddon. Go back and look at the synchronicity regarding that 1987 event. Now, pretend for a moment that you're still in Israel at the Temple Mount in the old city, then expand your field of vision and understanding to encompass the entire Middle East. We want you to look around for a moment and feel the discontent that has simmered and cooked itself there for over a half century. It has festered into a hatred that's affecting all of you at the moment. It's the center of the reason for your worldwide terrorism. It's creating the polarity that's on the planet right now that so many are experiencing.

It has polarized brother against brother. The Jew and the Jew supporters stand on one side, and Islam and their cultures are on the other. And the core of the challenge is in Israel! It was supposed to be the trigger for your Armageddon, but something happened instead. It became the trigger for your spiritual winter – a time on Earth that we spoke about: a large shift of civilization, a time when there could be no more fence-sitting about where you stood, a time for the Lemurians to return, a time for the Lighthouses to be built for the coming storm, a time where humanity decided to continue or not.

So here's the logic question, dear Human Being: In this day and age with all that you have before you, and with all the modernness of your thinking and all the leadership and ancient wisdom on the planet, show us the peace plan! In that place where everyone knows that an explosion is simmering, where's the solution? There is none. No plan. And if you think about it, that simply doesn't make sense, does it? How is it that everyone can see the problem, but no organization on Earth has the solution? Where are the wise men? Where are the peacemakers?

It's because you're in a winter where no one can think of what to do, since they've never seen anything like it. *"Go to the source and solve it!"* some would yell out. Doesn't that make sense? Isn't that logical? But you see, the trees of logic are dropping their leaves. You're in a spiritual winter where things aren't making sense. There's no peace plan for the very thing that continues to fuel the fire of hatred, create the wars, and perpetuate the terrorism that's at the core of old energy versus new energy on your planet.

Now, there are those of you who are saying, *"Well, there's going to be one. We have great hopes for leadership shifts on the earth. We're working on it, Kryon. It will be in this election that's going to be in the United States. There would be new leadership, and there would be new life, and then we will have a real peace plan."* We have bad news for you. Your American election won't make a bit of difference.

We gave you information in the year 2000 that it would be eight years until 2008 before you saw the potential of the temple being rebuilt. There's four more years of this, Lighthouse, so strengthen the foundation and keep the lamp lit. *"So, Kryon, that means that there will be no shift in the United States leadership."* We didn't say that. It won't matter who wins the election. You still have free choice, but take a look at what you have to choose from. The leadership of both choices is old-energy leadership. They're cut of the same cloth. Understand that it's appropriate for the larger plan that your time line will remain this way. Again, do not despair. Instead, send light to your leadership, no matter who it turns out to be.

You won't see miracles for a while. You won't see the peace plans yet either. Oh, there may be talk about it, but there will not be pure intent from any side. Does it make sense to you that Israel and Palestine would choose the two leaders they have now? Did you ever think of this synchronicity: Here are two leaders in the hot spot of Earth, where what happens ignites wars, and the people have chosen two old-energy men who have been trying to kill each other for over 25 years! Does this make any sense to you? Peacemakers?

All of what's before you will only serve to perpetuate the spiritual winter that is, at this moment, appropriate to continue. Let us ask you another question: If you haven't noticed, where are your heroes? There are none. There's not one on the horizon. Can you remember a time like this, where there weren't any bright spots of hope? There's no political or spiritual or "peace hero" in sight. "*Yet there always has been,*" you might say. But not in a spiritual winter.

Now, of course we speak metaphorically, but some of you are starting to get it. Perhaps what we're telling you is beginning to make sense, and you now understand why you're reading this. Listen: When it gets dark and you go into a spiritual winter, there's a whole group of you who have been placed here called the Lighthouses who are going to keep the ship of humanity from crashing against the rocks. And they're the readers and listeners and many, many more who are awakening.

Reader, are you getting this? There are tens of thousands of you reading this now. It's why you're here. It's why you exist, to hold that light during this spiritual winter. It isn't going to get better for a while longer. But don't despair. Hold that light. It's why you came, and why you're alive on the planet right now. Let us say it again and again and again: You'll never find a lighthouse built in a safe place, will you? The storm comes, and that's when you light the light. It's to hold the energy on the planet in a balance so that you can go through this *disconnection* and let it endure for the appropriate time.

In the Christian culture, the story goes that the master of love, Jesus the Jew, was being crucified. It's a story that is told over and over by several sources. He was in the process of what he thought was death. That's what crucifixion is. He was about ready to shift in dimensionality and go to the next level, whatever that meant to him, including the very real potential of ascension. But instead of this master looking up in peace for what was to come, it was reported that he called out to the heavens and said, "*Father, why have you forsaken me?*" Here he was... a Human whom some called "the Son of God, the Ultimate Divinity in a Human body," calling out in frustration. Why? Because he felt a complete and total severing of all relationship, and a total disconnection. He cried. *"Where have you gone? What has happened? Why have you forsaken me?"* The "third language" of constant connection to Spirit had suddenly left, and his spiritual lifeline was gone... and even "the Christ" was confused. This is common for dimensional and spiritual shifts, and you've got one going on right here on Earth. It's called the spiritual winter. It's the planet Earth's "dark night of the soul," and it's the first time any of you have seen it, but *all* of you came here knowing that it could happen.

Lighthouse, maybe you're getting an idea of why you exist on this planet? Listen: there is good news! There are heroes. The trees aren't dead, and the birds didn't stop singing. There are youngsters sitting here who have no concept of what they'll see in their lifetime, but the potential is that they're going to see the good news! Many of you will, too, but you'll just be a few years older.

Activation of the Eighth Layer of DNA

We're going to tell you what's going on: There's a potential of a new tune being sung on this planet by birds you've never seen before [another metaphor], and it's going to be sung if you'll activate certain layers of your DNA that are becoming interdimensional. The new tune is the consciousness of what you call the new children of the planet. Some have called them Indigo; some have called them crystalline. The crystalline designation is one that would emphasize the Crystalline Grid that's now being rewritten. This rewrite is literally the history of Earth. We know that you can't understand that. How can you rewrite history? Yet we will say it again: It's not about changing the facts; rather, it's about changing the consciousness of humanity when the 4D history took place. Think: If the facts created hatred and strife, a rewrite won't change the actual history, but instead, a rewrite of the reactions to history by humanity will change the entire scheme of your existing polarities and current feelings about the past and what to do next. That's going to tie right in to what we're going to tell you next.

We told you sometime ago that you're in "the dispensation of eight." We said that it is a dispensation of *responsibility*. Reader and listener, this activation is truly an important one. You are the staple of humanity, Lemurian, and that's why you came back. That's why you'll come back again and maybe even again. After all, why stop the cycle just when it starts to show results?

The winter is upon you. Look around you. Do you see anything really hopeful? The answer is no. Everything around the creation of peace or stability is either postponed or is simply not happening at all. Don't despair! (This is something we said before and will continue to say.) You've been groomed to hold the light. This is why you went through many of the things you went through, so that each lifetime you'll have a little more wisdom so that when this potential was manifested, you'd know what to do. There's purpose in all of this, and it's not a great mystery. Your life is a culmination of many expressions (lifetimes) on the earth, and they all build energetically on themselves to a focus, which is this spiritual winter.

We want to talk about Layer 8 and what it is. This layer is the individual Akashic Record of your divine entity. There are many of you who are aware that there's a divine Hall of Records on the planet that we've talked about for many years. This place keeps track of the comings and goings of all entities called Human Beings on planet Earth. It's a place that none of you will ever see except when you come and go. Call it a "spiritual accounting of Human balance on the planet" if you wish. It's called the "Akashic Record."

Now, if you were able to visit this place, you would find that in crystalline form is stored the memory of who you've been on the planet... all of it. Right now, in this room of more than 200 people, there is not one new being. There is not one here who's experiencing planet Earth for the first time! We would say this to you: This is unusual, Lemurians – old souls each – make no mistake. It's no accident that you would form and come together in this reunion to hear about this winter that you've planned.

Layer 8 is ready to be activated, and we're going to tell you about it. Layer 8 is your own personal, crystalline Akashic Record. Layer 8 in your interdimensional DNA contains the full record of every single Human lifetime you've ever had on the planet and everything that you've experienced. Up to this point, with you walking around in 4D, this layer wasn't really important past the obvious energies it provided for your contracts and karmic attributes. It kind of floated; it didn't matter; it was good for past-life readings, and that was about it.

It also gave you some phobias, if you've noticed! Some of you were born with abnormal fears related to things that have no connection to your life experience this time around. This is a safe place to talk about these things... it really is. Now the potential is that it all starts to make sense, and you can have an understanding of all these things. What are you afraid of? Are you afraid of light? Perhaps there are those here who don't want to take this activation step. They might be saying, *"I'd like this discussion to be over soon; let's not hear any more of this."* Done this before, have you?

What happens if you take that step? What's going to take place? Some still have the "seed fear of enlightenment." There are those in here who've taken vows of celibacy and who've married God. Suddenly, as you become interdimensional and Layer 8 is starting to vibrate, you're waking up at three in the morning. There are those here who know what we speak of because when you wake up at that time, there's a whole lot of entities in your room! [Laughter] It's irritating, to say the least.

Not all of you have this experience (of awakening often), but enough do, and so you will now know what's going on when it happens. Layer 8 is being awakened. You can't go into an interdimensional shift without your private Akashic Record waking up! Everything that ever was *you* is starting to vibrate. Anytime in the past where you gave a vow to God, you're going to be reminded of it. This Akashic Record will wake up and poke you about three o'clock and say, *"I couldn't help but notice you're married. What happened to that vow?"* [Laughter]

There will be other parts and pieces of your past waking you up at different times, saying, *"Remember when we did this and we did that? Well, then, we'd better not go to that spiritual meeting, because it might start a ball rolling that you can't control, and you'll end up paying the price again."* Remember, you can't unknow things! Remember the last time you entertained certain spiritual passions, and you ended up being burned at the stake for it? You don't want that again, do you? No, you don't. Memories are forever at all levels.

The Human attribute of an old soul is that he has many, many lifetimes and many of them are profound and wise. Especially if he goes all the way back to Lemuria. Lemurians are the core race of the planet. They were there when the Pleiadians appeared and gave humanity the seed biology, which included an extra dimension, did you know that? Did you ever have dreams where you were real tall? That's a pure Lemurian trait. We'll talk more about that another time.

But let us tell you, your Akashic Record is before you, and this represents lifetimes that sometimes number in the hundreds, if not more. These are lifetimes that you had on this planet, many of them profound, that are all coming together and are becoming an irritant to you because they all want to know what's going on! When you broach interdimensionality, this Akashic awakened consciousness will occur at some level. So we're giving you instructions regarding what's taking place.

It's time for you to throw away the idea of a *past* life, or at least what you thought of were the energies of a past-life experience. When you become interdimensional, there's no more linear time, and time and distance are irrelevant. In this new Earth energy, all of the *yous* of your past lives are together in the now, representing one energy in this lifetime. This is the *now* lifetime. Therefore, you cannot even say the words *past life*. Your current life is one that has attributes of everything that ever was, and the potentials of everything that can ever be. Welcome to what the masters felt! For this is the same thing that's the precursor to the DNA activation that they all had.

Now, what are you going to do with all of these awakening *past* energies that are sitting there tapping their feet due to a displaced dimensionality? This represents all the history that you had with all that you've experienced on the planet. So we give you these instructions before we close: It's time to unite all these energies together and speak to them out loud. Find a place and a time where there's no one else around, for we guarantee that they won't understand what you're doing! Interdimensionality is that way.

Speak to them out loud and say, "*This is what we've waited for! It represents all of the lifetimes we've ever lived, culminating in the one that we have now. Our purpose for being is truly being realized. Like a past school, all of us together are awakening into one being. You're my support; you're my team. Now, line up and get behind me and push! I need all of you to be as one in this new energy that allows for such a thing.*"

Take from all of them, the wisdom, the knowledge, and the experience that they gave to you in other expressions on the planet. Also, remember that they are all *you!* See it as the wisdom of the ages... a profound history book that you actually lived sequentially.

Then inform all the *yous* that there's a new vow on this planet that supersedes all the others. Then give the new vow: Create one for yourself that tells about your magnificence and your divinity and why you're here. For example, *"I vow to take the energies of all of the past that's being rewritten on this planet and pull them into the middle of my passion. I promise to marry myself so completely that I'm as comfortable with my own being as I am comfortable with God. I now have thousands of my own lifetime experiences behind me that are supporting me. I have the wisdom of the ages to apply to sending my light to dark places. Therefore, I vow to claim my place in this new energy and use all the attributes of each of my lifetimes that I carefully stored in Layer 8!"* Then do it.

Send your light right now as you sit, reader and listener: Send it to the Sudanese. It's time to stop the old-energy behavior in that place. They need your light! When the darkness of that situation is truly revealed, humanity will act!

Send your light, reader and listener, to Palestine, and give them hope for what we see is a peaceful state that's run intelligently by those who have a real goal for them, and not just a vengeful spirit. See them wishing to create peace with a neighbor who's been their enemy for half a century. See miracles in their future, with smiles on the faces of their children… in this decade!

Israeli, don't give up hope, for there's light being sent to you – no matter what language you speak, no matter what culture you're from. In an area that is small, yet so profound, called Israel, there can be peace with your neighbors. Drop the past energies and look to new possibilities. Look to the young people for what is to come. There are seeds of peace there regardless of the spiritual winter that you're seeing.

Lightworker, send your light to the continent of Africa. See those who can do something in the south create possibilities for the whole that have never been considered as a reality… a system of health that might cure a whole continent! A dream? We'll tell you this: We wouldn't ask you to send your light for this purpose unless that potential literally was written as a strong potential in your future!

Finally, we tell you this. In the heavens at this moment, there's a song being sung – a timeless and historic one – and it speaks of a beautiful place in the past called Earth. It speaks of the entities there who did something amazing on their own, on *the only planet of free choice* – the only one that has the power to choose a higher dimension. They brought upon themselves The New Jerusalem… peace to a divided planet. It's a story that will go down in the history of the Universe and be marked on the walls of the most divine places that exist. Entities will meet you all over the Universe, and they'll see by your colors who you are and what you participated in. This is the potential of what you're creating right now. In some aspects, the tune is already being sung, since you're well on your way to accomplishing a task that many of you came for. It's the reason you're here, Lighthouse. You're the light in the darkness of this spiritual winter. You may be the only light until the spring arrives! You exist for this storm.

And that's why we're at your feet, celebrating the Human entities you call *ordinary*, because in 4D you simply don't know any different. Some of you are starting to acknowledge it, waking up and seeing that it is so. After the winter will come the spring. And when you hear those birds and you realize the trees are not dead and the countries start to bloom with wise leadership, you will see that indeed peace on Earth is possible. Oh, there'll always be strife. There will always be discontent. There will always be those who have different opinions and ideas, but all of this can exist on a peaceful planet.

This is the potential we've always seen. These are the end times we spoke of 15 years ago, and you're right where you belong, holding it all together!

And so it is.

"'Kryon, what is mastery?' I'll tell you what it is, Human Being: It's when you walk around and you're not afraid of life. It's when you're peaceful when others are not. The situations that would cause drama in others do not in you. It's when the world around you is in chaos yet you walk into it and you don't feel chaos.

Instead, at some level you feel the wisdom of the ages. You absolutely know it doesn't have to affect you, and it doesn't have to touch you. It's when somebody yells at you and calls you a name and your first reaction is to wonder if they're right!

That's mastery"

Choosing to Dance

Newport Beach, California

December 2004

Photos at: www.kryon.com/newport04

Chapter Sixteen

Choosing to Dance

Newport Beach, California

Chapter Sixteen

Greetings, dear ones, I am Kryon of Magnetic Service. If you are one of perception, who sees the colors, look at them now. They come pouring into this place and represent parts that are greater than the sum of the whole. You see? They represent the healing entities, some of who have been here all day and some of who have been waiting for this moment to arrive.

Imagine that the roof in this place isn't here. It's a beautiful, clear night... warm, just the temperature of this room. A stadium surrounds this place and it's filled to the brim with tens of thousands of entities looking at what's going on in this room. If you can fathom such a thing in your mind, then you have a small idea of the truth, and the truth is that you're all connected to the family at a level that you don't easily comprehend.

Although you feel alone, which your duality postures very well, you're not. Spirit is at your shoulder. God knows all about you and looks upon you and smiles and doesn't judge. For you're a piece of the whole, designed to be this way. We understand that you're filled with questions, but for these moments I'm going to ask you to suspend your linearity and your 3D lives, yet anchor in such a way that you don't float away. Because you're being examined, as you speak, by those who love you.

You think there are tens of thousands of entities in this stadium above you? Now expand that stadium to billions, all over the Universe. If you understand that you're connected at a quantum level to all of these, that means that in all the multi-verses, they know about this meeting. And you might say, *"Is this meeting that special?"* Yes, it is. You're that special! This fact hides from you and you can't fathom it. You're a piece and part of an "interdimensional soup" – something that isn't complete without you. Therefore, your activities are all part of the God energy that you feel is apart from you, but it isn't. The Universe knows of this meeting because the angels who sit in the chairs, pretending to be Human, are part of the whole. And what are these entities doing? They're celebrating... they're dancing. Spirit speaks to Humans this way, so let the colors show it to be so. Let the auric energy of my partner expand to 27 feet so you who are here now may see it. Let it be known that the proof is here for you to look at, interdimensional seer, if you choose to. Then you'll know what's taking place – this meld between my partner and myself called channelling.

We want to tell you today about health and healing. We're going to bring you some premises that we have discussed before, but then enhance them. Then we're going to give you things we've never spoken about, because now it's time. We are becoming more scientific and also more esoteric regarding DNA. We've spoken about the layers; we've spoken about the Hebrew names that they contain. We've given you their purposes. We've also spoken about how they mix together. We haven't identified all of them yet, but we will.

We've given the layer information in a linear fashion, even though they're not linear. When you as a Human speak of DNA, you speak of all of it together, even though there are billions of parts. Interdimensional DNA is far more complex even than that, yet we give you the names of the layers as though they're in boxes that you can open and look at, rather than the energetic "soup" that they actually are. But it's the best we can do. So let's start at the beginning: Let's discuss a big one.

What's happening right now to the Lightworkers of this planet? So many of them are discovering things within their own biology that might seem fearful. Logically, a Lightworker might think that this moment would bring an energy where he would be so much better off than before, because the energy is starting to be commensurate with that of the planet. In other words, the Lightworker has been waiting for this energy! Yet it seems that the opposite is happening.

Relationships are falling apart, both personally and internationally. Human bodies seem to be disintegrating health-wise, and things you never thought you'd see, you're seeing. It's the challenge of the time, and we told you to expect this. Now, we can't say that these challenges all exist in this room, but it applies generally for you, plus for the tens of thousands who will read this message.

Let me speak to the room and the readership – the two eyes that are on the page multiplied many times. We say again: In an interdimensional way, listener, do you understand that the readers are here, too? And reader, as I speak to you now, do you understand that this small group of people who you call your brothers and sisters – in this December time, sitting here with the decorations all lit, the chilly evening outside – are with you right now? Even if you're reading this in August, they're with you! You're all connected. This is the interdimensional attribute of reality that you never realize. So greet each other now!

Again I will remind you: Lighthouses were built for storms, and you know what I'm speaking of. It's not a time of testing, it's a time of adjusting. It's not something you've done that brings you these problems and these challenges; rather, it's a time of shift. So dear Human Being, as your DNA begins to shift, a change of your comfortable past reality is what often happens. Don't despair. There's reason for all these things, and if you're one of those who decides in the face of this fear, *"I choose to dance,"* then you're going to make it through.

It would seem odd, would it not, that there seems to be an epidemic of challenge with Lightworkers? After all, it's the Lighthouse that's the strongest element in the storm! Take a look at the messages that I've given you just in these last few months as I spoke about a "winter of spirituality" [Kryon channelling, September 2004 – *The Winter of Spirituality*]. There seems to be a darkness over the land. It's a shift, and a time of scraping the foundation clean before the new building of civilization can be built, which will be called "peace on earth." And it takes Lightworkers to do that! The Lightworker is the one who's doing the scraping!

That's why it's often the Lightworkers who are the ones going through shifts and changes, and that's what some of you are experiencing. Indeed, this shift takes on many forms, but it's still a challenge, isn't it? Within this challenge we [Spirit] get asked many things: For instance, "*What's happening to the health of those especially in North America regarding food allergies? There seems to be so much of this.*" And so we'll answer that very clearly so that you can hear it, for it has to do with your health. It has to do with a changing consciousness, believe it or not, and it's very esoteric.

Food Allergies

Did you ever notice that for the most part, the children on small farms aren't allergic to milk? But children in urban areas often are. The children in the areas that you call home are often allergic to many things. Why would there be this difference? I now say things that we haven't literally put into transcription in this way before: If you don't honor the animals, you're not going to get the nutrition! But this fact hasn't been put together yet by those who are responsible for producing your food. In fact, it sounds very silly to them.

Here's the premise: Those who want efficiency and try to create a factory-farm approach to food will put the cows so close together that they touch all the time – all their lives. They're strapped in containers or small spaces and are milked and fed… and you wonder why you're allergic to milk? But the farm that has one or two cows that are cared for correctly will create milk that your body sees differently. This requires an interdimensional realization that you and the earth and the cows are very connected. Your cellular structure knows the difference and reacts.

Some take chickens and put them in containers so that all their lives they get two square feet – no light except when they're supposed to have it – just to produce many eggs. If this continues, soon you may have a population of Humans who won't tolerate eggs! And it has to do with something that we're going to mention a little later on in this channel, something that you don't expect that's starting to occur… even more than an interdimensional consecutiveness.

The reason is mainly because you're now free and clear of the Harmonic Concordance – the bookend of a measured energy time – that started with the Harmonic Convergence. After the Harmonic Concordance, by your own design, we started delivering energy to this earth that will literally change Gaia. One of these energies was the Venus Transit. At that time, we asked you to look back and see the kind of energy and balance that is delivered to the planet, for this shift is changing many things. [Kryon channelling, June 2004 – *The Venus Transit Gift*]

This new energy is going to accelerate certain things, like allergies to foods, unless you decide to change how foods are developed and collected and preserved. Almost everything you buy that's canned is bad for you, yet the whole idea of canned food is to keep food from becoming bad for you! Yet these are your storehouses, are they not, in case of trouble? You have all the canned food on the shelves. You open a can and you'll find what's in there seemingly to be fresh, tasting very good – but there's a price to pay for this.

And when you consume it, know this dear Human Being, you're putting a substance into your body that has never been seen before in nature. And how can you do that – at the same time expecting that through your veins will surge awareness, understanding, wisdom, balance and peace – when your biology is working overtime trying to balance the foods that you're eating? Maybe it's time to take a look at this for what it is. Make some choices that will take you away from factory foods. In certain cultures, it will require some work to do this, but after all, that's why you're here. [Kryon smile]

Vaccinations

Here's a question that may seem to have nothing whatsoever to do with the subject, but it does because of the way Humans connect it. They ask this question: *"I have children; I have grandchildren, and they're about to be vaccinated. What do you say, Kryon, about vaccination? We've heard many different attitudes about this."*

The premise of vaccination is accurate. It works for biology and it has for many years. It has voided and almost completely eliminated certain killer diseases from the planet and has saved countless lives by now. It works. However, will vaccinations continue to work? I'm going to say this, and as I do, some will understand and some won't: In the spirit that it was developed, and in the form that it was brought to you as many as 50 years ago, it will continue to work. However, there's been an attempt to put medicine with the vaccinations, which are also supposedly helping to stop other diseases, as many as 17 or 18 of them, instead of the seven or eight of the original design.

Here is our advice: Doctors, rewind time and go back to the seven or eight substances. Don't put the others into the vaccinations. Treat the others separately and give parents choices as to which substance they want: the original formula, or two formulas at different times. What you don't yet "see" in your science is that there is indeed an energy of consciousness when you combine too many of these together. It can actually void the purpose, and some cellular attributes cancel them completely if they're given together. And yes, there can be problems that won't show for years when you give these substances together, simply because they're not doing what you asked them to. They open a door for later imbalance.

For Healers: Enhancement in the New Energy

I have some advice for healers. My partner [speaking of Lee], you've never given some of this before, so get this right. [Kryon admonishes Lee, with a smile, to go slowly.] Here they sit – many healers. But many more are reading. Some use energy, some have physical facilitations, and they know who they are.

I have some advice for you if you're a healer. Would you like to make your healing abilities more profound? Well, first of all, let's discuss what's actually happening. Some of you have stopped your healing work because things aren't working the way they used to. There's often a question, in this new energy: *"Will my past healing modalities still work?"* The answer is yes – in fact you will, by intuition, be able to use them even better than before – but there is some advice also. The first is this: It's time to do something that not all of you are doing: Practice mastery! If you're going to be the vessel for balance, be balanced! Gone are the days when the healers can have the information and the knowledge, open the book, do the work, then go on and do whatever they choose with their own bodies. For the first time I'm going to tell you that your healing abilities will be connected to the work you're doing on yourselves – physically and spiritually.

You are a pure vessel for balancing others, and that's going to be "seen" at the cellular level by those you work on or advise. And if you want to stop a healing practice immediately, then I'll tell you it's easy. All you have to do, healer, is become unbalanced and everything will grind to a halt. And it didn't used to be that way.

Healer, in the old energy, the principles worked no matter what you did when you were alone. Over and over you may have put the crystals or needles in the right place, or created the correct colors and practiced the ancient ways. Perhaps you would visualize the right symbols and give the correct energy focus. Then you might get a healing in front of you! Not anymore.

So here's the advice: Tune yourselves up! Do you have a habit that's killing your own cells? And you think you can hide that from the one you're working on? In the old days, yes. But since the Venus Transit, no. Remember, the attributes of the Venus Transit are a balance of masculine and feminine. Part of that balance was a creation of intuition abilities at the cellular level for humanity. It's starting to work, and that's why so many are "awakening." The Human body is no longer "unaware" of what's around it, or what's happening to it. It's starting to react to frequencies of consciousness, and that's often you. That's number one.

Now the second one also has to do with tuning. The frequency of your reality has changed. Oh, your healing modalities will still work, but they're going to begin to fall flat unless you start searching for the new frequency where they will be activated. We know this isn't 3D information and is difficult to describe. So think of it like this: Your favorite radio station has increased its power and is slowly changing to a new place on the dial [a new frequency of transmission]. If you keep the dial set at the old frequency, gradually it's going to go away. Pretty soon there will be no music and you're going to have to reach down and turn the dial and actively search. *"Where's the new channel?"* you might ask.

It's not a mystery where the frequency is going, but don't let this take you by surprise after the fact. Flow with it now. If you're aware of this, you'll receive the information intuitively and gradually. But you must understand the premise. What worked yesterday may not work tomorrow unless you tune up yourself and also find the new frequency that everything is shifting to. Now, we speak metaphorically and generally. The reason we do this is that it's impossible to communicate each detail of the many attributes facing each of you personally. So we give the overview. But healer, you know what I speak of.

Perhaps you've discovered a premise and you've worked with it for a long time? You've done scientific research – perhaps you've even proved it in your own healing parlor. Now it starts to evade you. Things aren't working quite as well, and you might say, *"Well, that's because the population is no longer as receptive. They're denser now."* No, they're not! It's the opposite. It's time for you to make a shift. The population has been given new tools and they're starting to awaken and know the difference.

Bizarre Stuff

Here's one you may not understand: Healer, as you make this shift, look for the bizarre! There are some premises waiting for you to discover within your own work, which you think you know so well, that you haven't discovered yet. Look for the bizarre. I'll give you an example: The master acupuncturist will treat the 12 meridians of the body. And there are only 12 – that's ancient science that has stayed the same, since it's the way the body works energetically. That's the process they'll stay with. Now, I'm going to tell you how many meridians there really are for this time. For a starter this year, there are 24! *"Kryon do you mean that we are gaining meridians? Isn't this something that either 'is' or 'is not'? How can a health practitioner even begin to treat a Human if the rules of how health works shifts all the time?"* If you asked this question, then you're very astute! Yes, the Human is changing. The answer to your question of "how" is to *change the healer!*

Is the Human Being suddenly adding meridians? Not really. They were always there. But now in an energy where you're becoming balanced and interdimensionally aware, *what was always there, but invisible* is starting to show itself more clearly. The result? Enhanced healing! But it requires an interdimensionally aware healer. Interdimensionality is bizarre to a 3D Human! Don't let some of the intellectual 3D questions that you may have stop your search. For instance, where are the other 12 meridians? Don't look for them in physical places on the body. They're above the original 12!

"What?" you might say. *"How are we going to do accurate acupuncture and insert needles into open space?"* And that's where it gets bizarre. What about the intent of the healer? You put one in, and intend it be two! Does it work? Indeed. If you understand and recognize that that particular meridian exists above the ancient one, then you're on the right track. The one above is an interdimensional meridian that starts to tune the bodies in interdimensional ways, but which relate to the physical ones purpose also.

If you can understand this, then you're way ahead of the game.

Remember that acupuncture is an energy science: It's about the movement of energy within the body. When the energy of the planet is shifting and affecting everything, did you really expect that the Human Body would not also shift in the way it deals with energy? Just by acknowledging that, you've increased your knowledge and your potency as a healer. And when you insert the needle into the meridian that you always did, make it two needles in your mind. Now, perhaps you understand why the health of the healer's mind and body is important? A healer who is just "walking through the process" can never go beyond the 3D of it all. All of this, by the way, is for what? Is it healing? The answer is no. It's for balance. Acupuncture is a system of balance. Energy healing is a system of balance. Healers don't heal, they balance. The individual Human reaction to a balancing by a balanced healer is what heals the Human.

Involve the Patient's Consciousness

We gave you instructions over a decade ago and we're going to practice this premise even tonight with the listeners here. We can't get away from this basic premise and we encourage every healer in here to do what we are about to review every single time they see a patient. Interact with your patients in a specific way: Ask them if they give permission for a healing that day. Don't let a situation take place where they come to you thinking you're going to do something for them where they simply lay on the table and you supply magic, then they leave. No – instead make them participate in the process.

Before they ever lie down, look upon them – look in their eyes and ask them if they give permission for their own cellular structure to change. It has to do with intent. Perhaps you might say, *"Do you give permission today to have your DNA changed?"* Make them verbalize yes or no. Of course they'll say yes. After all, they probably paid to be there. But just the sound in the air when their own body hears that they're giving permission sets the stage for their own healing. If you want to carry it a little further, you might even ask them the second question: *"Do you understand that only you are responsible for what takes place in your body?"* Now they've got to think a little. *"Yes,"* they may say. Then do your work. This is profound, healer. You need to understand that it's part of the package of healing… truly part of the package. Make them responsible with you, and as a team, do your work. And here's something we recently have mentioned, but never in channel: We know a secret about healers – one that even they won't admit. You see, when they're alone and nobody's looking, and they can think about all the things that are going on, many of them feel guilty. They're feeling guilty about the ones they couldn't help – the ones that they couldn't heal. Their self-worth suffers due to it!

Healers are Lightworkers who literally have the gift of touching people physically and energetically and helping them in their lives, yet when they're alone, they feel so small. They often wonder whether they're doing any good on the planet. Oh, they know better at some level, but in 3D they suffer from negative self-worth. Healer, if this is you, you've got about a trillion entities who want to put their arms around you right now and say, "*You have no idea how you're helping the planet!*"

Did you know, dear one, that when a Human gets off your table, and this person has had an improvement in their biology, it actually changes Gaia? Did you know that? Did you know that every step you take with integrity and spiritual awareness helps Gaia? Say you may make a trip to the store and on the way you make a little prayer. You've helped the planet! Yet you feel so ordinary and you wonder whether you're doing anything. Let us take a moment to dance and to celebrate you! For the veil keeps you from seeing your own results!

Imagine walking through fertile lands for years. Everywhere you go, you plant seeds. These seeds are planted automatically, because wherever you step, your very presence leaves them. Years pass and you sit at home wondering if you've done anything at all for planet

Earth. You agonize over your seeming nothingness since you never get to return to the place where you walked and take a look. If you could see it, you'd see forests and giant plants, spectacular flowering fields, all with your name on them. Such is the way it works when you're in duality.

New Esoteric Information

Now we get into the esoterics. There will be those who will leave this place of hearing and reading and never absorb anything we're going to say in this last section, because they're not ready for it. The last time we were together we spoke technically about DNA. We gave some revelations even about the structure of DNA. We told you that your science will eventually prove what we told you, and it won't take that long. Let us review this big premise.

Imagine a racecar is in front of you and it's, metaphorically, your own DNA. It sits there idling and you can barely hear the engine. It's filled with three billion parts and they all work perfectly; that is, until something goes wrong. And when something goes wrong, the engine sputters and it knocks a little, and indeed, if it isn't taken care of and there's no understanding of it, the engine will eventually stop.

So it seems like the whole purpose of the study of DNA is to find out how it works so that it won't stop. How does this engine idle? How does it run so smoothly? This is what you're in doing now, studying this. The encyclopedia of DNA is before you and the Human genome has been revealed. You now can examine the parts and all the resources around the parts. It's the first time in the history of humanity that this attribute lays before you. Yet all the efforts for this are going into what? They're going into discovering how this engine idles so well. And that's it. That's it!

But what did we say is in front of you? It's a racecar. And every once in a while a Human Being in history will sit behind the wheel, step on the gas, and go around the circle at a blazing pace. And all the other Human Beings remark, "*That is absolutely astonishing. That's a master!*" There have been many masters on this planet who have stepped into the racecar and pressed the pedal. And whereas you are content to study an idling engine, what we are telling you is that DNA is *built for speed! It's built for mastery!*

This is the time we're inviting you to step into the car and press the metal to the floor. It's not about an idling DNA; it's about what else is there that it was built to do. Did you understand that even the prophet of your culture, Jesus the Jew, had the same DNA you have? But His was in *mastery mode*. He knew what was there and activated it. When the great Jewish master, Elijah, with his aid, Elisha, watching, decided to ascend, the best Elisha could do was to give the description of his master's ascension as that of a chariot coming down – the "wheel within the wheel." Elisha really was unaware or ready for what actually took place that day. And if you could have seen this, we'll tell you that what happened was that Elijah decided to turn into light! That's what masters do. That's what ascension often is.

In this day we give a message that ascension has not changed much, except you turn into light and you *stay here!* How would you like to run that racecar around the track – be an ascended one – and discover mastery? Remember, go slowly at first so you don't crash into the wall and have to start over. [Laughter] We talk metaphorically, don't we? Elisha went on to do great works. Some say they were even greater than his own master. But Elisha didn't vanish when it was his time. He took the mantle of his master, but then he added to it. When Elisha ascended, he stayed on the earth. His ascension didn't have anything to do with leaving or death; it had to do with staying here and dancing!

The Energy of Gaia and Your Own Biology

Now, my partner, I'm going to ask to go slow and make this correct, even though there is the commotion [Pause], tune them out. [A band starts playing in the next room!] There is an energy going on within this planet that we call planetary life-force. It's the very energy you call Gaia. Gaia is a combination of entities, but which has a feeling of only one energy, much like what you call the Kryon. It's not singular and it's not linear. But Gaia is related to you and you are related to Gaia.

In general, what happens on this planet regarding consciousness literally changes the cellular structure of your body. You're connected way past what you understand or expect. You're about to have something very, very interesting take place. The potential is for the life-force of this planet, the Gaia force, to shift in such a way that it will change the diseases that humanity is used to dealing with. And you might say, "*Wait a minute! That's just biology. We catch viruses, we spread AIDS, or we have tuberculosis... these things are just Human biology. They don't have anything to do with the dirt of the earth.*"

Let me tell you, this above statement represents an older energy Gaia, where you were blocked from full participation with the vibration of the planet. You're about to see shift and change, dear one, and you wonder why you're so tired? Some of you are actually detoxifying an old Gaia energy! The life-force of your planet is going to change and literally put a lid on some of the diseases that have been uncontrollable. The reason is because you have chosen to change this planet, and with it, you're going to change "planetary health consciousness." Get used to it. There's a consciousness of the planet that allows for certain kinds of disease to even exist. Remember that your biology is part of the dirt of the earth. You can't separate the two. Therefore, the planet is a major player in what diseases ravage humanity, and you are about to change that. Time will show a slowing of certain kinds of viruses, and the time has come for AIDS to be conquered.

An Unbelievable Tool

I told you earlier that Lemurians were interdimensional. The Lemurians had an attribute that you do not – a fifth-dimensional awareness. They understood much of what I'm about to tell you and this is the reason that the Temples of Rejuvenation worked so well for them. This is also the reason that this particular race, which has never even been validated or discovered, had so much going for them. In an interdimensional state, Lemurians knew something I'm about to tell you. They understood it and they practiced it. There's only one more premise to give you, and it's very esoteric.

We want you to appreciate what's happening in the next room. They're dancing! [The band is playing and people are having a Christmas party.] So celebrate them and listen to this, for it is the final, and the best.

Never before have we broached this, yet it's been before you for a very long time. Some have even studied it. I speak to the many females in this room and reading the page. Many of you live in fear of something that you're going to contract because your genealogy says you will. It's a very 3D thing – that your mother had cancer and your sister had cancer and they died. And you consider it just a DNA ticking clock and eventually you're going to get it, too. It "runs" in the family.

You can change this! You can rewrite the DNA and make that race car rev up and start moving this attribute and literally take that away. Now, that's old information and we've given it before. What we wish to tell you now is something unbelievable to some, and that's because it requires interdimensional attributes of reality. Again, listen carefully and get this right, my partner [a further admonition for Lee not to rush simply because there is a party next door and a potential distraction].

Dear one – in this audience, reading this – if you're one who's going to work on your particular genealogy and stop this disease from occurring in you, I'm going to tell you what the potential is down the line, *both past and present.* I'll try to be succinct if I can in an interdimensional way, but it's simply not explainable in 3D. When you void this potential within your own DNA, the whole lineage – your existing daughters, the daughters that they're going to have, and the daughters that they're going to have – will also be cleared. It's a clearing of your DNA that literally will change them all, no matter how far into the future you go. It's a total restructure of your DNA in that regard to that disease potential – one that actually changes your family history, and your karmic group from now on.

Then the questions begin: *"Wait a minute Kryon. You've told us many times that we can't heal others. They must do it themselves as we help balance them. So how could we change an existing daughter's DNA? I understand that if I change my actual DNA, that my unborn children will inherit this attribute and be clear, but how does it work with a living daughter?"* Let us say that in already living female, the propensity for the genome to have that problem may remain, but the surety that it's going to occur will vanish. It's going to be about choice within the female. Think of it this way: Your action will plant a seed in her DNA. It's a seed that will grow only if watered, but it's a divine seed that can, with her permission and understanding, change her, her children, and so on.

"Kryon, this is actually changing the past! She is already born, and has the potential." Yes, dear one. Exactly. See how this might be confus-

ing? But in a reality that is beyond your single-digit dimensional existence, time isn't in a forward linear fashion, and these things are not only possible, but very real. The Lemurians knew it well. Did you think all the rejuvenation in those temples in Lemuria were just for individuals? No. They were for families, represented by one individual! Think about it.

Now, dear ones, this is for the men. If you are one who has a lineage of certain kinds of cancers and your father had it and your brother had it and you have it, you need to hear this: When you work on yours, when you accomplish the eradication of it and stand free and clear of it, the sons of your sons of your sons won't have it either! And this, dear Human, is part of the new energy of Gaia that is being developed. We wouldn't say these things unless they were so. This should make you dance!

We're going to do something we've never done before in closing. We're going to declare this a healing meeting. One of the advices we gave for healers was this: Involve the one to be healed, verbally. And so I'm going to ask the question to all of you, reader and listener: Is there anyone here who gives permission to be healed? [Audience answers verbally with a strong *"Yes!"*] Let those responsible for enhancing the healing process, who have come here for that person, place their energy upon you. Let their weight be known, that you would feel them here, for you've given the answer that we expected. It's a cooperation and a new partnership with the new energy of Gaia that some of you are beginning to feel.

Permission has been given, and the reality is understood. Oh, there's a lot more, but the concepts are complicated, so we'll wait. Let's just say this: More will be given to you as we go. Did you say yes [referring to the question a moment ago]? If you did, that means some of you aren't going to sleep well tonight. Consider the challenge to be the angelic disco ball that will be your bedroom! There's a lot of dancing going on, isn't there? [The crowd in the next room is getting noisier as they dance to the increasingly loud band.] It may be the first time you ever gave that kind of permission. Maybe it's the first time you ever said it aloud? If it is, then it's not too late to say it again, if you wish. Right now as you read these pages.

And that's today's message. It's time to take your power… the power of a new Earth. Time to dance.

And so it is.

Who You Really Are

Crystal Lake, Illinois
August 2005

Chapter Seventeen

Who You Really Are

Crystal Lake, Illinois

Chapter Sixteen

Greetings, dear ones, I am Kryon of magnetic service. Some of you expected another voice, didn't you? The one on the page perhaps, which, of course, is yours! How many of you understand and realize that as you read the messages of Kryon, you are reading aloud with your Higher-Selves for emphasis? The Higher-Self of every single Human Being knows what I know. It is your Higher-Selves that we've asked you to collect together and channel with me tonight.

When you read the words of Kryon, you don't read anything new. Nothing is new, and yet everything is discoverable to those without full knowledge. When you read the words of Kryon, you read the truth as given by someone who has a relationship with you that I'm going to talk about tonight. I'll call it the Hidden Relationship. It's a relationship that is so strong that your Higher-Self can actually channel along with me since it knows what I'm going to say. When you read the books, you read along with your Higher-Self. That is the voice you hear. It's a divine voice; it's beautiful, and it's yours.

So, for those of you in the room, you can get used to this voice for a little while… the Human voice representing the Magnetic Master from the Great Central Sun. "Kryon, what exactly is the great central sun?" Well, I'll tell you. The answer is "yes." That's all I can tell you. The Great Central Sun is not a place at all. It is a metaphor, and it is the only thing that we can describe which would be the center core of the love of God. You know it very well. It's not a place of origin, but rather a condition. More than that, it describes the relationship between us. Oh, there is so much that is hidden from your immediate consciousness while you're here! Even hidden to those who would open the door and reveal the Akash of Earth, and who would then be able to look into your DNA and see all of your past lifetimes. Even a person like that wouldn't know what I'm going to tell you today. For what I'm going to tell you is not recorded in your Akashic Record. It's not in the earth, and Gaia doesn't have it either. It's not even in your DNA.

Your DNA and the Akash of the planet, that energy which lets you literally move into ascension status, only goes back as far as the earliest thing that happened for you on Gaia. Now, that's a lot! But that's where it stops. Your DNA and the Akashic Record can only give you information about past angelic-Human expressions. We've told you so many times who you are, and we're going to tell you again this night, but in a different way... an enhanced way. You see, there's a whole lot more than you think.

The entourage who is arriving in this place will surprise you. It's not who you think it is. You fail to see this. It's the obvious entourage of Kryon, whatever that means to you. It is those who come to wash your feet. But there are many more. Some of you will relate to this and some of you will not. Dear Human Being, all of those who you have loved and lost on this planet, in this lifetime, are now in the room. There are children in the room and you know who I'm talking about, don't you? Brothers and sisters and moms and dads; cousins and uncles and aunts. The room is filled with Human Family that some of you have put into the ground and said good-bye to. They are here.

Some might say, "Well, why would that be? Why would they show up just for today?" And I will tell you. They don't just "show up" today. Dear Human Being, so many have been with you all along, but you don't want to see them. They're vertical and you see horizontal [a reference to the study in perception given earlier in the day]. They are not in your perception. Your belief system doesn't support the information that these departed loved ones are still with you and part of your guide structure, and will be with you all of your life. Did you know that? It's part of the system... a well-hidden one.

Did you know there's an agreement between what you would call souls? Oh, you're so linear and so singular! You look in the mirror and there's one Human Being. There's one Higher-Self. There's one soul and that's what you seem to carry around. What a concept! Well, it's wrong. There is much more here to see. You are in many places at the same time. If I even begin to broach the subject, you won't understand. It's at this point that the Human intellect is insulted and shouts, "Tell us anyway. We are intelligent enough to understand anything." It's not about intelligence, dear ones, but rather about your trained perception in a dimension that is limited. Even the most intelligent Human can't comment on something he doesn't see or perceive.

Did you know there are multiples of you on the other side of the veil? Multiples of you! They are energetic ones... but multiples never-the-less. Did you think you took all of your power, angel, when you came down here? No. It wouldn't fit in your body. So, what did you leave behind? How do you think co-creation is done? Let me ask you that again. If you co-create something for yourself, and you're in a society with other Human Beings, what about the other Humans? Did you just blast your way through the puzzle with your own intent, right into their lives? If so, did you have permission? If not, where is the integrity of co-creation? Did you ever think of that? When you asked to be removed from a situation or to be placed into a new occupation, what about those who were affected by this event of yours? Did you just steamroll over them? I have some news. Every time you co-create, you're fulfilling somebody else's co-creation. Every time you successfully co-create, there is immense, complex planning going on. Did you know that? It's a system, you know?

The Higher-Self—a part of you on the other side of the veil—is doing work you can't conceive of. Call it a great planning session that is going on all the time as you pray, as you move, as you send light. But the session involves many others too. It involves the Higher-Selves of the ones you are interfacing with, and they're working together to create what you're trying to do on the planet, since it also enhances them. It's very complicated. When and if your intention, your creation, finally manifests, it's a win-win solution for all of you, accomplished with permission and appropriateness. How do you think this works? Unexplainable and hard to conceive of, isn't it?

I just told you that your loved one who passed on is a guide, one of many. What about you? Could it be, as my partner says, that you are somebody else's guide right now? When you passed over in a past lifetime, could it be that part of you stayed here to be with others? The answer is "yes." Perhaps they are still here and alive? How about that puzzle! Think of it. You reincarnated and here you are, but you might also still be with another Human as their guide. How's that for being multiple? That means you are in two places at once. How does that feel? It's true, you know, and when you ponder it, it explains much.

Ever wonder why, when you come into the planet, that you have psychological attributes that cannot be explained? Fears, remembrances, things you will or will not do, places that you want to go, all present themselves as though you had lived before. There is a connection to Gaia and other Humans. There's an actual relationship within all of it that is hiding. You're here on the planet as somebody else's guide! Not all of you, since this information is very specific. It depends on how old you are. The younger you are, the more it might be, for obvious reasons. It is complicated, but there is more going on than you know, and an even bigger item, a relationship, you don't know about that I'll reveal in a moment.

First, however, I want to do one of my favorite things. I would like to take you back to the wind of birth and I would ask you, for the first time, to visualize this with me in a 4D way. I want to give you a description of this so you'll know what I'm talking about, and so you can envision it with me, because I was there with you. I still am! I'm going to tell you something about Kryon that you didn't know. Who do you think I really am? Angel? Yes. So are you. Purveyor of Magnetics of the planet? Yes. So are you. You know how big the entourage was that helped me set the grids on this planet? There was over a trillion of you. Every single person who walks this planet and will be born in all the future of Earth helped to set the grids of the planet. You were there and helped to initiate it. Part of the relationship is that you took on the energy of the planet. Then most of you went someplace else, and I'm going to talk about that too, in a moment.

The wind of birth is the description of the time and place in 4D that you arrive into on this planet from a previous life, whether on Earth or not. First-timers are coming in and old souls are coming in. Picture, if you would, something the size of a stadium. Now, I'm just giving you this metaphor because this is partially in 4D and partially in multiple-D. You can't hear the light like I can, but you can see portions of it. Think of this stadium-sized object as a giant abyss. You're in another dimension and you're about ready to come into 4D [the Earth Plane's dimensional attribute], and you seemingly fall into that abyss. But there is this wind that is streaming out of that abyss like a cyclone. It's a silent one, blowing in an upward direction. It's multi-colored and beautiful; it sparkles; it has lights that go everywhere, but it's pouring from below to above. If you could lean into that wind, it would sustain and support your energetic weight until you literally remove yourself from the edge. Then, at the appropriate time, you would drop into what we call the canal of birth. The next thing you would know would be the doctor's hand, and you would hear your voice for the first time in the new life called Earth.

Don't ponder this too much, for the inevitable linear question will occur asking, "whose soul was in the fetus while it was growing? If I come in at Human birth, where does Human life really begin?" I have told you before—a subject for later, perhaps—that Human life actually begins with permission to create it, by both the parents and the child. It's a spiritual event, and not a physical one. It is only manifested by the biology of the two genders. The time spent in the womb by a soul is not as important as you have made it, for the actual angelic journey of a Human Being begins at actual birth. The "life process," however, is seen by God as precious from beginning to end... from spiritual permission to the deathbed. Humanity wants to compartmentalize it and assign spiritual aspects to the individual parts, instead of the whole spiritual process.

It's the wind of birth that I wish to examine for a moment. It's a portal and I'm always there. I'm there now. I'm with thousands every day that are making up their minds, and beginning the process to return to this Earth. Pieces of God, they are, examining what they're doing, coordinating with all of the workers, those multiple parts of themselves, (hard to describe) before they separate the biggest piece of themselves and come into the Earth. I was there when you came in. I'll talk about that in a minute. I'm there right now. I'm talking to every single one of them even as I do this communication. "Kryon, how can you do that? You're here channeling." Oh, if you think that's odd, I'll give you something else to think about. I'm also in the Hall of Honor! I'm greeting all of those I said goodbye to, in the wind of birth! To me, in the blink of an eye, they're back! And we celebrate every single thing that took place.

Hard to believe, isn't it? It's a system, you know? It's bigger than you think. Wait until you find out who you are. The reason you are having a hard time with my entity being in many places at the same time is because of your clock. It only allows for one thing at a time. I have no clock, and neither do you when you are here.

Who Are You?

So here you are on this planet. Biological beings haven't completely and total forgotten the angelic part of whom they were before they came. Some of you are tuned-in enough to actually read parts of the Akash. And this record will tell you about who you've been and some of the past lives that you've experienced. This record will give you an indication of some of the reasons why you feel the way you do this time around. It explains a lot about your current life when you know who you used to be. But who are you really? I'll tell you. I've told you some of these things before, but I'm going to tell you again.

The first thing is, you're a part of God and that means that you always were and you always will be—yesterday, today and forever. When you get out of 4D and time disappears, that's very understandable to you and it's a normal state of being. There is no beginning and no end. It's in a circle. Let me give you an example of the way I see things. What are you going to do tomorrow? You don't know that, since it's your future. Anything can happen since it's in the future. You can't know since it hasn't happened. When tomorrow arrives, it's the present and you will manifest it. In a way, you just manifested the future (as you saw it the day before). After tomorrow goes by, then it's the past. All it took was one day for the future to be unknown, known, and past. One thing becomes another. At what point does it transfer from the unknown future to the known past? The answer is "when you live it." Well, in my perception, you've already lived it! I see them all as one. To you, I say, "Live it daily." Therefore, you are always creating the future.

"Wait a minute Kryon. How can you say that? You told us that you don't know what's going to happen either, since we have free choice." Correct. I don't know what you're going to do, but I know all of the potentials that are possible of what you might do, and they lay out in front of me like a map. Every potential thing that you could possibly do is there. Which track you're going to take is unknown and will manifest itself with your free choice, but I see all of the potentials. Therefore, I already know one of the things you're going to do. This is the "now" and it's very difficult to explain when you exist on a linear time line.

"It doesn't make sense to me," you might say. It does when you're not here, dear ones. We see the potentials of the planet, and always have. Why do you think there's so much excitement from our standpoint? It's because we see the potential of Earth—all of the potentials together—and we see where you're taking it. And you're taking it right into the middle of The New Jerusalem! You're entering the cave that is so dark, and a great shift is before you, yet you enter with such courage! And you wonder why we love you the way we do?

When you were poised at the wind of birth, we asked you if you really wanted to do this again and you said "yes," and then you did! Who are you really? Ancient? All of you are beyond ancient. All of you have no beginning, but some of you are ancient on this planet. You've been here 50,000 years, some of you. To you, that's a long time. It isn't really. Thinking of what time it was when you set the grids with me, 50,000 years is just a fraction of a second on the world clock. 50,000 years ago, some of you were Lemurian, some Sumerian, some later become Egyptian. You choose some of the highest-tech societies that have ever been known on this earth, not defined by machines but by consciousness. You see, that's your perception. It's actually a cultural crutch! You think, "the higher tech it is, the better the machines must be." That's so funny!

High Tech: Let me describe what high tech really means. High tech is top science known intuitively by the Human Being and practiced every day because he has mastery over dimensional perception. It doesn't get any better than that. He doesn't need any computers. How was it that both the Lemurians and the Sumerians knew all about the Solar System? How can you do astrology without knowing about the planets, and yet it's the oldest science on the earth! Without telescopes, how could you know about astronomy? How could you know about the movements of the planets, yet this knowledge was well known long before telescopes. Give that a thought. There's more here than meets the eye [Kryon humor].

That's who you are. You are ancient. Some of you are indigenous to this area. Now, here's what I mean. You were the first to set foot on the dirt of the Earth right here. Want me to prove that? I can't, but you can, to your own consciousness. If you think you're one of those allied to the earth, one who really resounds to the land and the animals who are here, I challenge you go to the museum and check out the pottery that you made! You'll resound to it. I've said that before. That's who you are, old soul.

New Souls Coming to Earth

"Well, Kryon, something doesn't make sense. You say we come around and we go around, but the Earth has more Humans on it today, twice as many than when I was born. It doesn't make sense that the same entities are coming and going all the time. There have to be new ones coming in all the time." How perceptive. So, you want to know where you're coming from? Some of you aren't going to like this answer, but I'll tell you. Please be patient with my long answer. When you're on the other side of the veil, Human Being... how do I say this? There is so much excitement, if I can use the word; there is so much energy, if I can use the word; there's so much enthusiasm, if I can use that word, around who you really are.

Lightworker, if I ask you, "Who are you?" you would say, "I'm tired." That's the answer we get all the time. It doesn't answer the question at all, but it's what is on your mind the most. And how are you today, we often ask? "I'm tired" is the reply. You're tired when you wake up and you're tired when you go to sleep, and that's because so many of you are doing the heavy work. So tired are you that you feel you are spiritually wrung out.

How many of you are convinced that it's your last time here? [Many hands are raised] Well, guess what? You're wrong! "Kryon, I don't want to hear that. I've done my part and here I am. This is a very tiring thing... coming and working on Gaia. I don't want to do this again. I've earned some rest." But when I see you in the Hall of Honor, you can hardly wait to get back to the wind of birth! That's what you said the last time, during the last incarnation too! That's what the Human Being in biology experiences, dear one. You are so tired because you're putting out spiritual energy that is actually changing the planet. You get on the other side of the veil, to Earth, and it doesn't even occur to you about your real relationship and I'll tell you why, because you are specialists in this.

Haven't answered the question, have I? Where are you coming from? New souls are coming in all the time. Where are they coming from? This is the part that some of you are not going to like. You're coming from this same kind of a test in another dimensions, from other places and situations not called Earth, but very much like it. This test is always going on, and that's not what you wanted to hear. It's going on within multi-dimensional universes, and there's more than one of these tests at a time. There may be only one in this Universe but there are others happening in alternate universes and this is what you do... come and go from these tests as specialists.

There is a name for your specialty that I cannot give you because it is one that is only perceivable on my side of the veil. It's a name that you know so well, and it's pasted upon you because it's what you do. So, you have come from another testing place whether the test there was complete or not. When you arrive, you choose to come into this Earth test as a newbie. It's hardly the first time around for you. You've been doing it in some way since before there was a beginning! Now, that might tell you something if you haven't thought about it. There's a bigger picture going on. There's a system. Think of this: If there is a system which includes multiples of tests, and you have done this forever, that must mean that there's an engine of creation going on because of your very existence on this planet. Did you ever wonder about actual creation? Could you be a part of something far larger? And if you think that, the answer is "yes," There is a much bigger picture that you know about when you're not here.

I know all of you very well... all of you. There's not one entity here that doesn't recognize the name of your specialty. "Well, Kryon, this information makes me tired thinking about it." And that's the Human reaction we would expect, dear one. I'll tell you what our reaction is when we think about it. It's glorious; it's spectacular. Your specialty is known by all the angels. You carry the colors and the badges of where you've been and what you've done everywhere you go. This changes with every single lifetime. Speaking of lifetimes, they're quick, you know? You come and go very fast... very fast. That's who you are—specialists in universal creation.

Types of Comings and Goings

It's interesting the way this works for you. Many of you have seen these things, but don't know it. The first-timer. A first-timer is one who comes to the earth for the first time in his cycle. He comes from other biologies, other universes, other earths, (if you wish to say that) but not exactly. This test you call Earth is not a duplicate of something that's happened before or is currently happening. It's not about alternate selves. No. This test is unique, and all the testing places are unique. They're all about free choice, and what it specifically creates within the confines of a single universe. We know your potentials, but truly, what you actually may do is accomplished by free choice.

The first-timer: You can spot them—innocent they are—complete innocence and yet devastated by humanity in general. The first-timer is the one who will immediately go into nature because they can't stand Humans. "This doesn't work for me," they say. In normal conversation, they speak "A" and they get back "B." In their perception, conversation is very difficult. They often don't look you in the eye or respond the way you expect. They don't understand why Humans spin drama, either. "Why would Humans do that?" they say. "I don't like this place," they say. "I'll talk to the animals." That's a first-timer—very confused about the actual relationship between Human and Human. They must learn about this, and they always do.

A first-timer is one that's just a little out of sync. Some say they're a little bizarre, and that's just because they're so bewildered with the Earth and humanity. You've seen them. You know who they are, and they are gentle and precious... precious souls. But they seem so out of place with society, so honest, learning how it all works.

Then there's the opposite—the old souls. Some of you are 50,000 years old and nothing surprises you. You've "been there and you've done that." You've played all the roles within both genders many times and you're just doing another one... and you're tired. You're so tired! But to the ones who are convinced that this is the last time around, and you are not coming back, I have news: Yes, you are! Oh, yes, you are. [Kryon smile]

Then there's the pretender. The pretender, well, he's really a newbie. But he gets the spirituality bug quickly and easily. After all, isn't that the core of all of you? The pretender goes to what you all have in common, which is something he understands, and hides within it, pretending to be an old soul. You wouldn't know it, either, except that one thing gives him away. Have you ever heard the expression, "too spiritual to be any earthly good?" If so, he or she probably is a pretender. They're floaters—reality floaters. They don't want anything to do with the real world. These are the ones who you'll find in the communes. "There has to be a better way," they say. So they surround themselves with spirituality and try to mold their own reality. They also wish to ascend and "get out of here." They would love to be like the prophet Elijah... get spiritual enough, and simply disappear! That's their goal. They want out so they won't have to deal with Humans any more, or at least the ones who don't think as they do. They are as precious as the newbie, but in a different way, for they actually can see that divinity is real. They endeavor to crawl back up the wind of birth to find it. But they never see the humanity, or the test before you, as being sacred.

"Well, Kryon, if this is so, what is the goal of Humanity in general? I understand we are helping creation, but when are we finished?" Indeed! I though you'd never ask! [Kryon smile] The goal? I'm not sure if you're going to like this explanation either. The goal is to "do it until you're done." Right now you are really tired. But dear one, ask the soldier who does battle every day, "Are you tired?" You already know the answer. Oh, but it's so grand, what you are doing at this moment! If you could only see the system. If you could only see the relationship! You might be doing this forever. Tired yet?

Past Non-Human expressions on the Earth

Oh, there is so much love here! The system provides for it. Do you know why you do this? Because you're in love with the system. The system is you and it's also God (in your view), and it's also nature (in your view). You're in love with Gaia! What a beautiful energy. How many of you were aware that you have had past lifetimes without being a Human? Ahh. Now we're getting spooky. Do you dare think of it? A lifetime without being Human—how could that be? How about a lifetime within Gaia? How about being an actual part of the earth for a hundred years or so, then coming back? How about being part of the rocks, the plants or the trees? How about being part of the life in the air—interdimensional life in air? Did you know that this is the way of it? If you understand this, we'll tell you something else. Your non-human lifetimes are not recorded in the Human Akashic record. There are those spiritual readers would might say, "I read your Akashic record and it appears as though you disappeared for several hundred years, doing something else, then came back. I can't tell where you were, or what you did." I'll tell you where you were—you were in the earth in an energetic form! Your "readers" can only read what is within the scope of your humanness, for that is all there is to see for them.

When you don't have an energy imprint to read within your interdimensional DNA, no reader or seer can see "where" you are, or "where you were." Therefore, the assumption is linear: If you didn't come back to Earth as a Human, then you surely are resting somewhere on the other side of the veil, getting ready for the next incarnation. Then some of you envision your soul-selves in angelic rocking chairs somewhere, eating angelic food [probably chocolate] on an extended universal vacation—rolling around Heaven all day! [Kryon smile] Oh dear one, listen: It's a far larger system than you know. Your linearity gives you such neat and simple answers to such complex goings-on.

How could such a thing be, some ask. To give you an idea, let me ask you: Why does the energy of Gaia have consciousness? The answer is because it's part of who you are! Does it feel oddly like "home" to you? It should. It's a divine energy and now we're really getting out there to some of you, I suppose. [Kryon knows who is in the audience and there are some who are not of a spiritual mind, but attending never-the-less.] Your goal is to change, through free choice, the vibration of this planet and make it as high as you can. Because, at the end of the test (whenever you choose it to be over), the energy will be measured and applied to something else within the universe you don't understand now. Then, the universe shifts accordingly, actually using the measurement you created.

It's the engine of creation itself. It's what makes things work. It's as important to the rest of us as food is to you here on this planet. What you are participating in interdimensionally and universally is profound, It is important and you don't know anything about it while you're here. You can't, for where would the test of energy be? But there is purpose for all of it... and you wonder why we love you the way we do?

I'm almost finished. Now I want to take you back to the wind of birth. I want to take you to your own earth-entering experience this time around. I was just there, you know? So were you, too. Time is such a deceiver. Only in old age do you begin to realize the joke of linear time, when you can look back on all of it in a split second, and you begin to realize that you lived it in only a moment. Time is a construct that allows the system to be laid out in simplicity, while being accomplished with complexity.

My partner asked you this question earlier on: "Did you think about why you would ever have decided to be here now? You are at the crux of the big problem on Earth. You are here during the renewal of the energy of the planet, where the test gets hard." Now I'll tell you something startling: One of the easiest things you could have done is to have gone through the Armageddon. There's nothing to it; you simply die. You've done that before, many times. Almost everyone here has been burned alive. How about that one? It's almost a prerequisite for awakening spiritually, as presented by your religious history. Did you know that? It would have been easy for you to do that. You have experience doing that, and it's over in a moment... just a shift of energy. But you didn't.

Instead, you said, "Let's go and solve the big issue. Let's go and do something we have trained and trained for. Let's be the meek that inherit the earth. Let's change the actual vibration of the Earth. Let's have the battle of all battles, to be fought in the trenches of our own cultural exchanges, day by day. Let's go and start the hard work."

At the wind of birth I held your angelic hand and looked at you with my energetic sight—you were half angel, and half Human. You had one foot in 4D and the other in what we would call multiple-D. It's so different than you would imagine. I reminded you that this is a step like no other you've ever taken. I reminded you that you were about to go back to the planet of free choice without any knowledge of your grandness or your purpose or of the relationship. Every single one of you in the room, and reading this, was born in a time when Earth prophecy was different than it is today. And I said to you, "Do you mean it? Why go again? Why now?" I knew the answer, but I just wanted to hear the warriors of light that you are, claim it once again. Can angels smile at each other? Oh yes! They do it with light-energy to one another, intermingled in a beautiful way with gorgeous colors. And you said to me, every single one of you: "I know what I'm doing. I have spent a long time helping the Earth to get to this place, and now I'm going to go again and make a difference." And now, here you sit because you did what you intended.

I don't know what that means to you as you get up and leave and walk to your vehicles tonight, or put down your book and prepare a meal. I don't know if that means anything to you. I'll tell you, however, what it means to me, grand one. You changed the universe! That's what has happened on Earth… and you don't even know it. Even some sitting here don't even believe it. Impatient they are, as we close this communication. They are hungry and wish I would stop. So I say to them, isn't it interesting that none of the very time specific prophecies of the Armageddon took place? Isn't it interesting that you can't find anything that's going on today within the writings of the 400 year-old priest? [Nostradamus] Isn't it interesting that you have instead, and will have, events that will change world history, but which didn't seem to be on the "radar screen" of the best spiritual readers of the past? These are events that were never predicted, and now, even the "players" of the old prophecies are gone from your reality. Might that imply to you that there is something else happening instead? I'll tell you, doubter, what the biggest issue is: It's that when I saw you last, you were one of those who told me that you would go to Earth to change the energy… and today you are with others who believe they have. What a coincidence! [Kryon smile] I'll tell you something else, doubter: You are as loved by God as any Human on this planet, and will not be judged by your unbelief. You are actually holding a place for those you sit beside, allowing them to send light where it is needed. Therefore, perhaps… just perhaps, you are doing the very work you came to do, but you are now discounting it all as silliness. Such is the way things often work. You are as precious to me as any.

The "Relationship"

Finally, I'm telling you that this relationship that you don't know about is a profound one. When you leave this place and I see you in the Hall of Honor, magic occurs. An interdimensional shift happens and the entire energy of your being returns to who you are, and joins me. Listen and read the words... "Joins me." Because I'm a part of you! I don't know if you wanted to hear that or not. There's a relationship between the two of us, which goes way beyond brother and sister, or angelic partners, for these are linear and simple Earth terms. No. Instead, it's a piece of God that you become. Have you ever felt this... our relationship?

We've told you about the soup analogy before. It's the best metaphor we have for something outside of your full understanding. You look at a bowl of soup and you see soup. You don't see the molecules in it. You don't see the flavoroids in it; you don't see the salt and pepper or the ingredients. When you talk about God, you just imagine God... a singular energy that represents love to you, or perhaps authority? There is no insult in what I say next, just reality. Your perception of what God really is has a comparison to what your pet must think about you! Your pet seems shallow and doesn't see "the big picture." It can't, because it has a limited intellect. Your limitation is the same kind of thing. You wish to think you have great intellect. But your intellect is truly limited by your dimensional perception. It's designed that way.

The truth is that if you could examine God, and were able to "think beyond the box" you are in, you would find your name there! And I'm there with you... and so are the masters who walked the Earth, your friends, and all the ancients. The relationship is that I am you, and you are I when you're not here. We are one soup, and combine in a way not explainable to any of you. That's why, when you read these words on the page, you might feel something, because it is part of "you" who is actually giving the message. Some of the parts of you, who are not "with you" now, are giving this message! Because they are still part of me. How do you feel about that?

There is more to it than you think about being the piece of divinity that you are. God bless all of you for your work! Oh, the unbeliever is still here. I know you. There's nothing that says that by attending this meeting, you will become strange. Please don't fear the love of God. Maybe you think you're going to sit this lifetime out and just have a disconnected existence from all of this spiritual talk? Okay, then what brought you here? Think about it. It's really kind of humorous.

And that's why we wash your feet, Human Being... every foot that's here. Somehow you are in the dark, but with an enormous spotlight waiting to develop when you wish it to. And that's who you are. It would be a good time for a healing, you know? Ah, anyone come for that?

[Pause]

Now would be a good time. Reader, are you "listening?" [Kryon smile] Now would be a good time. Claim that connection in your own way. Open the door when you're alone. With pure intent say, "Dear Spirit, Dear Source of Love, Dear God... tell me what it is I need to know." Do you want to go to the next step or not? Some do and some do not. There is no judgment at all... only honor for the journey.

Part of the family, you are. Part of God, you are. Leave differently than you came. Some of you are not going to have the sleep tonight that you'd like. Seeds have been planted of knowledge and purpose, allowing you to ponder the unponderable. Perhaps you've made a decision? Perhaps it's about your biology, or about your self worth? Time for the shift, isn't it? That's why you're here. I promise you that if you will make that shift, I'll be there to hold your hand and help you through it. Not as an angel, but as a part of your own divinity. I challenge you: Stand in front of the mirror and open your eyes and look at yourself, and say, "I am that I am," which means I am God. Then go from there. And that's the truth. We would not bring you these things if they were not so. Grander than you think, the plan here, is. More beautiful than you can imagine, workers of the light, all of you. All of you.

And so it is.

"Many of you see 11:11 on your clocks, don't you? It's more than coincidence, isn't it? Why would this be? Every time you see that configuration on your clock, dear Human Being, I want you to say, 'Thank you, Spirit.' It is a reminder of who you are, Human Being, and why you are here. Did you ever notice that you didn't look at the clock accidentally and see 11:12 or 11:10? That's because that angel who taps you on the shoulder waits until 11:11 and then says, "Look now!" [Laughter] How does that feel to you? It's way out of the chance of reality, isn't it, that you would see it so often?

Eleven, in numerological terms, means 'Illumination and appropriate spiritual action.' This is a master number. Not coincidentally, it is also two 'ones' next to each other. The number one means 'new beginnings.' The energy around 11:11 is therefore a master number that means, 'the beginning of appropriate illumination on the planet.' Every time you see it, celebrate this new beginning!"

Kryon Products

Videos, CD's, Books
Website, Meetings

Information

www.kryon.com

Visit the Kryon E-Magazine

No subscriptions • No passwords
No disclosing personal information
No solicitations for money • Just FREE

FREE ONLINE
To read, download and
share with friends and family

In the Spirit Epublication

- Kryon questions & answers
- Indigo & inner kid
- Photo scrapbook of seminars
- Articles on travel
- Science & technology
- Music & Art
- Healing Techniques
- Laughter & Humor
- Archived articles for reference
- And much, much, more!

Drop By and visit our HOME - *page*

The award winning Kryon website allows you to find the latest information on seminars schedules, and Kryon related products. Browse through portions of Kryon books, read some of the most profound Kryon channellings, reference, inspirational and educational material. Read some of the hundreds of answers in the Kryon Q&A section. Also, enjoy the Kryon on-line magazine, *In The Spirit.*

Kryon's Website offers the latest in technology and is easy to navigate. Our main menu allows you to view in an animated or non-animated format allowing for maximum Internet speed.

Find the latest Kryon information at:
www.kryon.com

www.kryon.com

Audio Books, Music & Meditation CDs

www.kryon.com/store

THE JOURNEY HOME - KYRON BOOK 5 - on CD!
unabridged, and read by Lee Carroll

COLOR AND SOUND MEDITATION
(ENGLISH or FRENCH)
by Jan Tober
ISBN 1-888053-06-2

TEKNICOLOUR TAPESTRY
by Jan Tober
ISBN 1-388053-07-0

I HAVE THE FEELING I'VE BEEN HERE BEFORE
JAZZ! by Jan Tober
ISBN 15882-008722

THE WAY YOU LOOK TONIGHT
JAZZ! by Jan Tober
ISBN 34479-05472

THE JOURNEY HOME
Jan Tober and Mike Garson
ISBN 15882-01432

Books and tapes can be purchased in retail stores and by phone: **1-800-352-6657**
Also through our Website store at: **www.kryon.com/store**
Credit Cards Welcome

The Rest of the Kryon Book Series

- **THE END TIMES - 1**
  ISBN 0-6936304-2-3 • $12.00
- **DON'T THINK LIKE A HUMAN - 2**
  ISBN 0-6936304-0-7 • $12.00
- **ALCHEMY OF THE HUMAN - 3 SPIRIT**
  ISBN 0-9636304-8-2 • $14.00
- **THE PARABLES OF KRYON - 4**
  ISBN 1-56170-663-9 • $10.95
- **THE JOURNEY HOME - 5**
  ISBN 1-56170-552-7 • $13.95
- **PARTNERING WITH GOD - 6**
  ISBN 1-888053-10-0 • $14.00
- **LETTERS FROM HOME - 7**
  ISBN 1-888053-12-7 • $14.00
- **PASSING THE MARKER - 8**
  ISBN 1-888053-09-7 • $14.00
- **THE NEW BEGINNING - 9**
  ISBN 0-9636304-2-3 • $14.98
- **THE INDIGO CHILDREN (3 books)**
  by Lee Carroll/Jan Tober
  ISBN 1561706086 • $13.95
  ISBN 1561708593 • $13.95
  ISBN 978-1-4019-2317-4 • $14.95
- **A NEW DISPENSATION - 10**
  ISBN 1/888053-14-3 • $14.98

Books and tapes can be purchased in retail stores and by phone: **1-800-352-6657**
Also through our Website store at: **www.kryon.com/store**
Credit Cards Welcome

DVD Videos

KRYON IN SHASTA
Lee Carroll
DVD - 2005
69 minutes - $18.00
Kryon Summer Light Conference
See a sample video clip
[www.kryon.com/videos]

QUAD CHANNELLING
Lee Carroll/Fred Sterling
Pepper Lewis/Louise Jones
DVD - 2005
62 minutes - $18.00
See a sample video clip
[www.kryon.com/videos]

KRYON - THE WHOLE STORY
Canadian Documentary
DVD - 2004
47 minutes - $18.00
See a sample video clip of this
Peter Beamish Canadian Documentary
[www.kryon.com/videos]

PRAYER FOR EARTH
Jan Tober Meditation
DVD - 2002
18 minutes - $16.00
Beautiful channelled meditation
accompanied by photos of the power spots
of the planet.

Books and tapes can be purchased in retail stores and by phone: **1-800-352-6657**
Also through our Website store at: **www.kryon.com/store**
Credit Cards Welcome

DVD Videos

KRYON IN MEXICO
Lee Carroll
DVD - 2006
72 minutes - $18
(English & Spanish)
See a sample video clip
[www.kryon.com/videos]

KRYON IN MOSCOW
Lee Carroll
DVD - 2007
60 minutes - $18
(English & Russian)
See a sample video clip
[www.kryon.com/videos]

KRYON IN CHILE
Lee Carroll
2 DVD set! 0 - 2007
70 minutes each - $20.00
(English & Spanish)
See a sample video clip
[www.kryon.com/videos]

KRYON IN ARGENTINA
Lee Carroll
2 DVD set! 0 - 2006
72 minutes each - $20.00
(English & Spanish)
See a sample video clip
[www.kryon.com/videos]

Books and tapes can be purchased in retail stores and by phone: **1-800-352-6657**
Also through our Website store at: **www.kryon.com/store**
Credit Cards Welcome

Up Close

with

Kryon

Get together for a personal afternoon or evening with Kryon and Lee Carroll in the comfort of a cozy community center or intimate hotel conference venue with a small group of dedicated Lightworkers. It's the most popular way to join in the Kryon energy in the USA and Canada.

The special meeting starts with an introduction and discussion by Lee Carroll regarding timely New Age topics, then it continues during the day with profound, inspired teachings from the Kryon work. It finishes with a live Kryon channelling. Group size is typically 60 to 100 people. Often lasting up to five and a half hours, it's an event you won't forget!

To sponsor an event like this, please contact the Kryon office: e-mail <kryonmeet@kryon.com>. For a list of upcoming event locations, please see our Website page [www.kryon.com/schedule].

Kryon at the United Nations

Lee Carroll - UN visit 2005

In November 1995, November 1996, November 1998, February 2005 and again in March 2006, Kryon spoke at the S.E.A.T. (Society for Enlightenment and Transformation) at the United Nations in New York City. By invitation, Jan and Lee brought a time of lecture, toning, meditation and channelling to an elite group of U.N. delegates and guests.

Kryon Book Six, Partnering with God, carried the first two entire transcripts of what Kryon had to say... some of which has now been validated by the scientific community. Kryon Book Seven, Letters from Home, carries the meeting in 1998. All five of these transcripts are on the Kryon Website [http://kryon.com/channelling]. The 2005 and 2006 transcriptions are in this very book!

Our sincere thanks to Zehra Boccia for her help with introducing us to the presidents of this organization over the years. We thank the S.E.A.T for the invitations, and for their spiritual work, which helps to further enlighten our planet.

www.kryon.com

Free Audio online!

No subscriptions • No passwords
No disclosing personal information
No fuss • No e-mails asked for
... just FREE

[www.kryon.com/freeaudio]

Check out the many channellings and even some former Kryon audio books and discontinued audio cassettes at the above Internet address. Download these free MP3 files and put them in your iPod or just listen on your computer. These are full stereo, high-quality live recordings of some of the most profound Kryon channellings in an updated and growing library.

Free MP3 Download
Israel #1

Free MP3 Download
Israel #2

Free MP3 Download
Israel #3

Free MP3 Download
Parables 1

Free MP3 Download
Parables 2

Free MP3 Download
Parables 3

Index

Lifting The Veil

Index

Index

Index

Q&A ONLINE

See hundreds of questions directed to Kryon through four and a half years. They are all here, alphabetized according to subject matter!

www.kryon.com/questions

Find the latest Kryon information at:
www.kryon.com

www.kryon.com

"Now would be a good time. Reader, are you 'listening?' Claim that connection in your own way. Open the door when you're alone. With pure intent say, 'Dear Spirit, Dear Source of Love, Dear God... tell me what it is I need to know.'

Do you want to go to the next step or not? Some do and some do not. There is no judgment at all... only honor for the journey."